HINTON ROWAN HELPER: *Abolitionist-Racist*

W.R. Helper

SOUTHERN HISTORICAL PUBLICATIONS #7

# Hinton Rowan Helper:
## *Abolitionist-Racist*

HUGH C. BAILEY

UNIVERSITY OF ALABAMA PRESS

*University, Alabama*

Copyright © 1965 by
University of Alabama Press
Library of Congress Catalogue Card No. 65-16384
Printed in the United States of America by Paragon Press, Montgomery, Ala.

To Joan

# Contents

# Preface

HINTON ROWAN HELPER—a statistical fanatic, abolitionist, militant racist, Republican propagandist, ardent patriot, international railway projector, and promoter of inter-American co-operation—was a man of great paradox and tragedy. Born and reared a Southerner, he became a caustic and potent critic of slavery, who sought to "liberate" his people from its burdens. Unlike many of his Northern abolitionist friends, however, he loathed not only the Negro but most "non-Anglo-Saxon peoples." It is shocking to read Helper's violent pleas for abolition and to know of his contempt for the Negro.

Helper was fascinated by statistics and by quantitative evaluations, but for too long he has been regarded primarily as a statistician concerned only with calculations. He was that, but much more importantly, he was a member of the relatively small mechanical and clerical class of the provincial, Southern back-country who came to grips with the fundamental question of economic survival. In this light his racist attitudes, while deplorable, are understandable and suggest that the views of abolitionism have been too greatly conditioned by the study of New England figures.

In some ways Helper's racism is the least of the many paradoxes in his career. Born in poverty, he acquired a moderate sum of money, only to spend it in promoting an abortive international railway. With relatively little formal education, he developed the ability to write brilliantly, if often stiltedly, and to move with decorum (when he chose) among the international leaders of his day. Violently anti-Catholic and anti-Latin in outlook, he married an Argentine woman, probably in a Catholic ceremony, and in the thousands of words of his extant writings scarcely ever referred to her again.

One should not assume, however, that Helper had a whimsical personality. He was clever, driven by ambition, constantly scheming and planning. Highly romantic and idealistic, he had the misfortune to see near success extinguished by practical-minded men. An intense patriot, he centered all of his dreams around the advancement of his country. He was consistent to his prejudices throughout the years and exhibited doggedness and determination that have seldom been equaled in his efforts to collect claims in Latin America and obtain the construction of an inter-American railway. In its behalf, as in other areas, he exhibited an idealism and a visionary faith in the unity of the Americas far in advance of his time.

Part of Helper's tragedy lay in the fact that he was a dreamer with unlimited self-confidence. In the slavery struggle he believed that he had only to reveal the truth and others would act to attain the results he foresaw. Unfortunately for him, the limited success of *The Impending Crisis* confirmed this view and led him to overvalue his words in print. He never recovered from the delusion that he need only write a book or pamphlet to obtain what he wished.

For years the author, conscious of the need for a detailed study of Helper, collected materials in hope of writing a biography of him. Unfortunately, he was forced to conclude that the sources for an adequate biography are simply unavailable. Many questions presented themselves which proved unanswerable including details of Helper's youth, education, courtship and family life, and his ability to remain economically solvent while scarcely ever holding a job. The author's extensive research, however, revealed aspects of Helper's personality as an abolitionist, racist, and patriot which proved not only interesting but illuminating. A study of Helper's career and published works led him to broaden his own views of abolitionism and to hold a new concept of nineteenth-century racism in America. Because of this enlightenment, he concluded that the results of his research should be shared with others.

HINTON ROWAN HELPER: *Abolitionist-Racist*

# Chapter One

# Youth and Adventure

HINTON ROWAN HELPER was an incurable romanticist. Born of provincial parents and early left to his own resources, he traveled over much of the Western Hemisphere seeking recognition by his fellow-man. When acclaim was not attained, he became increasingly egocentric and radically condemned the social orders in which he lived.

The tradition of rebellion was a familiar one in the North Carolina region of Helper's birth. Rowan County, in the heart of the back-country, was a center in the Regulator Movement staged in protest to the underrepresentation of the Western counties in the legislature and their proportionate overtaxation and abuse by the Eastern ones. When the movement failed, Rowan did not humbly accept its inferior role. His county became a Federalist stronghold following the creation of the Union and the emergence of political parties, in an era when Eastern North Carolina and most of the South were Republican. In the 1830's it moved into the Whig ranks, as the region it opposed became Jacksonian. Not until 1835 did Rowan and the other Western counties receive equal representation in the state legislature, and political equality was denied until 1857, when property qualifications for senators were removed.[1]

It is easy to understand why the farmers of Rowan County had to struggle so long to obtain equality in a planter-dominated state.

In 1860 only one of the county's 14,589 people owned as many as one hundred slaves and only thirty-seven held more than twenty. Only one-eighth of its people possessed enough real and personal property to be taxed, and of these, only sixty paid more than thirty dollars in taxes.

The failure of slavery to develop in the Rowan region was partially attributable to the attitude of its numerous Quakers. Here, as elsewhere, they were devoted manumissionists who, so far as the laws and their wealth would allow, bought slaves and liberated them. After legal changes in the 1830's restricted manumission, they either persuaded those slaves who were purchased to go into free territory or held them only nominally, allowing what amounted to personal freedom.[2]

The Quakers were one of the few American groups fighting slavery when Hinton Rowan Helper's grandfather, Jacob Helper, came into Rowan County shortly after the American Revolution. Little is known of Jacob's background. There is a legend in North Carolina, denied by Hinton Helper, that his grandfather was a Hessian soldier of Lord Cornwallis, named "Helfer," who, like many others, became enamored with America and chose to make it his home.[3]

Jacob's son, Daniel Helper, lived and died on a two hundred-acre farm on a tributary of the South Yadkin River. Like his neighbors he traveled no more than twenty miles from home and scarcely heard of the railroad, the steamboat, or the telegraph. Yet he became the owner of a slave family, a man and wife and their two children, and was referred to as "captain" before becoming a militia officer in the War of 1812.[4]

Like most of his neighbors, Daniel Helper's wealth was limited, and his early death from mumps in 1830 left his wife and seven children, five boys and two girls, near poverty. At that time the baby in the family, Hinton Rowan, born December 27, 1829, was less than a year old. His mother, the former Sally Brown, successfully provided for the children and kept them together, caring for them at home until their teen years, and Hinton Rowan, at least, was sent to the Mockville Academy.

Study at the academy proved a major influence in Helper's life.

Its teachers were the Reverend Baxter Clegg and Peter Ney, a man so renowned in his area that some felt him to be Napoleon's great general, Marshall Ney. The academy's physical facilities were crude, but the students received excellent training. Helper had no additional formal education, yet from his days at Mockville he had a high regard for the life of the mind. He was impressed with the forces which shape history and fascinated by mathematical comparisons. He had some knowledge of literature and an affection for Columbus and Washington, the heroes of innumerable other young Americans of the time. In a beautiful script he expressed himself with clarity and vigor, if often in a stilted fashion. Indeed, he early became aware of his literary ability and enjoyed using extended metaphor, alliteration and other devices to overwhelm his readers.

Though his training at Mockville proved an asset, Helper had received only a good preparatory education. If he could have obtained additional schooling, he undoubtedly would have avoided some of the weaknesses of evaluation which are notable in his writings.

Instead of going to college after graduation from the academy, Helper was subjected to an experience common to many of the poorer classes of his region, indenture to a Salisbury storekeeper—in his case, Michael Brown.[5]

While serving a three-year apprenticeship, Helper grew to manhood. Physically he was attractive, with coal black hair, blue eyes and a six-foot frame of athletic proportions. He carried himself with an almost military bearing which enhanced his over-all appearance.

Helper did not readily accept his role as an apprentice and rebelled against it in the one way he could without jeopardizing his security. He allowed himself to be persuaded by the son of one of the wealthiest men in the area that all apprentices supplemented their meager fare by stealing small sums of money from their employers. Though he continued the practice for years, the prevailing Puritanism of his personality prevented him from enjoying the fruits of his thievery. He kept a careful account of the money taken and resolved to repay it once he was independent.

Much to Helper's delight his term of indenture ended in Feb-

ruary, 1850. True to his romantic nature, he gathered all his resources, most of which were probably taken from Brown, and
moved to New York City in search of the wealth and recognition
rumor held it afforded. He was accompanied by his troubled
conscience, and in the fall of 1850, when Brown came to the city
on a shopping expedition, Helper called on him and confessed his
thievery. Brown was astonished, but sympathy for the young man's
dilemma led him to accept Helper's note for $300 and to assure
him that he would never reveal the indiscretion. This promise was
kept for seven years, until Helper's abolitionist views offended
Brown's proslavery conscience.[6]

Burdened by the need to repay Brown, Helper unsuccessfully
sought suitable employment in New York City for several months.
When work did not materialize, he became increasingly intrigued
by stories of great wealth to be taken in California. By late 1850 he
had decided to try his luck in the wonderland of America and, by
some inexplicable means, obtained passage on the clipper ship
"Stag Hound," which sailed January 31, 1851, for California via
Cape Horn.

This first trip to sea convinced Helper that land transportation
must be the mainstay of American development. He became
slightly seasick at once and markedly so when tempestuous seas
were encountered the fifth day out. For three weeks he scarcely
ate anything. In late March the "Stag Hound" reached Patagonia
and for a week struggled desperately in the passage around the
Horn. At last, short of water, the vessel arrived at Valparaíso on
April 8, 1851. Here Helper made his first contact with Latin
Americans, and his reaction reflected the provincial outlook of
the western Carolinian of his day. He would have been surprised
had he known that he was to spend much of his life working in behalf of such people.

A few days before the "Stag Hound" docked at Valparaíso, a
severe earthquake had rocked the city. The ever curious Helper
was so anxious to see its results that he rushed ashore within half an
hour of sunset, only to be forced to return to the vessel. Early the
next morning he was abroad again. Everywhere he met crowds of

natives "making a great hubbub with their clamorous tongues and noisy actions." Though they seemed to be "an inoffensive, simple-hearted sort of people," he felt them to be "inexcusably ignorant and abominably filthy." The majority of their houses looked to be built of mud or straw covered with tile and seemed "upon the whole inferior to the negro huts upon a southern plantation."

When a slight tremor occurred while Helper was being shaved in a barber shop, the barber abandoned him, joined others in the street, knelt, and crossed himself. To the militantly anti-Catholic Helper, this action seemed superstitious and was the final clue to the people's stupidity.

Within the framework of his prejudices Helper could recognize value, and he was quick to concede that the Catholic college was one of the two attractive sites in the city. Perhaps his views were influenced by the fact that he was well received at the school by "a kind-hearted and well disposed" priest, who insisted on giving him some delicious grapes. After four days the "Stag Hound" cleared for San Francisco, arriving May 25, 1851, 113 days out of New York.

The San Francisco which greeted Helper was the "grand mart" and nucleus of California, a position he believed that it would retain as long as the people depended on imports for their subsistence. He was impressed with the harbor's size and the numerous ships in port, but the rough frontier aspect of the city came as a shock to him. He had grown up in a frontier environment but one in which the influence of evangelical religion had subdued the rougher elements. Unprepared for the lack of moral and social inhibitions of many of the people, he came to form an unduly severe opinion of all California.

Helper's inspection of San Francisco left him with mixed emotions. He was depressed by the "motley" crowd of all the world's races which met the passengers at the wharf. The streets were crowded with scores of children working as news vendors and fruit sellers, and the teetotaler Helper was amazed to see them enter the numerous grog shops at will. Both the gentile and Jewish merchants appeared to be "the shrewdest rascals in the world."

Respected Easterners seemed to deal shamefully in their business relationships, and Helper surmised that "a straight-forward, honest man" could not negotiate with the San Francisco trade people.

Equally bad was the fact that the most respected leaders of business and society frequented the bawdiest saloons, the center of the city's social life. With the shortage of women, those establishments with female barkeepers enjoyed exceptional favor, and the numerous gambling houses seemed to stay open continuously. The "Diana," extending from Clay to Commercial streets, was particularly shocking with its display of nude female paintings. Here professional gamblers rented tables by the month and were ready to take any one who came their way.

The square between Washington, Clay, Kearney and Brenham streets seemed "a cow-pen" to Helper. Enclosed by unplaned planks and devoid of vegetation, the square boasted a center which contained a rostrum "for lynch-lawyers and noisy politicians." Nearby was the city hall where, if one were content to rest a few minutes, he would see an officer bring in a drunken woman in a wheelbarrow. This was true on Sunday as well as every other day, since the population, if they kept the Sabbath at all, did so as a day of "hilarity" and "sport." The tippling houses and billiard halls did a bigger business than ever.

Helper hoped to get a better perspective of the city from Telegraph Hill but was much disappointed. The absence of shade trees and grass because of the dry season made nature wear "a repulsive and haggard expression." Even the city's hotels offered no solace, as they were mere "human-stables."

Helper utilized his time in San Francisco in studying its people as well as the physical surroundings, and in writing of them, he gave distinct expression to the racist views which were to characterize his entire career. He was amazed at the estimated 40,000 Chinese in the state, their presence offending his strong Anglo-Saxon prejudices. Their clothes, features and deportment were so similar that they all looked alike to him. He could not imagine how all of them made a living. Their contentment with their own culture and their reluctance to work for Caucasians also disturbed him. He wondered if they would ever "discard their clannish prepossessions, assimilate with us, buy of us, and respect us," and felt their immigration was most undesirable. He found it unthinkable that they were allowed to come to California to work and be subject only to a small state tax. "I cannot perceive what more right or business these semi-barbarians have in California than flocks of blackbirds have in a wheatfield." But fate was against the Chinese, he reasoned. "No inferior race of men can exist in these United States without becoming sub-ordinate to the will of the Anglo-Saxons, or foregoing many of the necessities and comforts of life." So it had been with the Negroes in the South, with the Irish in the North, and with the now extinguished Indians in New England, "and it will be so with the Chinese in California."

The Mexicans were almost as undesirable in Helper's opinion. He had received extravagant reports of the beauty of Mexican girls, but after observing them, he could not concur. "Their pumpkin hues and slovenly deportment could never awaken any admiration in me, even in California," he wrote. Bonnets appeared to be almost unknown among the women, but most seemed to feel that a shawl was an indispensable item of apparel. Morally there seemed to be a lack of consistency among them. "Notwithstanding they engage in the lowest debaucheries throughout the week," he observed, "they may be seen any Sunday on their way to Matins, Mass, or Vespers."

The Mexicans seemed to be very fond of frequenting bathing establishments, and Helper assumed they maintained a number in San Francisco primarily to indulge their moral depravity. He was told that it was the custom of the proprietor "when a gentleman retires to take his bath, to dispatch a female servant to his room to scour and scrub him off!" Since he resided near an American bath house, he never became acquainted with the Mexican practice in this situation.

On close scrutiny, bull fights, another favorite Mexican custom, seemed equally unwholesome. The press of the crowds, the presence of large numbers of women and children, and the pain suffered by the animals were all disgusting to Helper. They were yet another sign of the decadence of California. He knew of "no country in which there is so much corruption, villany, outlawry, intemperance, licentiousness, and every other variety of crime, folly and meanness."[7]

Holding this attitude, it was not surprising that he approved the activities of the Vigilance Committee. It was the institution of the country, he wrote, which struck terror into the hearts of all evil doers. "Like all energetic associations, it was capable of being abused and sometimes ran into extremes," but even its worst enemies could not deny "that it was the only thing which could suppress crime at the time it was in power."[8] There is no question that, in the early 1850's, much of California society "was reckless, drunkenness common, and [that] everyone went armed with [a] knife or pistol." In fact, "all of California, the mining regions, as well as every other section, was compelled to fight out the old battle between law and disorder which every frontier society has had to face."[9]

In the summer of 1850 a voluntary meeting of San Francisco citizens chose twenty-two men to break up a group of desperadoes, known as "The Hounds," which had operated mainly in the foreign quarters. But the next year new, secretive groups of gangsters organized themselves into efficient forces. By the time Helper arrived, the terrorized people were afraid to go outdoors at night; many patrons of the gambling houses came at dusk and stayed until dawn. In June, 1851, the first of two Vigilance Committees was formed, comprised of 128 of "the wealthiest, most prominent men in the city." Legal formality was sacrificed, but San Francisco came to know the greatest security in years.[10]

San Francisco's example was followed in other areas of the state, and Helper personally witnessed the functioning of the Sacramento committee. When a rather naïve miner was attacked and robbed, the alert Sacramento committee apprehended the two guilty men and brought them to immediate trial in a stunted oak grove on the outskirts of the city. Helper joined a large group to witness the proceedings. "There was an expression of calm determination on the faces of the committee, of angry excitement on the rest of the crowd," which, viewing the culprits, cried, "Hang them!" The committee impaneled a jury, and statements were taken from those witnesses who had seen the assault. The accused men looked the jury in the eye but refused to speak. Almost instantaneously a verdict of guilty was handed down, and with solemnity, the judge announced that after one hour for religious preparation the convicted men would be hanged. At the appointed time a man who identified himself as a Methodist minister came forward and tied the hands of the doomed men, while the crowd renewed the chant, "Hang them." Within a matter of seconds both men were strung up, and the mass of people began quietly to disperse. An hour afterwards no one would have supposed the incident had occurred.

The streak of steel in Helper enabled him to watch approvingly. None of the disgust he found in the brutality of the bull fight was present when he saw swift justice administered to renegade human beings. "Such proceedings as these," he wrote, "produced order throughout the state. Indeed, it was the Vigilance Committee alone that ever has enforced obedience to law in California." He noted (1855) that the state attorney in San Francisco stated 1,200 murders had been committed in four years and only one criminal had been convicted. It was not surprising some people still cried for the days of the Vigilance Committee![11] Their desire for action led, in 1856, to the establishment of San Francisco's second committee.[12]

Although Helper was interested in the social and political life of California, he came to the state to make a quick fortune with relatively little physical labor. Therefore, armed with the usual accouterments, he joined the trek to the gold fields, his first expedition being to the territory along the Yuba River. He went by coach to Maryville, an all-day journey from Sacramento, arriving at Park's Bar the following afternoon. The entire area belonged to the United States government, but each miner was governed by the laws a majority of his colleagues saw fit to impose. Helper pitched his tent on his bar—as the small plots available to the individual were called—and, like most of the other prospectors, slept under the stars. Pork and beans were the main article of his diet, since he could eliminate daily cooking chores by cooking a pot twice a week. Those miners who had good claims worked them seven days a week, but Helper, like most of the others, took Sundays off to wash and mend his clothing and to rest.

The surface digging in which Helper engaged was the first truly hard work he had ever done, and he found it to be opposed to his taste. When the temperature hovered between 90 and 105 degrees, he was completely miserable. No wonder he could lament, "This is the hardest work in the world," and that many of the miners seemed contentious. Despite the fact that personal disputes were frequent in the field, Helper found more honesty to exist among the miners than any other class in the state, especially when they were beyond the influence of city gamblers and speculators.

Fate decreed that Helper, like the vast majority of prospectors, was to fail in his search for gold. At the end of three months on his bar, his returns above expenses amounted to precisely 93¾ cents, only a fraction over a penny a day for the hardest labor he had ever known. "This was building a palace with a vengeance," he wrote. So he gave the money to a neighbor and temporarily shook the dust of the fields from his feet.[13]

But Helper was an incurable optimist where his own career was concerned, and time healed his disgust. A few months later he and a chronic drunkard, named Shad, left San Francisco for the fields near the base of the Sierra Nevada, reportedly the richest in the state. They first went to Stockton, a supply center for the Southern mines, which Helper preferred above all other Californian towns except San Francisco. It seemed to have fewer "drones and desperadoes" than other cities and was located in the valley which could, in Helper's opinion, become the richest agricultural section of the state. From Stockton passage was obtained in a lumber wagon to Columbia, where Helper and Shad began to work a new bar. They daily collected more and more dirt, but the usual winter rains failed to come, and Shad turned to drink. The land became baked; "not a shrub, not a leaf, no not even a blade of grass could be seen in any direction." "Men and animals dropped. . . ." When Helper's money ran low, he and Shad had no alternative but to return to San Francisco.

A second failure was too much for Helper, and he decided to leave California. For three years he had unsuccessfully sought his fortune in the state and was disgusted and longed for home. What troubled him most was the ability of some Mexicans, whom he despised as an inferior people, to make finds. "These delving countrymen of Santa Ann," he wrote, seemed "to have a peculiar knack for discovering the veins of gold".

Having once experienced the horrors of a voyage around the Horn, Helper chose the Nicaraguan route for his return trip. For some years it had been known that the Central American state afforded a possibility for an isthmian canal. After the gold rush anxious Americans developed a crossing between the oceans utilizing Lake Nicaragua and the San Juan River much of the way. This route shortened the east-west journey but, as Helper was to learn, it had disadvantages. The first portion of his trip was splendid; only thirteen days out of San Francisco he and six hundred others aboard the steamer "Cortes" arrived at San Juan del Sur, the Western terminus of the Nicaraguan route. From the time the woefully inadequate harbor was sighted until the luxury of an Atlantic steamer was gained several days later, life was miserable. Twenty years later Helper remembered the crossing vividly and became one of the earliest champions of an isthmian canal.

At San Juan del Sur passengers had to be carried ashore through the shallow water by native stevedores. A fifteen-mile journey through a beautiful but dangerous tropical rain forest followed before the group arrived at Lake Nicaragua. The water of the San Juan River was so low that the passengers had to change boats a number of times and walk along the shore a great deal. Even when aboard the packed boat, everyone had to prepare his own food and sleep on deck in the ever present tobacco juice.

Helper's party arrived at San Juan del Norte, or Graystown, April 1, 1854. From here, it was relatively simple to take the steamer, "Star of the West," which cruised to New York City in eight days.[14]

Immediately after arriving in the East, Helper set out for North Carolina, where he owned an interest in the small farm left by his father. He settled in the near-by town of Salisbury and began

to write *The Land of Gold, Reality Versus Fiction,* which gave
expression to his frustration from the unfruitful California years.
In some ways it was a vilification, as the worst features of California
were overplayed; nevertheless, when Helper's friends saw his
first draft, they insisted the work should be published for the
public's benefit. Helper agreed and added chapters on the Nicaraguan route before seeking a publisher.[15]

The purpose of *The Land of Gold* was not merely to provide an
interesting travelogue but to reveal the difficulties confronting a
California emigré—his slight chance of acquiring wealth, the personal discomforts to be endured, and the moral dangers to be
encountered. Moreover, it sought to evaluate the new state's contribution to national life. In three years in California Helper
felt that he had become "too thoroughly conversant with its rotten-
ness and its corruption, its squalor and its misery, its crime and its
shame, its gold and its dross." Not surprisingly, he entitled his first
chapter "California Unveiled."

Helper believed that propagandists aroused false dreams of "El
Dorado" in the minds of thousands of Americans and lured them
west to "delude and destroy them." His personal observations convinced him that California's gold fields and arid hills were its
poverty, while its fine harbors and geographical location were the
true basis of its wealth. Its greatest hope lay in the construction of a
transcontinental railroad which would enable the United States to
tap the commerce of the Orient. Without this railroad, Helper felt,
the state would become the poorest in the Union.

To prove this assertion, he launched into the first of the statistical
arguments used throughout his career. Without revealing his
sources, he calculated that until January, 1855, the state had produced $245,000,000 in gold. If adequate allowance were made for
the transportation and labor of its approximately 215,000 men, the
state was laboring under a deficit of $98,230,000. This did not take
into consideration the purchase price of the area nor the phenom-
enal losses incurred by acts of God in the state. To Helper this was
evidence that, economically, the "golden state" was destitute. He
did not realize that his statistics were paper figures and that the cost

of labor should be considered profit rather than loss; neither did he concede that some individuals had made great fortunes in the state.

Helper's experiences convinced him that obtaining gold required "a greater sacrifice of moral and physical wealth than a single exchange of it afterwards can possibly restore." While the outlook was better for those pursuing agriculture or the mechanical arts, he was still pessimistic. The fertile California valleys were so few in number that they could be compared to oases in a desert, and probably manufacturing would never flourish as long as much of the machinery, raw materials and fuel had to be imported.

In the light of his later works, Helper's attitude toward Indians and slavery were significant. Over much of California he encountered the Digger Indians, a group which, rumor held, John A. Sutter had used in building his famous fort. Apparently the most filthy and vermin-infested of peoples, these Indians seemed to pollute the cities and could be seen everywhere standing around kitchen and slaughter-house doors, begging for food. "Too indolent to work, too cowardly to fight," they will "melt away before the white man like snow before a spring sun," Helper wrote.

In *The Land of Gold* Helper did not contend that slavery was economically unprofitable for the white man in simple, agricultural economies, as he was so forcefully to do in his later works. However, he did predict that slavery would become unprofitable in an advanced economy. In a state like Nicaragua, where the climate was oppressive for white laborers and the most primitive agriculture was only beginning to be systematically followed, he felt slavery could serve a useful purpose. "Nothing but slave labor can ever subdue its forests or cultivate its untimbered lands," he wrote. "White men may live upon its soil with an umbrella in one hand and a fan in the other; but they can never unfold or develop its resources."

In a philosophy later developed more fully Helper foresaw the day when slavery would no longer be profitable in the United States. Then it was highly probable that "the descendants of Ham" would find themselves "toiling under the control of new masters, in the fertile wildernesses and savannas nearer the equator." Surely if Louisiana and Texas ever found it to their interest "to adopt the white slavery system of the North," Mexico, Central America, and the countries farther south would become the "outlets and receptacles of the discarded American Negroes".

Helper noted the few permanent Negro residents of California and believed those present, like free Negroes in New York and Massachusetts, were primarily slaves to the community. Like their Northern cousins, they lived in filth and degradation in the worst areas of the towns. The small number of Southern Negroes in California refused to claim their right to freedom because of their attachment to their masters. Helper knew personally of Southern Negroes, enticed away by "meddling abolitionists," who became so disgusted with a valueless freedom that they returned.

The applicability of slave labor was becoming a theme of discussion in Southern California. Helper believed that, if the legislature were to divide the state, Southern California would legalize slavery under laws similar to those of Virginia and Louisiana.[16]

When later indicted for his compromising attitude toward slavery in *The Land of Gold,* Helper replied that in the original draft he had contended talent and capital are necessary for city life, and since the Negro had neither, slavery should be discontinued in cities. Moreover, he had been so impressed with the accomplishments of free society in the North that an antislavery spirit crept into the entire work. Still, he conceded, "I was not yet wholly emancipated from my original pro-slavery predilections and proclivities," since he would have allowed slavery to exist, for a time at least, in the rural areas.

His antislavery views failed to reach print, Helper later explained, because *The Land of Gold* was published by Charles Mortimer, a strong proslavery man, at the office of *The Southern Quarterly Review.* On reading the original draft, Mortimer condemned some of its views as those of "a deluded Abolitionist" and refused to have anything to do with their publication. Articles of agreement had already been signed, and Helper had paid him $400. He did not feel that he could afford to lose his investment and, with it, his chance for recognition and perhaps wealth. Therefore, he sacrificed his views to his burning ambition and relinquished all control of the manuscript to the publisher. Mortimer removed the antislavery sections but, in Helper's words, "kept the few which I had written in passive recognition of slavery in the country."

The finding of a publisher even under these conditions greatly encouraged Helper, and he returned to his family in Salisbury with new hopes for a literary career. Determined to write a major work which once and for all would earn him the reputation he felt he deserved, he conceived the idea of comparing statistically the achievements of free and slave societies to demonstrate the blight of slavery. Residence in the North undoubtedly convinced him that his great opportunity lay in such a work. Even before leaving Baltimore, he obtained some of the discarded sections of *The Land of Gold* and began to plan *The Impending Crisis*. "I at once assumed toward slavery an attitude of more direct and determined hostility," he recalled. "I had ceased to be the submissive victim of an unmitigated despotism."

Helper's racist views also served as a motivation for *The Impending Crisis*. Like many of the poorer whites of his native region, he loathed the Negro, as his later works indicate, and wished to see slavery destroyed, not only to improve the economic lot of the small farmer but also to remove the Negro from American life. With his limited formal education and contacts, it was highly presumptuous of Helper to attempt to speak for a large segment of American society. His tremendous ego, his burning ambition, and his limited outlook contributed to the assumption of this role. Again he was realist enough, however, to conceal some of his basic concepts in an effort to find a publisher and an audience. In this case, to appeal to the antislavery element, he rigorously suppressed the racist views which were a major feature of *The Land of Gold* and all of his postwar works.

After the experience with his first work, Helper realized that there was no press in the South which would publish any work that did not treat slavery with the most "positive security and aggrandizement." As he read the *Southern Literary Messenger's* review of *The Land of Gold,* he knew that such kind words from a Southern journal would not greet *The Impending Crisis.* The *Messenger* considered his views of San Francisco to be "freshly and vividly drawn" and agreed with him that gold-producing countries do not "rise in the scale of moral and political greatness."[17]

Regardless of what the Southern press might say, Helper continued his work on *The Impending Crisis.* A few days before John C. Frémont's nomination for the presidency in June, 1856, he sold his interest in the farm inherited from his father for $280 and headed north to seek a publisher. In Baltimore he stopped long enough to aid in the formation of one of the South's first Republican associations, but shortly afterward its activities were ended by the intrusion of what Helper described as "a pro-slavery, pro-negro mob."

In Baltimore and New York City Helper had difficulty finding a publisher. Maryland publishers considered his work incendiary and protested that state law would prohibit publication. In New York no regular publisher would take it, even as a gift. After consultation with his partners, the abolitionist, James Harper, announced that the publication of the work would cost his company twenty per cent of its business. An appeal to the editor of the *National Anti-Slavery Standard* was equally unrewarding. For seven or eight months Helper went from publisher to publisher without success. At last he accepted the offer of A. B. Burdick, a book agent, to issue the work, with Helper securing him against any loss, and in June, 1857, the first edition was available at one dollar a copy. Few realized at the time that a literary weapon of the first magnitude had emerged.[18]

*Chapter Two*

# The Impending Crisis

PUBLICATION OF *The Impending Crisis* marked something of a climax in the thought and reaction of the Southern mind toward slavery. Before 1830 the strongest antislavery sentiment in the nation had been found below the Mason-Dixon Line, apparently reaching a crest in the Virginia debates of the early 1830's. Afterward, a procession of Southern writers forged "the dialectic weapons" to defend slavery. The Northern counterpart of this movement was the abolitionist crusade, which served as a constant stimulus to those who sought to save the South through conformity.[1]

Absolute conformity was never achieved, although the dissenters retained their right to criticism only by suffering the punishment meted out for violation of a Southern taboo. From Washington, D.C., in the 1840's Daniel Reaves Goodlow, a native of Louisburg, North Carolina, delivered a forceful attack on slavery as an economic institution. He contended that capital invested in slaves was unproductive and its returns were an appropriation of the wages of the Negroes. Abolition would free capital to develop commerce and industry in the South, and towns and cities would arise.[2]

Also in the 1840's the west Virginian, Henry Ruffner, contrasted the economic conditions of the North and South and urged Southerners to rebel. Angelina Grimké of South Carolina marshaled arguments against slavery effectively enough to write her way into Northern exile. Cassius M. Clay, through the columns of the Lexington *True American,* published the works of Goodlow and other antislavery writers and sought to organize the nonslaveholding whites against the slaveholders. In his contention that slaveholders were the natural enemy of yeomen and poor whites, he was the forerunner of Helper.[3]

The existence of Goodlow, Ruffner and Clay, to say nothing of the more numerous Southerners who supported the American Colonization Society, indicates that the South's convictions on slavery were not as solid as they have been portrayed and raises the question as to the number of conformists who suppressed their moderate antislavery beliefs. One cannot avoid the conclusion, however, that, as individuals, their influence was limited. Yet Helper, following in their tradition and drawing on their ideas, produced an antislavery work the political and social significance of which was exceeded by no ante bellum publication with the possible exception of *Uncle Tom's Cabin*.

Through the years historians have been aware of the significance of *The Impending Crisis* while differing as to its reliability and effect on events. James Ford Rhodes accepted its statistically supported reasoning and held that, if the Southern poor whites had been able to read it, slavery would have been doomed. Because of the influence of *The Impending Crisis,* Clement Eaton termed Helper "the most noted antislavery man that the old South produced." While noting Helper's selection of many of his statistics and an oversimplification in his conclusions, Avery Craven conceded that in *The Impending Crisis* he "struck a heavy blow in a vulnerable spot at a crucial time." As another critic expressed it, the book "dealt with the question of the hour; its style was as keen as a scalpel and as smashing as a sledge-hammer." What else could be expected of "the most caustic attack upon slavery ever written by a Southerner"?[4]

The historian of the North Carolina secession movement believed that *The Impending Crisis* "omitted no argument, no expression, and no condemnation which in any way tended to belittle slavery

and slave-holders." Nowhere else could he find as apt a description
of the economic dependence of the South on the North. No wonder
the work caused profound disturbances in North Carolina immediately before the war.[5]

A major historian of the American Negro found that only *Uncle
Tom's Cabin* exceeded *The Impending Crisis* in "sensational interest." This was true because Helper, a "son of the South" and
representative of the Southern whites of limited means, dared expose the Southern economic system.[6] Two modern students of race
relations stated that Helper "burned the truth into the minds of the
southern people with the red-hot iron of his statistics, and made the
whole South writhe under his withering sarcasm."[7] Some agree that
this pronouncement was an overstatement, yet Allen Nevins wrote
that, had the depression of 1857 proved more severe in the South,
Helper's ideas would have spread to the "suffering yeomanry" and
at least a portion of his program would have received implementation.[8]

What was the nature of *The Impending Crisis* that enabled it
to create such an impression? It was both an economic comparison
of Northern and Southern society (based on fifty-eight tables and
numerous spot checks on life in sixteen Northern and Western
states with that in thirteen Southern ones) and a militant abolitionist document demanding uncompensated emancipation. In order
that the reader might understand the delight and horror with
which the work was received, *The Impending Crisis* will here be
closely and uncritically examined, after which the work's reception
and its validity will be considered.

The preface to *The Impending Crisis* foreshadowed its later development. Among others, it was dedicated to "THE NON-
SLAVEHOLDING WHITES OF THE SOUTH." As if to pre-
pare his readers for the attack he was to launch, Helper proclaimed
that no narrow political or economic doctrines or early prejudices
influenced his writing, but only "the long-settled convictions" of his
heart. He did not desire to cast "opprobrium" upon the slaveholders
nor to display sympathy for the blacks, but he was concerned with
the economic aspects of slavery as they related to the whites. The

religious and humanitarian implication of slavery, he held, had been well treated by Northern novelists. He was content to let Yankee housewives give the fiction of slavery; he would give the facts. In so doing, he hoped to elevate the South to a powerful position among the enlightened regions of the world.[9]

Above all, *The Impending Crisis* is a statistical study of the economic effects of slavery. Therefore, in chapter one Helper plunged into an economic comparison of the free and slave states. To initiate his parade of statistics, he contrasted New York and Virginia in 1790 and 1850. In that sixty-year period the population of the Northern state had increased almost ten-fold, while Virginia's had doubled. Between 1791 and 1852 Virginia's exports had increased fifty per cent and New York's had risen forty-three-fold. In both cases Virginia had previously excelled New York (by approximately one hundred and fifty per cent). The Southern cause was even darker when imports were considered. From a basis of approximate equality in 1790, New York in 1853 had attained imports valued at $178,270,999 contrasted with Virginia's $399,000. At the same time New York's real and personal property came to be three times that of Virginia (slaves excluded), and the value of her farms and farm machiney was twice as great as that of "the Old Dominion."[10]

To demonstrate that this condition was not limited to one Southern state, Helper compared Massachusetts and North Carolina in the same period. He demonstrated that the Southern state had slipped from an excess of 20,000 population to a position 135,000 less than her Northern neighbor (this included North Carolina's 288,548 slaves). During the period Boston's imports and exports made her the nation's second commercial city, but Helper was ashamed to mention those of Beaufort, North Carolina. In 1850 Massachusetts' manufacturing was over nine times that of North Carolina, and her personal property (exclusive of slaves) was twice as great.

The contrast of Pennsylvania and South Carolina was equally impressive. At one time Charleston imported fabrics for the Philadelphia trade, but now South Carolina was "sick and impoverished." According to Thomas Hart Benton (in his *Thirty Years' View*) in 1760, Charleston's imports amounted to $2,662,000, but in 1855 they were only $1,750,000. In 1854 Philadelphia's stood at over $21,000,000. Pennsylvania's returns from mining and manufacturing in 1850 were over twenty times those of South Carolina, and her farm properties were five times as valuable.

From swaddling clothes to marble tombstones, the South looked to the North for many of its goods and services. Helper believed that Southern society was ill, or it would not have become so dependent. Why should this be? In the author's opinion, it could be traced to one source, SLAVERY. It was then his duty to convince his readers that "the peculiar institution" forced the more industrious to migrate, prevented the bold and enterprising from coming into the South, and produced inertia in every phase of life.[11]

Since the South prided itself on its agriculture, Helper felt that it would have nothing of which "to boast" if he could demonstrate that the North was superior in this field. To prove his point, he contrasted the 1850 production in sixteen free and thirteen slave states of certain bushel-measure products (wheat, oats, Indian corn, potatoes, rye, barley, buckwheat, beans and peas, clover and grass seeds, flax seeds, garden products, and orchard products). He concluded that the Northern exceeded the Southern production by 17,423,152 bushels, to the value of $44,782,636. To those "who are not too perverse, or ignorant, to perceive naked truths," this should demonstrate the superiority of free labor, Helper wrote.

To make certain this end was accomplished, Helper proceeded to demonstrate to his own satisfaction that the Northern hay crop was worth much more than all of the tobacco, cotton, rice, hemp and hay produced in the slave states. He valued hay at $11.20 per ton, the price given by the Bureau of Agriculture, a figure less than half the current market return. Valuing cotton at $32.00 per bale, tobacco at ten cents a pound, rough rice at four cents a pound, sugar cane at seven cents a pound, and hemp at $112 a ton, he calculated that the Northern hay crop exceeded the Southern products by three and one-half millions of dollars. He hoped that the "lords of the lash" would learn from this report "the utter inefficiency and despicable imbecility of slavery."

A South Carolinian reported that many cotton planters were realizing less than one per cent from their investments. As short crops occurred, slaves had to be sold. This was vivid evidence, Helper moralized, that slavery was an unprofitable institution which fed upon itself. "At one time children are sold to procure food for the parents, at another parents are sold to procure food for the children." What else could be expected from such an unproductive system?

A contrast of the returns from the principal pound-measure products (hay, hemp, hops, flax, maple sugar, tobacco, wool, butter and cheese, beeswax, honey, cotton, cane sugar, and rice) provided another exhibition of the superiority of free society. Statistics revealed that the free states, in 1850, had a superior production of 24,539,694,241 pounds, with an excess value of $59,199,108.[12]

Helper tabulated the value of Northern farms, farm implements and machinery, and live stock as approximately twice that of the slave states. "No figures of rhetoric can add emphasis or significance to these figures of arithmetic," he wrote; they prove "the great moral triumph of Liberty over Slavery." Could "the slavocracy" ever think of cotton again? He wondered if they should not, as an expiation for their evils, clothe themselves in sackcloth and, after reasonable contrition, follow the example of Judas Iscariot and hang themselves.

Helper was unable to find sufficient figures to compare gallon-measure products in the North and South, but he was so persistent in his determination to present his case that he estimated the free states exceed the slave states annually in the value of these products by fifty million dollars. Although he could obtain no figures for the lumber industry, the widespread use of Northern lumber products indicated Northern superiority in this field also. Here, as elsewhere, it was evident that in "the North everything is turned to advantage . . . while at the South everything is either neglected or mismanaged."[13]

On the evidence marshaled by the Southerner, James D. B. DeBow, in the census of 1850, Helper demonstrated that the value of all property in the free states was three times that of the slave states. Southern property was evaluated at $1,366,090,737 (exclusive of slaves), or only one-third that of the free states. Some Southerners realized that slavery was to blame for this condition. Virginia's Governor Henry A. Wise, for one, faulted a reliance on agriculture, a result of slavery, for the relative decline of Southern commerce. As early as January, 1832, Thomas Ritchie, editor of the Richmond *Enquirer,* warned that the percentage of Negroes in Virginia must be reduced if the state were to become a garden spot.

No one ultimately benefited from slavery, Helper held, if for no other reason than it depressed the value of Southern property. In 1850 the average value of Northern lands was $28.07 an acre, while the Southern average was $5.34. Helper believed that slavery alone had depressed the value of Southern lands $22.73 per acre. Should abolition take place, he felt every acre in the South would immediately increase in value by this amount. Therefore, the slaveholders owed the nonslaveholders $22.73 for each acre the nonslaveholders owned, or a total of $7,544,148,825. Only with the payment of this debt could the nonslaveholders forgive the many injustices under which they had been forced to live. Abolition was the simpler answer, however, since the slaveholders' lands would increase in value more than enough to compensate their loss in Negroes.[14]

Despite these economic actualities, slaveholders contended that slavery was their exclusive concern. Helper denied this claim, contending that slavery was as vicious as any disease and equally to be condemned. Slaveholders were probably "less amenable to the moral law" than thieves, since those who stole deprived no one of physical liberty nor fettered the mind. The thief rarely stole from more than one man in a hundred, but no one escaped the slaveholder. "Thieves practice deceit on the wise; slaveholders take advantage of the ignorant."

Yet, numerically, the slaveholders were an insignificant part of the population in 1857. The census indicated that in 1850 there were 347,525 slaveholders, but because of multiple entries, Helper believed that there were fewer than 200,000. He could not conceive the Southern masses forever tolerating domination by such a small despotism.[15]

The pernicious effects of slavery could be seen in scores of other areas, and Helper set out to reveal them. In 1850 the value of Northern manufactured products and the number of Northern workers were five times as great as the South's. In the mid-1850's over three times as many miles of canals and railroad were completed in the free states as were built in the South. In both bank capital (1855) and militia forces (1852) the free states exceeded the South by approximately two hundred per cent.

In 1855 the free state post offices and their returns were three times those of the South, although there were only about three hundred thousand dollars difference in the cost of transporting the mails. The free states, in 1850, had three-and-one-half times the number of public schools and teachers and over four times the number of pupils of the slave states. The same year there were 14,911 public libraries in the North, with approximately six times the number of volumes as in the 695 libraries in the slave states. In 1850 there were 704 newspapers in the South, with an annual circulation of 81,038,693, compared to 1,790 newspapers in the North, with four times the Southern distribution.

The year 1850 found the South with over twice as many native illiterate white adults as the free states. Considering foreign immigrants, there were approximately ninety thousand more adult white illiterates in the South than in the North. In political power the North's superior numbers gave that section 144 seats in the House of Representatives in 1857, as compared with the South's 90, and in the popular votes for president in 1856, Northern states cast twice as many votes as the slave states. The value of Northern church buildings in 1850 was over three times that of the South. Northern ingenuity kept pace with physical progress, and in 1856 her citizens obtained seven times the number of patents granted Southerners.

Statistics indicated that the free states were as far advanced in philanthropy as in material things. Northern contributions to the Bible and Tract Cause in 1856 were four times those of the slave states; contributions to the Missionary Cause in 1855–56 were almost five times that of the South and to the Colonization Cause, almost twice the Southern toll.

Certainly these statistics were overwhelming proof to Helper of the superiority of free labor. He felt that slavery, alone, was to blame for Southern inertia and that it could be shown statistically that climate was not responsible. In 1850 the ratio of deaths to the number living was 72.91 in the North and 71.82 in the slave states. Dr. Josiah Nott, the noted slavery apologist, admitted that, for a six-year period, the annual mortality rate for the blacks exceeded that of the whites. Furthermore, a study of the birthplace of Americans indicated that slavery excluded the most productive white labor. In 1850 there were approximately three times as many natives of the slave states in the free states as Northerners in the South. Professor B. S. Hedrick stated that over half his friends left North Carolina upon realizing "free and slave labor could not both exist and prosper in the same community." Because he did not conceal his opinions, he was dismissed as Professor of Analytical Chemistry and Agriculture at the University of North Carolina, "ignominiously subjected to the indignities of a mob, and then savagely driven beyond the borders of his native state."[16]

Not only would many be denied their civil rights, but equally distressing, Helper held, the South would never develop a great commercial city on the Eastern coast as long as slavery continued. Without such a city, where the funds, talents and energies of the people could gather, the South could never develop her resources. By the tabulation of a series of replies from city officials, Helper calculated that the population of nine leading Northern cities was 2,083,000, with an average wealth per capita of $754, while that of nine Southern cities (including Baltimore and St. Louis) was only 787,000, with an average per capita wealth of $477.[17] Under these conditions it was understandable why the citizen of the slave states was dependent on the North for manufactured products and transportation. The rural nature of the South contributed to a grinding poverty for the nonslaveholders, Helper believed. Wages were abominably low, being about half those in the free states. Many Southerners never owned five dollars in cash and died without knowledge of the invention of the alphabet; they looked for super-natural signs and gave themselves up to sensuality and intemper-ance.

Such a society could not support a Southern literature. Truly, compared with the North, Helper found that the "South has no literature." Though she had some talented authors, she lagged in publication and purchase of written works. Experience showed, Helper believed, that the intellectual activity "which expresses itself in books, is measurable by the mechanical activities engaged in their manufacture." In 1850 the free states had two-and-one-half times the number of periodicals with almost four times the circula-tion of those in the slave states. In rural areas there were not half a dozen journals equal to the Northern country press. Three-quarters of the publishing houses of the United States were in New York, Philadelphia, Baltimore, and Boston, and nine-tenths were in the free states. Traditionally, the Southern school child had read North-ern texts, and even *DeBow's Review* was printed in New York City.

Helper contended that slavery paralyzed Southern talent. The "oligarchs gabble" about a Southern literature, he noted, but they do not mean "a healthy, manly, normal utterance of unfettered minds without which there can be no proper literature; but an emasculated substitute therefore from which the element of free-dom is eliminated." This opinion was borne out by the Duyckinck *Cyclopedia of American Literature,* which listed 569 American authors, 403 of whom were Northern and 87 Southern-born. Of the Southern writers listed, none compared favorably with Harriet Beecher Stowe, Henry Wadsworth Longfellow, George Bancroft or John Greenleaf Whittier. Helper felt that Edgar Allan Poe ranked below first class in a narrow field, and although William Gilmore Simms had a literary reputation, he did not compare favorably with James Fenimore Cooper. Only when the South had a free, prosperous people, educated in schools and true "colleges" comparable to those of the North, could she produce great literature, Helper believed. "Where free thought is treason, the masses will not long take the trouble of thinking at all."[18]

In *The Impending Crisis,* Helper hoped to forge a literary weapon which would lead the Southern white masses to overthrow slavery and establish freedom in which both intellectual and physical progress would take place. His statistics were not the musings of an intellectual, but they were the working materials of a man who hoped to produce dramatic action. Therefore, *The Impending Crisis* was an abolitionist document which, while reflecting an acquaintanceship with Northern abolitionist literature, was itself unique. A sense of personal and class injury breathed throughout its pages, which was in keeping with the style of Southern attacks on abolitionism.[19]

Essentially Helper was seeking to stimulate the small farmers and laborers of the South to conduct the type of revolt which the Tillmans, Bleases, and Longs led in later generations. To attain this objective he analyzed Southern society and attributed the South's backwardness to the aristocracy's oligarchical rule, the chief aim of which was to maintain slavery and a stratified society. Helper felt that he had "only to speak out boldly," and the people would rise in indignation. He did not perceive that the average Southerner who read his book would consider it a villification of Southern society. He was gambling that his class appeal, the most dangerous in a partially stratified society, would arouse the masses to action. If his arguments failed, some factor other than a lack of zeal in their presentation would be responsible.[20]

Since Helper had no doubt that free labor was "more respectable, profitable, and productive" than slave labor, he was confronted with the question of why slavery continued to exist. His answer was that it was a crime perpetrated on the masses by the oligarchy. They had succeeded in making the nonslaveholders slaves themselves. All labor was held to be disrespectable, and the white worker was treated "as if he was a loathsome beast, and shunned with the utmost disdain." Politically, the masses were kept in a state of impotence; for all practical purposes they were disfranchised, although they were allowed a "shallow and circumscribed participation in the political movements that usher slaveholders into office." Yet the aristocracy had the audacity to maintain that slavery was the bulwark of freedom and to attribute all of America's achievements to it. At the same time they kept an "iron curtain" around the Southern people. Nothing was done to combat "unparalleled illiteracy" and misinformation about Southern achievements and those of other sections of the United States. All who propagated the truth and cast any doubts on the "gospel of slavery" were forced to become either "heroes, martyrs, or exiles."[21]

The Southern people had to be told that, though they had given the slaveholders all the offices, the masses had not received the benefits of legislation. While the plain people fought the battles of the South, the aristocrats had lolled on their piazzas or played "the tory" and endeavored "to filch" from the people their "birthright of freedom." The oligarchy had absorbed the wealth of their communities for selfish purposes. They sent their children to Northern schools or imported Yankee teachers for their own families while refusing the people the privilege of common schools. They "have scorned to patronize our mechanics and industrial enterprises," Helper wrote, and have passed to the North for every "article of apparel, utility, and adornment."

Annually the South poured $120,000,000 into Northern coffers, but it was only after the North ridded herself of slavery that she began to absorb Southern wealth. In the stratified, slavery South there was no hope for progress. The slaves themselves were cowards; the slaveholders were tyrants; and the slavehirers were "lick-spittles." No apologist for the South could explain away the fact that in the free states "wealth, intelligence, power, progress, and prosperity are the prominent characteristics," Helper wrote, while in the slave states "poverty, ignorance, embecility, inertia, and extravagance are the distinguishing features." For one to defend slavery, Helper charged, he must be either "a fool, a knave, or a madman."[22]

Ignorance explained the acceptance of the institution by the majority of Southern people. Slavery made the masses poor, and poverty produced ignorance. Therefore, "nothing short of the complete abolition of slavery can save the South from falling into the vortex of utter ruin," Helper concluded. Some Northerners thought that, by checking the expansion of slavery, they were doing their share, but Helper believed that they were remiss "in their *National* duties" by being only freesoilers; he held no man could be a true patriot unless he was an abolitionist. For too long the oligarchs had molded the "passions and prejudices" of the Southern people and induced them to act in direct opposition to their interests. They had taught the masses to hate the abolitionists, their "best and only true friends."[23]

It was the "first and most sacred duty" of every informed Southerner to become an unqualified abolitionist. A sense of obligation to the South, if nothing else, would lead him to do so, just as a feeling for the Negro would induce him to be a colonizationist. He would no more desire to force Negro presence on white society than he would desire to retain slavery. "It is against slavery on the whole, and against slaveholders as a body, that we wage an exterminating war," Helper wrote. As the light of truth spread, Southerners would join the crusade. Every man must determine whether he would be slave or free. Nonslaveholders who did not oppose the oligarchy were enforcing compliance with its demands. "You must either be for us or against us," Helper stated, but the decision to oppose the oligarchs must be followed by action; the masses must not reserve their strength until they became powerless.

The oligarchy could determine whether the masses were "to have justice peaceably or by violence," but the masses would have it one way or the other. "Do you aspire to become the victims of white nonslaveholding vengeance by day, and of barbarous massacre by the negroes at night?" Helper demanded. Would the oligarchy bring upon their wives and children a fate too horrible to consider? Would the Massacre of St. Bartholomew's Day be replaced by the story of the South as an example of atrocity and carnage? The Southern aristocracy had the answer in its actions. The Southern masses, if given justice, would not pluck a hair from an aristocratic head, but if they continued to be abused, they certainly might rise against their oppressors. Undoubtedly they would be joined by the black slaves, also the cruel victims of the system. Although, in many cases, the slaves received better pay than did the whites, slavery was an even more immediate threat to the Negro's life. In fact, it was "a perpetual license to murder." Slave lives were often taken with impunity and without punishment. Unlike the white slaves, the black peons could not raise their voices in testimony against the pernicious institution, but they could fight should the occasion present itself. "In nine cases out of ten," Helper observed, they would be "happy to cut their masters' throats."[24]

Helper fervently hoped that abolition could come without bloodshed and felt it could, if the oligarchy granted freedom of speech and fair elections. He incorporated his ideas in a specific eleven-point program:

1. The non-slaveholding whites must be organized for independent political action.
2. They must then exclude the slaveholders from political power. Never should there be another vote "to the Trafficker in Human Flesh."
3. The non-slaveholders must cease all co-operation and fellowship with slaveholders in every phase of society—politics, religion, etc.
4. All patronage of slaveholders and slaveholding establishments such as slaveholding merchants, lawyers, doctors, hotels, must cease, as well as receiving and granting audiences to slaveholders.
5. No recognition must be granted to pro-slavery men except as "Ruffians, outlaws, and Criminals."
6. All subscriptions to pro-slavery newspapers must be abruptly cancelled.
7. The greatest possible encouragement must be given to "Free White Labor."
8. All employment of slaves by non-slaveholders must cease.
9. "Immediate Death to slavery," or if this is impossible, there must be an "unqualified Proscription of its Advocates" during the period of its existence.
10. A tax of $60 should be levied on every slaveholder for each

slave that is in his possession or that he holds between the present time and July 4, 1863. The returns from this tax should be used to transport the "Blacks" to Liberia or to colonize them in Central or South America or in some "Comfortable Settlement" in the United States.

11. An additional tax of $40 per year should be levied on every owner for each slave he holds after July 4, 1863. The returns from this fund should be given to the Negroes held in slavery or their next of kin to be used as they see fit. (This should be raised to $100 per year if complete abolition has not taken place by 1869. If this does not end the institution in one to two years, the tax should be placed so high as to kill it before July 4, 1876.)[25]

While Helper conceived of abolition taking place on the state level, he hoped that within three years a general convention of nonslaveholders from all the states would convene and present "a digested scheme for the reclamation of . . . [the] ancient rights and prerogatives" of the masses. If such a program should be presented, Helper believed, slavery would be destroyed overnight. Then the Southern masses and the American people would be free of the "heart-sickening arrogance and bribery" which had given the Southern oligarchy control of the presidency two-thirds of the time and had prevented the re-election of any Northern freeman. The ill-bred Southern officials, whose delight was in duels and homicide, would be removed from Congress forever.

Upon the removal of slavery, Helper contended, it would take the South a quarter of a century to catch up with the North economically. Therefore, it was imperative that abolition take place at once. As instruments to achieve this goal, the older political parties had proved inadequate. The Democratic Party had been captured by the slave power, and the average Democrat in Congress had become noted for his ignorance and squalidity, while "his senseless enthusiasm" was disgusting. The Whigs deserved the defeat they had received because of their concession to the slave power. In the election of 1856 almost all states enjoying the benefits of free soil, labor, speech, presses and schools voted for Frémont,

Helper asserted. With one exception, all the states which had grown accustomed "to hating everything with the prefix Free" voted for James Buchanan. With few exceptions, the informed Southern non-slaveholders and the more reputable slaveholders voted for Millard Fillmore. If the Democrats would not repudiate their proslavery heresies, Helper believed their party was doomed. In supporting the Republicans, Helper was not loyal to the party for the party's sake, but to the group which could bring abolition most quickly.

Some had suggested that compensated emancipation was the answer, but Helper opposed it. Like Charles James Faulkner in the Virginia debates, he did not feel that the masses should be taxed for property removed because it was a menace to society. Yet he held the freedman should receive sixty dollars in cash. For 237 years they had been held in bondage in America, and from their hands and loins "the human-mongers of the South" had become "wealthy, corrupt, and tyrannical." Heaven would justify them in claiming one-half of the property of their masters, but Helper asked only twenty-six cents a year for their services.

It frequently had been held that a weaker race might be enslaved by a stronger one. Although Helper did not accept a belief in the unity of races, he conceded that all men were descended from Adam and Eve and were entitled to liberty. By emancipation of the slaves not only the Negroes but the white masses of the South would receive justice. To all classes slavery was a curse. Since abolitionism had worked in fourteen-fifteenths of the areas where it had been tried, it would work in America also. The entire world moved toward freedom, Helper wrote; the oligarchy might as well "attempt to stay the flux and reflux of the tides, as to attempt to stay the progress of Freedom in the South." It was merely a question of time.

The oligarchy threatened secession if abolitionists did not cease their crusade. This threat could never stay the march of freedom. If "treasonable attempts" should take the South out of the Union, Helper felt, "we will bring her back tomorrow," this time with aristocrats in their rightful place.

In espousing abolitionism Helper contended that Southerners

were living up to a great tradition. Throughout history nearly all of the South's "great sons" had been the friends of universal freedom. At the time of the Revolution and the formation of the Constitution they seemed to have a tacit understanding that the states would abolish slavery. Although Virginia refused to comply, some of the finest abolitionist expressions ever uttered were put forth by sons of the "Old Dominion" in the debate of 1831–32. At that time Charles James Faulkner noted that no "avowed advocate" of slavery had arisen to defend it as an institution. He compared the Virginia of his day with colonial Virginia, noted her declining position in relation to the Northern states, and ascribed the poverty and disunion of the Southern states to slavery.

Another member of the Virginia convention, Helper noted, described the South as being composed " 'of a sparse population of freemen, deserted habitations, and fields without culture!' " It seemed to him that even the wolf returned " 'to howl over the desolations of slavery.' " William M. Rives of Campbell County, said everyone in the house had observed the " 'curse and deteriorating consequence' " of slavery. Robert D. Powell could scarcely persuade himself that there was a member of the house who would not admit that the removal of slavery " 'if practicable, is a consummation most devoutly to be wished.' "

What paralyzed action by the Virginia Legislature in 1832? If the accounts Helper heard were true, one of the "blackest schemes of bribery and corruption" ever perpetrated took place. Virginia's Negro population was suddenly decreased by forcible emigration. "A large gang was driven farther South, sold, and the proceeds divided among certain renegades and traitors," who, like Judas, "had agreed to serve the devil for a price."

The Virginia statesmen, in this instance, betrayed the interest of their people and the heritage of the "Founding Fathers," as a golden opportunity was lost. Helper believed that, in the 1850's, there was scarcely a slaveholder between the Potomac and the Mississippi who would not "burn to pounce" upon the "Founders of the Republic." Certainly Washington would be mobbed and Jefferson dismissed, as would a college professor, should he attempt to teach. To demonstrate the antislavery opinions of the "Fathers," he cited numerous expressions of their opinions.[26]

Washington was quoted as saying he hoped never to obtain another slave and ultimately to see abolition by law. He described an abolition plan of Marquis de Lafayette's as a laudable enterprise and an example of the Frenchman's benevolence.[27] Helper cited the *Notes On Virginia* as proof of Jefferson's detestation of the institution. It led to the exercise " 'of the most boisterous passions' " and resulted in a contest of despotism versus submission. It led to inertia, since in warm climates no one would labor if he could have someone else do it for him. Well might Jefferson have trembled for the United States when he reflected that God was just.[28]

Madison held in the Constitutional Convention that where slavery exists, "the Republican theory becomes still more fallacious." Monroe in the Virginia ratifying convention held that slavery had preyed "on the vitals of the Union" and had harmed all states where it had existed. Patrick Henry found it surprising that any Christian should defend slavery and that slavery should consciously be introduced in any country in an enlightened age. John Randolph gave his slaves the freedom to which his conscience told him they were entitled.

Helper cited other Southerners who joined the chorus of protest. Addressing the Kentucky Colonization Society in 1829, Henry Clay contended that nowhere in the farming sections of the United States would slaves be used generally, if the owners were not tempted " 'to raise slaves by the high price of the Southern market.' " Francis P. Blair charged, before the Maryland Legislature in 1856, that slavery resulted in slaveholders monopolizing the soil and state governments. Lieutenant Matthew Fontaine Maury stated that, unless something could be done with the excess slave population, there would be a " 'death struggle for the mastery' " between the races.[29]

With such testimony from their own people, Helper felt that the Southern masses should support the Republican Party as the tool of abolitionism and hold it strictly accountable for that mission.

Helper found that Northern testimony for freedom was equally eloquent. The best was the 1,300,000 votes given Frémont in the presidential election of 1856, achieved only by the pleas of countless human voices and the strokes of numerous pens. Among these was the pen of John Jay. In 1819 Jay stated that slavery should not be allowed to expand and should be abolished where it existed. There was no question in his mind as to the authority of Congress to prohibit the importation of slaves into the states. Helper found the *Diary of John Quincy Adams* to breathe abolitionism. The former President held that slavery tainted everything with which it came in contact by destroying human reason and Christian ethics. Daniel Webster thought the moral and political evil of slavery to be unsanctioned by the thesis that the Negro was the weaker race. Christian conduct would require protection of the weak.[30]

Spokesmen of other nations were cited by Helper as being gifted contenders for freedom. In England the prevalence of a doctrine of natural law made slavery intellectually indefensible. John Locke asserted that every man had a property in his own person. Dr. Samuel Johnson held that no one, by nature, was the property of another and that only by a forfeiture of natural rights could one be enslaved. Sir William Blackstone contended that society's main purpose was to protect the individual in the enjoyment of his absolute rights of nature; hence it must be the primary purpose of human laws to protect those rights. Sir Edward Coke asserted that an act of Parliament could be overridden by the rights of nature.

The Irishman William Burke held slavery to be so degrading and improper that it should not be allowed to exist. In France Charles Montesquieu stated that slavery was contrary to the fundamental principles of society. Since the slave was not a member of society, what civil law would govern him? Jean Jacques Rousseau asserted that the terms " 'slavery' " and " 'right' " were contradictory. Lafayette said that he would never have drawn his sword to aid America if he had conceived that he was founding a slave land. The Dutch jurist Hugo Grotius proclaimed that to steal a man is the highest form of theft, and Martin Luther held that unjust violence could not rightly commend obedience.

Helper also invoked the voice of the ancients. Cicero believed the law of all nations prohibited one man pursuing his advantage at the expense of another. Socrates contended that slavery was systematized outrage and robbery. Aristotle said that all men were alike, and Plato asserted that slavery was a system of complete injustice.

In his citation of authority Helper next turned to the churches and Holy Writ. Albert Barnes, a Presbyterian minister of Philadelphia, said that slavery was against the spirit of the natural law and the New Testament. The General Assembly of his church condemned the institution as early as 1818. Episcopal Bishop Clement Moore Butler declared that slavery was injustice unjustified by the consideration of polity. He particularly condemned the spiritual ignorance in which many slaves were kept. A former South Carolina slaveholder turned Baptist minister, the Reverend William H. Brisbane, taught that, when St. Paul spoke of the law being made for man-stealers, he was speaking of slaveholders. The Reverend Francis Weyland asserted that slavery should be destroyed, since it was founded on the belief that the Negro is a brute with a separate creation from the rest of mankind.

Helper quoted John Wesley, the founder of Methodism, as saying that American slavery was the vilest form ever to exist. Methodist discipline, as amended in 1784, provided that every owner of slaves in the society must emancipate his holdings within twelve months. Those who refused to comply were not to be admitted to Holy Communion. Among Roman Catholics, Pope Leo X held not only Christianity but nature itself cries against slavery. In Helper's eyes, Gregory XVI "immortalized himself" by urging all Christians to subject no man to slavery.

The Bible, Helper held, was the only complete antislavery textbook. The slavery practiced "by those venerable old fogies, Abraham, Isaac, and Jacob, was one of the monstrous inventions of Satan that God 'winked at.' " To assert that man, created in the image of God, was authorized to hold slaves is to question the justice and goodness of God. There were numerous passages in both the Old and New Testaments which, Helper believed, advocated freedom. In the Old Testament were found: "Let the oppressed go free." "The wages of him that is hired shall not abide with thee all night until the morning." "Proclaim liberty throughout all the land, unto all the inhabitants thereof." "He that stealeth a man, and selleth him, if he be found in his hand, he shall surely be put to death."

In the New Testament were found: "Call no man master, neither be ye called masters." "All things whatsoever ye would that men should do to you, do ye even so to them." "Stand fast therefore in the liberty wherewith Christ hath made you free, and be not entangled again with the yoke of bondage." "The laborer is worthy of his hire." "Where the Spirit of the Lord is, there is liberty."[31]

Thus, Helper contended that the highest moral law and the most gifted minds in all ages and areas cried for abolition. To achieve it he advocated a compromise between Southern and Northern Republicans by which, in 1861, John C. Frémont, Cassius M. Clay, James G. Birney, or some other Southern nonslaveholder would be elevated to the Presidency. In 1865 he should be succeeded by William H. Seward, Charles Sumner, John McLean or some other Northern Republican. If in the process of their assertion of political power the Southern masses were confronted by forces raised by the oligarchs, "the first battle between freedom and slavery will be fought at home," and there could be no doubt of its ultimate outcome. God, Himself, would defend the right.[32]

*The Impending Crisis* was unique in ante bellum Southern literature. As Helper presented Southern society, the presence of slavery produced the caste system on which was based the exploitation of the masses by the favored few. With him the "popularization of the poor-white theory" received a mighty stimulus, apparently backed by undeniable statistics.[33]

The later myth of the poor whites found classic expression in the work of a French visitor. To him the masses of the ante bellum Southern whites were the *plebs romana* who, while supposedly citizens, found their only privileges to be those exercised in "blind subserviency to the great slaveholders," the country's real masters. Without slavery, the "poor whites" could possibly have developed into sturdy yeomen and small proprietors, but they were doomed to idleness by slavery.[34] In somewhat different phraseology, this was Helper's contention: slavery was not merely unprofitable, but it was "The Heart of A Class Problem." Firmly convinced that their society insured stability, that ultimately it would be emulated all over the world, the leaders of the South closed their eyes to the weaknesses of their economic system. In viewing the economic status of the nonslaveholder, they either pointed out the opportunity for him to become a planter or appealed to his keenly sensitive race pride.[35]

Helper was a Southern yeoman, and his prejudices were those of his class,[36] but the importance of *The Impending Crisis* was in no small measure due to the vibrancy with which he subdued his race consciousness and pursued his central theme. Instead of trying to counteract the Southern rationale, he overwhelmed it with statistics. But his figures were of significance only as they constituted arguments on which to base his social philosophy. Therefore, an overemphasis on the inaccuracy of Helper's reasoning and the illogical nature of some of his statistical comparisons misses the main import of the volume. Helper's assertions were all-encompassing. Every phase of Southern life was demonstrably inferior to that of the North, due to slavery and oligarchical rule.[37]

The zealous, aggressive nature of Helper's indictment of slavery and the slaveholders accounted for much of the fear the volume engendered and its failure to reach a wide Southern audience. The castigation of the Southern upper classes, undoubtedly, weakened his arguments in the minds of moderate men.

His concept of the struggle between the slaveholders and the non-slaveholders was the most fully developed of any writer, and well might it have frightened those who desired to preserve the status quo.[38] For one unfamiliar with the generally loyal character of the slave and the overriding race identity of the masses and aristocracy, Helper's plan of revolution could have induced panic. He had the misfortune, however, to address a severely limited lower-class Southern audience which was not sufficiently class conscious to appreciate his propaganda.

*Chapter Three*

# The Crisis Projected

HELPER'S PERSISTENCE AND his insight into the dynamics of American politics prevented *The Impending Crisis* from remaining a virtually unknown work. Settling in New York City in 1857 and devoting all his energy to the promotion of his work, he cultivated the leaders of the Republican Party and lost no opportunity to impress on them the political significance of *The Impending Crisis*. After two years of struggle his efforts culminated in unusual success.

The first and most significant New York Republican with whom Helper became friends was Horace Greeley, editor of the New York *Daily* and *Weekly Tribune*. Helper spared no effort to convince Greeley of his work's importance, realizing the critical influence of his publications. As a result, on June 26, 1857, the day *The Impending Crisis* was published, the *Daily Tribune* endorsed it, stated that it was destined to be a best-seller, and urged ambitious book agents everywhere to contact the publisher. Quoting the Boston *Daily Traveler,* it asserted that the work was the "most remarkable" antislavery publication since 1854 and marveled at the " 'immense number of facts' " Helper had gathered.

On July 13, 1857, the *Daily Tribune* gave a thorough and laudatory review of *The Impending Crisis*. Greeley felt that, in Helper, the Southern white masses had found "a spokesman—one who utters no stammering, hesitating nor uncertain sound, who possesses a perfect mastery of his mother tongue, who speaks as well from a long study and full knowledge of his subject as from profound convictions, and in whose vocabulary the words fear and doubt seem to have no place." He assured his readers that *The Impending Crisis* was anything but boring. Helper's "heavy artillery" of statistics was relieved "from anything like monotony or tedium by being interspersed with rolling volleys and dashing charges of argument and rhetoric." Of the slaveholders' character and criminality, Helper spoke "with scarcely less plainness and severity than Mr. Garrison himself." Since Greeley was not an abolitionist, he rejected Helper's plea for uncompensated emancipation; yet he rejoiced in the new work's publication. He felt that it indicated the seeds Jefferson had sown were taking root and that the South would have a literature of its own.[1]

Helper was gratified that other publications beyond his personal influence also gave appreciative reviews of his work. *Hunts Merchants' Magazine and Commercial Review* applauded Helper's sincerity and held that he had made an excellent statistical case. The *New Englander* said *The Impending Crisis* was "the most complete and effective" antislavery work. From its unquestionable facts flowed "a reliable 'sociological' study of slavery." The New York *Evening Post* agreed that it was "the most compact and irresistible array of facts and arguments to the impolity of slavery."[2]

The abolitionist publications were equally warm in their praise. *The National Anti-Slavery Standard* (August 22, 1857) felt *The Impending Crisis* in its demands for immediate abolition was the most remarkable work of the age. The Boston *Liberator* (July 29, 1859) wrote that Helper's arguments were unanswerable and "unimpeachable in testimony."[3]

Helper welcomed all recognition *The Impending Crisis* received, even the unfavorable Southern reviews. He was quite disappointed, however, that most of the Southern press ignored the work in 1857 and 1858. Only two newspapers, the Washington *Union* and the *Carolina Watchman,* ran reviews, because they had carried adver-

tisements before learning *The Impending Crisis* was an abolitionist work.

In its issue of June 23, 1857, Helper's hometown newspaper, the
*Carolina Watchman,* commented editorially that Helper was "a
ready and agreeable writer," and wished him success in his literary
endeavor. When the editor learned that Helper had written "an
abolition book," he proclaimed the author had been persuaded to
do so in order "to pick a fortune from the pockets of the fanatics."
Shortly afterward, the *Carolina Watchman* inaugurated a campaign to prove Helper a complete scoundrel. It began to spell his
name "Helfer" and resurrected the story of his youthful indiscretion. It found particularly deplorable the fact that he was an active
member of the Presbyterian Church at the time and castigated
him for concealing the nature of his forthcoming work from his
friends while obtaining their endorsement of bank loans. Helper
was distressed by this personal attack but was, undoubtedly, amused
that the *Carolina Watchman* conceded him to be a gentleman until
his abolitionist work became known.[4]

Helper was even more distressed when the strongly pro-Southern
Washington *Union* unleashed false charges against him. It contended that in 1850 he had been sent to New York by Michael
Brown to purchase books but, instead, changed his name and fled
to California. It also incorrectly held his attitudes toward slavery in
*The Land of Gold* and *The Impending Crisis* were diametrically
opposed. In the *Union's* opinion Helper's latest work had been
written to please the fanatics of New England and the New York
*Tribune.*[5]

Despite the early attention given *The Impending Crisis,* the
work did not receive the sustained consideration which Helper felt
it should. He envisioned a national circulation which would change
the nature of American life and earn him a just fame. As he studied
the sales reports, Helper increasingly turned to the Republican
Party as the one hope of a substantial subsidization. His friendship
with Greeley gave him entree to Republican leaders, and by late
1857 he had convinced John Bigelow, publisher of the New York

*Evening Post,* and William M. Chace, treasurer of the Republican Party, of the desirability to publish a cheap 100,000-copy edition of a compendium of *The Impending Crisis.* Before this plan could be executed, the depression of 1857 forced its postponement.[6] Despite this setback, Helper continued to meet with Republican leaders in New York and to make needed revisions for a new version of his great work. His persistence alone prevented interment of the enterprise.

*The Impending Crisis* played its first prominent role in politics before the compendium was issued. On March 20, 1858, Senator Henry Wilson (Massachusetts), in a Senate speech, cited Helper's work as an authoritative picture of Southern society. Then, on April 5, Senator Asa Biggs (North Carolina) replied with a personal attack on Helper, repeating with slight variations, the usual charges against him.

To exonerate himself, Helper sent Senator Wilson evidence proving that his theft had become known by self-confession and had been fully repaid. An affidavit by three citizens stated they had seen Daniel Helper's family Bible and all the names in it were spelled "Helper." This evidence convinced Wilson that Helper had been maligned by Biggs. The Massachusetts senator felt that it was significant that Michael Brown waited seven years before indicting him.[7]

The castigation by Senator Biggs angered Helper to the breaking point. He felt he was being persecuted because of his writings, not his conduct, and believed that the Salisbury district congressman, Burton Craige, was behind the attacks.

A week after Biggs's speech Helper went to Washington and sought Craige in the House chamber after adjournment. When Helper attempted to question him about his part in the affair, a fist fight occurred. Before grave damage could be done on either side, the men were separated, and Helper was arrested and placed under $1,000 bond, his bondsmen being the prominent Republican leaders, John P. Hale of New Hampshire and Montgomery Blair of Washington. (Blair had recently served as counsel for Dred Scott and later was to help obtain defense counsel for John Brown.

In 1861 he became Postmaster General in Lincoln's cabinet.)

Although the incident was understandable, it would have been better for Helper and his cause if it had never occurred. It was a typical reaction and in keeping with Helper's impulsive nature. When arrested, he was carrying a Colt revolver and a bowie knife, which gave Southerners additional grounds for feeling that he was a revolutionary planning violent action. A common Southern reaction was that of Representative Augustus B. Wright (Georgia), who believed Helper wished to provoke Craige to assault him so that he could kill the congressman.[8] Helper lost no Republican friends because of this incident, and many were amused at seeing a Southern congressman attacked by a Southern Republican.

Following the Washington episode, Chace, Greeley, Helper and others continued to plan a compendium of *The Impending Crisis*. Previously, A. B. Burdick, the publisher of the parent volume, had offered to publish a compendium of 100,000 copies at 18½, 18, 17½, 17 and 16⅔ cents each, wholesale, but every offer had been refused as too high. In September, 1858, as "a last and final offer" to several propositions made by Chace and Helper, he agreed to furnish 100,000 copies of a 200-page compendium for $16,000.[9]

In November, 1858, Helper persuaded the Rhode Island Republican Committee and a number of New York Republican leaders to join him in accepting Burdick's offer and to conduct a national appeal for contributions to make possible gratuitous distribution of *The Compendium of the Impending Crisis of the South*. Helper proposed that a number of prominent Republicans in New York, Boston, Providence, Philadelphia, Wilmington, Washington and St. Louis sign a circular explaining the project and calling for contributions. These men were to collect and forward gifts to the treasurer of the fund in New York City.

Helper sought the aid of Francis P. Blair, Sr., of Silver Springs, Maryland, "as the one most likely to have proper weight and influence in the latitude of the Potomac". However, the venerable leader would not agree to become a sponsor because he felt the work contained some objectionable features, even though Helper sent Daniel R. Goodlow to persuade him.[10] Francis P. Blair, Jr., did become one of the eight sponsors and served as its promoter in the St. Louis area.

By December 1, 1858, Helper completed the circular, outlining the compendium project, and it appeared in the New York *Daily Tribune* December 4. He was disappointed at not being able to announce that Governor E. D. Morgan of New York was treasurer of the fund. Earlier Morgan accepted this position but resigned, probably due to political pressure. Helper's choice for the job was the prominent New York attorney (and father-in-law of the future Secretary of State Hamilton Fish) William Henry Anthon, and in late November he wrote Anthon, "Mr. Greeley . . . concurs with me in the opinion that your name is an excellent one for the position." Fortunately, he accepted the appointment and worked closely with Helper for months.

Helper had labored on the circular presenting the compendium project, attaining an eloquence very seldom equaled. It held that "no course of argument so successfully controverting the practice of slavery in the United States . . . has equalled that of" *The Impending Crisis* and urged all who could to make contributions for the extensive circulation of *The Compendium*. Contributors of ten dollars or more were entitled to receive copies of the work equal to their donation (at sixteen cents a copy) and to have their names printed in the volume. The "prominent Republicans" who signed the circular, in addition to Anthon and Blair, Jr., were Samuel E. Sewell, Boston; William B. Thomas, Philadelphia; William McCaulley, Wilmington; Lewis Clephane, Washington; and Cassius M. Clay, Whitehall, Kentucky.[11]

The New York *Tribune,* to Helper's satisfaction, gave the warmest support to the project, as could be expected since Greeley was one of its architects. The *Daily Tribune* noted that Helper was a Southerner who saw slavery for what it was. When he was lured by gold to California, he was unprejudiced enough to see that slavery was "the curse and blight" of the South and, as a result, produced a masterful attack on it. "Could it be read around every American fireside," the *Daily Tribune* wrote, "the present century would witness the death and burial of African Slavery." The publication called for greatest attention to be given to placing the proposed compendium in the hands of the Southern white masses, who were completely unacquainted "with the truths so well presented" by Helper. "In their dense ignorance" the white masses were "artfully misled by the ruling class to detest, not slavery, but negroes, as the cause of their keenly felt depression."

In his contacts with Greeley, Helper was careful to conceal his detestation of the Negro. They found mutual agreement in the belief that slavery fettered the masses of white men and that the white nonslaveholders of the South were unaware of their true condition. Helper, then, convinced Greeley that a campaign of communication and education such as the one envisioned in the mass distribution of *The Compendium* was essential. Greeley warned that the slaveholders would not permit its free circulation, but he felt that attempts to suppress it would result in a greater demand for the work.[12]

By December 15, 1858, Anthon had received $574. Helper was encouraged by the comments of many of the contributors. Lemuel Jewell, a 78-year-old resident of Guilford, New York, believed that the original work was too large a volume for widespread circulation and *The Compendium* was the "only one to reach the masses." After reading about it, he hastened to send Anthon one dollar before going to bed lest, he wrote, "I might leave the world ere I had done anything for the success of so good a cause."

Another notable early contributor was Benjamin S. Hedrick, who expressed great faith in the usefulness of a compendium and sent fifty dollars from his exile residence in New York City. He said, "The facts and arguments [of *The Impending Crisis*] are all drawn from such sources that they come home with great force to the people of the South." He foresaw impediments to a compendium's circulation in the South and predicted that Helper would be even more detested than he, since Helper claimed the nonslaveholders had rights which should be respected.[13]

Despite widespread publicity, Helper was dissatisfied with the contributions which were received during the months immediately after the plan's presentation. His self-confidence and zeal led him to assume personally a much more dominant role in the program and to write a number of Republicans and known opponents of slavery expansion throughout the country. With each letter he included a copy of *The Impending Crisis* and explained the plan to publish *The Compendium*. He suggested that twenty men pledge one hundred dollars each to insure early success. As a result, numerous contributions were made or pledged, which confirmed Helper's belief that his project was destined for success.

One of the contributors, D. L. Gregory of Jersey City, forwarded his pledge of one hundred dollars and wrote Helper, "You have so arranged . . . facts in tables that there can be no mistake in understanding their bearing on the future of this great continent." He believed that a cheap edition would diffuse a knowledge of the institution which prevented prosperity for all.

Edward Harris of Woonsocket, Rhode Island, replied the same evening he received Helper's letter, pledging one hundred dollars, in order that he might "have the reflection after retiring to rest, of having endeavoured to contribute in some degree for the relief of suffering humanity."

Gerritt Smith of Peterboro, North Carolina, one of the few Southern contributors, was able to pledge only twenty dollars. He felt that the burden which fell on him was very great since there were few in his area to unite with him in an attack on slavery. "My work is that of a oldline abolitionist," he added, "not of a Republican."[14]

Some Republican leaders worked with Helper in promoting the project. Chace, for example, reported two subscriptions of one hundred dollars from Rhode Island and expected another. Before March, 1859, however, it was Helper's diligent pleas which brought in most of the subscriptions. Bradford R. Wood of Albany, New York, originally contributed fifteen dollars but, at Helper's prompting, sent an additional eighty-five dollars and suggested three men to whom Helper might appeal. One of these, John Norton of Farmington, Connecticut, responded in a week with one hundred dollars.

Helper's characteristic persistence was nowhere better illustrated than in his appeal to Samuel May of Boston, who ignored his first request. In a second letter he suggested that May join Samuel E. Sewell in raising five hundred dollars in Boston. May was favorably impressed by Helper's determination and forwarded his personal pledge for one hundred dollars at once, assuring him that four hundred dollars would follow. "It would be disgraceful to the City of my Birth & residence if the sum you mention ... could not promptly be obtain'd here." He was sure Helper's work would be taken to completion since " 'tis the cause of God."[15]

When contributors could not give one hundred dollars, Helper suggested they give less, and they often did. E. G. Dudley of Boston gave fifty dollars and assured Helper, "Rather than have the enterprise fail, I would pay a good deal more than $100, for I think a cheap edition of your excellent book circulated all over the South would do more toward ridding the country of Slavery than all things else combined." He did not believe slavery would endure twelve months once the contents of *The Impending Crisis* became known in the South. E. M. Davis forwarded fifty-five dollars to Helper as contributions of four men, and W. A. Buckingham of Norwick, Connecticut, promised to add a "small sum" to the treasury of so worthy a program.[16]

Despite Helper's campaign, only $3,177 had been obtained from about a hundred men by March, 1859, not one-fifth of the sum needed. Then Helper, Greeley, and the leaders of the program in New York, through the New York *Daily Tribune,* launched an extensive program to raise the remainder of the $16,000. They issued another circular describing the plan, adding separate endorsements by Republican leaders of Congress and leading citizens from New York State. This strategy ultimately succeeded but not in the manner foreseen. Nine months later it projected *The Impending Crisis* into the heat of political controversy and made it a best seller.

In the new attempt to obtain support for *The Compendium,* the *Daily Tribune* described the use the Republican Party could make of *The Impending Crisis* in the months ahead. To a great extent this plan became the blueprint which was faithfully followed. By bringing the whole nation to "understand fully the nature and influences" of slavery and "the views and purposes" of the Republican Party, the great struggle of the age would be ended and a Republican would be elected President by the votes of both the North and the South. Frémont was defeated in 1856 because the legitimate Republican case could not be presented in half the states of the Union. The proponents of slavery spoke throughout the North, "while throughout the Slave States," the *Daily Tribune* wrote, "our speakers were allowed no hearing, our journals were destroyed in the post offices, or their circulation obstructed by terrorism, and even our ballots were not allowed to be distributed." It was not surprising in such a police state that the great majority came to feel *"the Republicans are hostile to the South."* In vain, Republicans proclaimed that they sought "her renovation, not her ruin." Now, in Helper's work, they had, "in part because of its Southern origin," the best instrument to circulate to counteract the false impression forced on the Southern masses. The *Daily Tribune* stated, "No man can candidly persue it and not be convinced that Slavery is an enormous blunder as well as a cruel wrong, and that its abolition is the indispensable basis of Southern advancement and prosperity." Only a large, cheap edition of *The Impending Crisis,* with many copies distributed gratis in the border, slave, and free states, would provide the proper means "of inaugurating the canvass of 1860." Thereafter, particular attention should be given to the gratuitous circulation of the work in Pennsylvania, New Jersey, Indiana, and Illinois which, many felt, was "to decide the next Presidential contest."

The congressional endorsement was gratifying to Helper, who felt his work, at last, was receiving due recognition. It read: "We, the undersigned, Members of the House of Representatives, do cordially endorse the opinion, and approve the enterprise, set forth in the foregoing circular." It was signed by sixty-eight of the ninety-two Republican members of the House, including all the prominent ones, except Nathaniel P. Banks. Ominously the thirteenth signature was that of John Sherman.

Helper gave careful consideration to the selection of the New

York committee appointed to aid in the circulation of *The Compendium* and to receive subscriptions, among whom were some notable men: Charles W. Elliott, David Dudley Field, Charles A. Peabody, R. H. McCurdy, William Curtis Noyes, Edgar Ketchum, Abram Wakeman, James Kelly, Benjamin F. Manierre, and James A. Briggs. An endorsement of their mission was signed by Horace Greeley, John Jay, Henry Anthon, Thurlow Weed, James Kelly, William C. Bryant, Marcus Sprino, E. Delafield Smith, B. S. Hedrick, John C. Underwood, R. H. McCurdy, John A. Kennedy, Abram Wakeman, and William Curtis Noyes.[17]

This well-laid plan proved severely disappointing to Helper, for the two months after its release only $523 were subscribed, and by June 15, 1859, only $3,700 were available. Of this total, $2,400 came from $100 subscribers, among whom were Burdick the publisher, Helper, Greeley, John Jay, Governor Morgan, and Lewis Tappan.[18]

With this sum of money Helper and his associates had approximately one thousand specimen copies of *The Compendium* published in July, and about five hundred of them were distributed in the summer and early fall.[19] Following the first edition of his work, Helper continued to collect statistics and revise his materials. In 1859 his revision for an 1860 edition was almost complete and *The Compendium* was based on the revised manuscript. Not only were later statistics used in a number of areas, but the fifty-eight tables of the 1857 edition appeared as thirty-four in *The Compendium* and thirty-six in the 1860 edition.

Of greater significance was the markedly less radical tone of both the 1860 edition and *The Compendium*. Although Helper did not abandon a single basic contention and reproduced the same fundamental statistics, he eliminated some of the more radical language and charges. For example, the indictment of Thomas R. Ritchie for supposedly bribing the Virginia Legislature in 1831-32 was deleted. The severity of the castigation of slaveholders was muted. A two-page essay which proved "the gentlemen" worse than murderers was omitted. Also, the demand that slaveholders never again hold office was removed. The target date for attainment of abolition was moved from 1860 to 1870. Above all, the milder tones of the later versions of *The Impending Crisis* were shown by the deletion of Numbers 5, 9, 10, and 11 of Helper's eleven-point program to destroy slavery. Together they had urged immediate action against slavery including nonrecognition, proscription, and taxation of all owners.[20]

Later, when various politicians were indicted for endorsing *The Impending Crisis,* it was pointed out that they approved only the milder version.[21] The more vehement charges and plans in the first edition were shocking to so many that expediency demanded they be eliminated. Republican leaders probably suggested these modifications, but there is no reason to believe that Helper was averse to them. Though at times he became highly romantic, generally he was a practical man. He did not wish to retain anything which would prevent his work from accomplishing its purpose. In two years of Northern residence he had ample time to decide for himself what portions of *The Impending Crisis* should be changed or deleted to make it the most useful tool for crushing slavery.[22]

After all his care in revision and preparation of *The Compendium,* Helper was extremely disappointed with the failure to get large numbers of the work in immediate circulation. Two men, Holmes and Underwood, were appointed as commission agents in July but met with little success. In September John B. Brown of Alexandria, Virginia, who had gone "thro the fire" as a Republican elector in 1856, called to see Underwood to purchase five dollars worth of *The Compendium* at cost—sixteen cents each. Burdick, however, asked him twenty-five cents each, and when Tappan brought this happening to Helper's attention, he was very upset. "Between a publisher whose business it is to make all the money he can out of the book (a clever enough fellow though)," Helper wrote, "and a tardily acting committee, I find that while comparatively little good is accomplished in any way, a bad impression will get out among the people in regard to the management of the enterprise." Helper immediately provided copies of *The Compendium* for Brown at cost.[23]

When Jesse Wheeler of Guilford County, North Carolina, received a request from Helper that he aid in abolitionizing his area, he replied at length outlining his position and that of his region. He rejected Helper's suggestion that he become a member of the Republican National Committee, for he considered himself "an old line Whig" and hoped that the Whigs or Americans would unite with the Republicans at the next election. He informed Helper that, without the formation of a coalition, the Republicans had no chance in North Carolina, and he believed it "would be useless to make a Republican demonstration" in the state. He advised "let the Southern States alone except Delaware Maryland and Missouri and let all your energies be directed to securing the doubtful Free States for should a Republican candidate be elected our people would acquiesce without a murmur."

Wheeler, ordering one hundred copies at cost, assured Helper, "Your book is eagerly sought after by many men." As protection, he suggested that his copies be sent "as merchandise not books" to the railway station at Wilmington.

Wheeler's letter spurred Helper to attempt to get more copies of *The Compendium* printed, and he directed that orders from the South, such as Wheeler's, be filled at once. "I have labored long, and labored hard to reach the South with the facts of free labor as well as those of slave labor," he wrote, "and now, that some of them at least are eager to learn, and willing to pay for the information, I hope that the truth will not be withheld from them." Helper felt it was time to consummate the "slowly progressing enterprise." It had been "so long and so prominently" before the public that "the *honor* as well as the success" of the Republican Party depended on it being "speedily carried out in its full extent."

In October Helper and Greeley discussed means to raise additional funds, deciding that a meeting of New York endorsers was needed. " 'For God's sake,' " Greeley urged Anthon, " 'get us together again, and let us do something.' "

The meeting was held, and the "something" resorted to was an agreement with Burdick to publish 25,000 copies of *The Compendium* for five thousand dollars. The publisher agreed to wait for one thousand dollars of this sum.[24] Under this plan backlogged orders began to be filled, and copies were available when the book came into political prominence in December, 1859.

The attempts to raise money through subscriptions before *The Compendium* was available to the subscriber were generally unsuccessful. William Garrison of Baltimore wrote Helper in November, 1859, that he had no doubt 1,000 copies of the book could be "judiciously distributed" in his locality, but he could not obtain the money in advance. The attendance at the monthly meetings of the Baltimore Republican Association was so poor that he felt unjustified in trying to obtain money there. Moreover, he felt John Brown's raid had made it much harder to gain support.

Cassius M. Clay held the same opinion of the influence of the Virginia invasion, reporting that the Republicans of his area in Kentucky were getting started with "a fine prospect of a fine organization, when the Brown affair dashed all our hopes." The Westport Convention was a failure, and only "by great firmness and conciliation" did Clay and his friends escape being mobbed. In two delightful, consecutive sentences Clay wrote, "Few will venture to circulate your book here! Send me 100 copies." He also ordered 350 copies for other Kentuckians and gave his opinion that "any proceedings against slavery [other] than legal and conservative and practical is undesirable and will be disastrous." He vowed, "We shall not fail to work however because fanatics injure our cause—or insurrection threatens our lives also." He felt, "The work before us is the cause of Providence to be done."[25]

The Brown raid did not have an adverse effect in the North, and plans to circulate *The Compendium* as a Republican campaign document continued apace. Joseph Medill, editor of the Chicago *Press and Tribune,* had written Helper in May, 1859, advocating that thousands of copies be distributed in the Midwest during the following winter and spring. He felt Helper's book to be "the ablest work of the kind that has yet appeared," although he advocated an addition of a dozen pages dealing with Southern impositions on the North.

Medill wished the Republican Party to distribute 50,000 copies of *The Compendium* in the Northwest by September, 1860. He wrote, "We have a strip of territory commencing opposite Wheeling via north of the Ohio river, to a line drawn from Wheeling west thro Zanesville, Columbus, Indianapolis & Springfield to Quincy and from Burlington to Council Bluffs, in which a majority of the adults (natives) over 21, are from the slave states." In this area *The Compendium,* written by a Southerner for Southerners, would be the finest available work to win Republican votes. To start the ball rolling, Medill ordered one hundred volumes "to send to friends in Southern Ill. as *seed* copies."

In November, 1859, Medill gave his estimates of the number of copies of *The Compendium* that would be needed in his region before May, 1860. Only a few hundred copies would be needed in Minnesota, Wisconsin, and the Northern halves of Illinois and Iowa, but 22,000 to 30,000 copies could be used in Southern Illinois. Medill advised Helper to contact Indiana leaders as to the number needed there.

Helper shared Medill's views, and when William Pickering offered aid in distributing *The Compendium* in Illinois, Helper ordered as many copies be sent for his distribution "in Egypt" as he could use. Anthon was instructed to give this request top priority.[26]

Hearing of the extensive plans being made for *The Compendium* and realizing their threat to Democratic victory, the New York *Herald* unleashed an overwhelming campaign of vilification against it in late November, 1859. In biting satire, two and one-half columns of its first page described *The Impending Crisis* as an "Abolition Revolutionary Scheme." It held that the book was an incitement to treason and civil war and that it contained the theory which John Brown had practiced. The article contended Republican support of *The Compendium* was an abolitionization of the Republican Party, which was engaged in a treasonable effort to crush the South. Editorially, James Gordon Bennett proclaimed that the revelation of the union of leading abolitionists and Republicans in support of *The Compendium* was the most extraordinary disclosure to be "brought to light in this country since the treason of Benedict Arnold was detected at Tarrytown." The *Herald* felt it unthinkable that the governor of New York and sixty-eight Republican congressmen should endorse such a work. Speaking to the endorsers, the paper charged, "Hinton Rowan Helper proclaims you as revolutionists and traitors, and your fellow citizens wait to hear your own plea of guilty or not guilty." While condemning Helper, the *Herald* believed that he was a front for the New York *Tribune*. It wrote, *The Impending Crisis* "smells so strongly of the shop that every one who examines it is led to the inevitable conviction that the workers of the *Tribune* have had their hands deeply in its preparation."[27]

Helper was amazed, not that the ardently pro-Democratic *Herald* should attack him but at the aggressive nature of the attack. He had little time to contemplate this development, since one week after the *Herald's* assault the first session of the Thirty-sixth Congress opened, which gave *The Compendium* national publicity and made it a best seller. December 8, 1859, W. B. Thomas wrote Helper from Philadelphia that his city would need a large number of copies since *The Impending Crisis* had received so much advertisement in the Congress, and "I could sell hundreds daily in this city if I possessed a supply of them." On December 12 the Pennsylvania Anti-Slavery Society requested five hundred copies, writing, "We could wholesale them very fast now." The society would not think of wholesaling any of the fifty copies it had received that morning, however. J. A. Hopkins ordered "a few hundred" copies for distribution in Virginia. "Despite the rigor of Uncle Sam's agents," he knew that he could sell them along the south bank of the Potomac and throughout Fairfax District.

Discussion of *The Impending Crisis* in Congress, S. B. Beman wrote Helper from Waterforce, Pennsylvania, "has made many of our Republicans anxious to see the work." He asked that one hundred copies be sent him, since almost every subscriber to the New York *Tribune,* in his area was determined to have a copy.[28]

Once the demand for *The Compendium* became overwhelming, the New York *Tribune* assumed responsibility for seeing it was met. By December 26, 1859, with Helper's blessing, it was sending out five hundred copies a day and hoped to increase this to one thousand. At the same time Burdick had a brisk sale for the 1857 version of *The Impending Crisis* and was preparing the 1860 edition for publication.[29]

Helper was delighted by the tremendous reception his work was obtaining, but he was saddened that it could not be widely distributed in the South, the area for which it was written. In many Southern localities it became a crime even to possess the book. Charles T. Crem and Charles T. Dixon of Church Creek, Dorchester County, Maryland, obtained forty-five copies of *The Compendium* from William Garrison and began their distribution. Dixon was arrested and held for $10,000 bail on grounds that he was distributing incendiary documents. Thomas Crua purchased a number of copies from Lewis Clephane in Washington and distributed them to Virginia slaveholders and nonslaveholders. He did not dream that he was violating the law as long as he "did not interfere with the colored population." Much to his surprise he was arrested and freed only under $2,500 bail. To avoid further trouble he fled to Sturgis, Michigan, from which he wrote Helper for fifty copies of *The Compendium*. In his travels everyone Crua met who had seen the work wanted a copy.[30]

Some of the most notorious instances of suppression of freedom came in Helper's native state. North Carolina law made it a felony to bring any publication into the state which would make the slaves discontented or excite them or free Negroes to insurrection. For the second offense the penalty was death.

In 1859 Helper, in New York City, personally presented copies of his work to Governor John W. Ellis and former Governor John M. Morehead of North Carolina and sent Representative John A. Gilmer, an old-line Whig, a free copy. Subsequently, Gilmer and the radical Democrat, Ellis, stated that they had received copies without their permission and Ellis declared he had used his copy to light his pipe.[31]

Six men were arrested for circulating the work in Guilford County and several in Mecklenburg and Randolph counties. At least three were driven from Guilford and Randolph counties by mobs, and in Greenville, South Carolina, copies of the work were burned before the county courthouse. Representative John D. Ashmore, addressing the Congress in 1859, stated that Harrold Wyllis, who had been apprehended with seven copies of *The Impending Crisis,* was in a South Carolina jail, but, the representative avowed, he would be hanged. From Arkansas came reports that three men had been executed for merely having the work in their possession.[32] The Southern reaction, because of the nature of American federalism, had even international repercussions. A representative, of the British government called on George M. Dallas, the Minister of the United States in London, asking his intervention in obtaining "the release of a foolish Briton, long resident in Fairfax Co. Va.," who had been circulating the Helper book. The wary American Minister refused to give advice.[33]

Helper was dismayed, but not surprised, when the Maryland Legislature forbade any endorser of *The Impending Crisis* from becoming a policeman. In the same spirit the charter of a Baltimore street railway prohibited supporters of Helper from using the cars. It was in North Carolina, however, that the most notorious case of persecution took place, that of the Reverend Daniel Worthy. A native of Guilford County, where he had been a justice of the peace before moving to Indiana, Worthy had served in the Indiana Legislature and, in late 1857 or early 1858, returned to the neighborhood of his birth to serve as a Wesleyan Methodist minister. He distributed much antislavery literature and believed it did " 'a work little inferior to the living preacher.' " In July, 1859, Worthy described his work in North Carolina as being most satisfactory; all was " 'peace and quiet' "; he had not been disturbed.[34]

After the raid on Harpers Ferry, however, Worthy was arrested for circulating Helper's book and on the grounds that he preached so as to make the slaves dissatisfied with their lot. He was imprisoned in Greensboro for several months, refusing on moral grounds to give a $5,000 bond to keep the peace. In the course of his trial sections of *The Impending Crisis* were read to demonstrate its subversive character. Several witnesses testified that Worthy had sold them copies for one dollar and urged them to read it closely and follow its teachings. The defense contended that the law only applied to the distribution of dangerous literature to slaves or free Negroes, not white persons. The jury, composed mostly of nonslaveholders, received the case at 11:30 p.m. and returned a verdict of guilty at 4 a.m. Worthy received a one-year jail sentence and, perhaps because of his prominent family connections and the fact that he was a minister, a suspension of the required public whipping.

The (Raleigh) *North Carolina Standard* was disappointed, since it wished Worthy's execution. The convicted minister, a man of spirit, appealed his case to the North Carolina Supreme Court. Although represented by James Morehead, a large slave owner, the court upheld his conviction on the grounds that incendiary literature could not be segregated from the blacks. Rather than go to prison, Worthy forfeited his $3,000 bond and, like Helper, took asylum in the North.[35] As the Worthy case illustrated, the South clearly regarded *The Impending Crisis* as incendiary literature and those who circulated it as enemies of the people, deserving punishment.

While persecutions of this type were taking place in the South, moderate men were thoughtfully reading Helper's work, and their thoughts were molded by it. Abraham Lincoln read a copy, brought from Boston by William Henry Herndon, his law partner, as he wrote his "House Divided" speech in the spring of 1858. As Lincoln read, he marked sections he felt unacceptable, among these being the later revised passages demanding immediate emancipation and holding that the "pro-slavery slaveholders" were criminals. "That the book should have been produced, that the non-slaveholders of the South and the poor whites should have found a voice, that so direct and fierce a challenge should be hurled at the rich planters who controlled the South, was a symptom and sign that Lincoln tried to analyze." His analysis came in the speech which began, " 'If we could first know where we are, and whither we are tending, we could better judge what to do, and how to do it.' " At the same time Senator Andrew Johnson read *The Impending Crisis,* and it became his *"vade mecum*—his arsenal of facts," for an attack on those who profited from slavery.[36]

Helper never doubted the significance of *The Impending Crisis,* and had he known the use Lincoln and Johnson were making of it, he would not have been startled in the least. Its use was not confined to the great or near great; by late 1859 it had directly or indirectly affected the thoughts and lives of thousands. It was then, however, when it became the center of a critical dispute in the House of Representatives, that it emerged as one of the most important books America has ever known.

# Chapter Four

# Political Import of

## *The Impending Crisis*

"It is a little known fact—an amazing one—" that *The Impending Crisis* had "the nation teetering on the edge of civil war ten months before Lincoln's election."[1] This was a result of its direct relationship to the speakership contest in the House of Representatives. From his New York City residence Helper followed this drama closely. Although he was upset by the personal attacks on him which the book evoked, he felt more than compensated by the publicity given *The Impending Crisis* and the increased demands for it.

The week following the execution of John Brown at Charleston, Virginia, the last of the ante bellum Congresses convened in a tense Washington. Sensing the gravity of the situation, former President John Tyler wrote that any indiscreet move could spell disaster, and above all, he feared the Speaker's election, which could induce great excitement.[2]

Tyler's fears were based on the knowledge that there would be no one majority party in the House and that internal divisions would strain party loyalty in all groups. The lower chamber was to be composed of 109 Republicans; 27 Americans or Whigs; and 101 Democrats, divided into administration and Douglas followers, Southern ultras, and anti-Lecomptonites. It was doubtful if eight of the latter, who owed their election to Republican support, would vote with the rest of the party. The Americans, four of whom were from New York and New Jersey and twenty-three from the South, and the Republicans were divided between moderates and those unwilling to compromise on the slavery issue.

Since, if all members were present, 119 votes were necessary to elect a Speaker, it was obvious that only by a defection from strict party lines could a choice be made. The regular Democrats were placed on the defensive because they could count on only eighty-six votes, while the Republicans could, perhaps, muster all of theirs. The Democratic reaction produced a crisis.[3]

At the opening session the Republicans chose Ohio's John Sherman as their candidate, and he received eighty-six votes on the first ballot, to the sixty-six of the regular Democratic candidate, Thomas S. Bocock of Virginia. Fourteen other candidates received many American, anti-Lecompton and some Republican votes.[4]

A stalemate was produced when John B. Clark (Democrat, Missouri) presented a resolution stating:

> Whereas certain members of this House now in nomination for Speaker, did indorse and recommend the book hereinafter mentioned,
> Resolved, That the doctrines and sentiments of a certain book, purporting to have been called "The Impending Crisis of the South—How to meet it," written by one Hinton R. Helper, are insurrectionary and hostile to the domestic peace and tranquility of the country, and that no member of this House who has indorsed and recommended it, or the compendium from it, is fit to be Speaker of this House.[5]

Clark, attacking the sixty-eight Republican endorsers of Helper's work, contended that previously no major party had advised a large portion of the country's people "to stop at nothing until they put out of public life, disfranchise, and murder" many fellow Americans. William Kellogg (Republican, Illinois), smarting under the attack, demanded that Clark cease his remarks and allow the endorsers time to study *The Impending Crisis* and avow or disavow it. Clark refused to yield; instead he had the clerk read the Helper program and the Republican congressmen's endorsement. In his opinion they had counseled treason and murder and deserved "a fate which it would not be respectful to announce in this House." When Clark concluded, John A. Gilmer (American, North Carolina) offered a substitute resolution which he felt would reduce tension in the chamber and would debar any Helper endorser from the Speaker's chair. The resolution stated that it was the "duty of every good citizen ... to resist all attempts at renewing, in Congress or out of it, the slavery agitation, under whatsoever shape and color the attempt may be made." This resolution was the only means of saving the House from mob-like confusion, according to Helper's hometown newspaper, the *Carolina Watchman.* To satisfy those who wished a more definite position, however, Gilmer added a provision that no one should be elected Speaker whose political opinions did not conform with his measure; in so providing, he felt he represented moderate men of every section.[6]

Ironically, neither the Clark nor Gilmer resolution came to a vote, but their introduction initiated one of the most important debates in American history. The Clark resolution gave the Democrats the initiative, which they retained throughout the contest. It couched their struggle for power in a moral garb, but it did not substitute sectional for party lines. The Southern members of the American Party did not coalesce with their Democratic colleagues until temporarily at the end of the struggle, nor did Northern Democrats embrace the Republican candidate. Instead, both sides settled to a verbal duel, with the Democratic spokesmen holding the floor much of the time.

The second day of debate Sherman defended his endorsement of *The Impending Crisis,* asserting that he was unaware of the book's contents. He recalled signing a general endorsement brought to him by Governor E. D. Morgan of New York, after he was assured that the book contained nothing offensive. With this apology Sherman moved to the offensive, maintaining the most numerous party should be allowed to select the Speaker, and if he were chosen, he promised to administer the House without trespassing on anyone's rights. As if to assuage Democratic fears, he avowed, "I am opposed to any interference whatever by the people of the free States with the relations of master and slave in the slave States."

For weeks after this, although frequently attacked, Sherman remained silent. He felt his lips were sealed by the Clark resolution, since it condemned all endorsers of *The Impending Crisis* and classified them as unfit to be Speaker. As a man of honor he would not dignify his assailants by defending himself as long as the resolution remained before the House. If it were withdrawn, he offered to express his views of the Helper book, page by page. In the interim, he declared that to charge the Republican Party with the book's doctrines was unworthy of the Democrats, and he personally pledged his support to "the Union and the Constitution, with all the compromises under which it was formed, and all the obligations which it imposes."

Thomas C. Hindman (Arkansas) challenged Sherman's statement on the grounds that he had advocated exclusion of slavery from the territories and had branded the new fugitive slave law "as a savage and inhuman" one. Sherman retorted, "In other words, I am charged with being a Republican. That is my offense; none other."[7]

Sherman's position was unsatisfactory to most of the Democrats and a number of Americans, and he privately acknowledged he had blundered in signing the endorsement. It was "a thoughtless, foolish act," he wrote his brother, William T. Sherman, perpetrated when he was under pressure of business in the House. "Everybody knows that the ultra sentiments of the book are as obnoxious to me as they can be to any one," he held, but the threat of Clark's resolution placed him in such a position that he felt he could not reply.[8]

As a mighty chorus, many of the Southern Democrats and their allies outside Congress charged that *The Impending Crisis* was conceived to promote violence, and as one orator saw it, any endorser was "not only not fit to be Speaker" but was "unfit to live."[9] As another phrased it, "The book recommended *direct* warfare on southern society, 'be the consequences what they might,' " and was so extravagant in tone and diabolical in design that it was, at first, "generally supposed to be the work of a fool or of a madman." The great surprise came when the Republican Party embraced the work.[10]

*DeBow's Review* listed the contents of the Helper abolition program so that its readers might know exactly what the "Black-Republican Members of Congress endorsed, and contributed funds to have in general circulation." It would have shared the views of the Raleigh *Register*[11] that, if the South could close its eyes to the "malignity of the conspirators" who endorsed *The Impending Crisis,* then it must "be given over to hopeless blindness and to that madness which goes before destruction."

The New York *Herald* prided itself on being the first newspaper to reveal "the horrible plot of abolition treason, rebellion, and bloodshed" embodied in *The Impending Crisis,* and many of the Southern congressmen probably had their opinions molded by reading it. William H. Seward was cited as the principal villain who had revealed his intentions in his Rochester speech, in which he had contended that there was an "irrepressible conflict" between the forces of slavery and freedom. The *Herald* proclaimed Seward's philosophy, the Brown raid, and Helper's work were "portions of the same programme to create a servile insurrection in the slave States." It charged that *The Impending Crisis* was compiled under the direction of Francis P. Blair, Jr., with the intention of elevating William H. Seward to the Presidency and contended that the House was in the position "of the French Convention just before the Reign of Terror commenced."[12]

The Richmond *Semi-Weekly Examiner* was astonished that even Republicans would aid the circulation of such "a treasonable and disunion firebrand" as *The Impending Crisis.* It warned that the work was designed to produce rebellion and overthrow government. The violent Washington *States and Union,* an administration newspaper, declared that the elevation of Sherman to the Speaker's chair would be the election of "an incendiary, bearing his lighted torch in hand for the conflagration of the republic." It urged Southern representatives to remain calm but, if Sherman were elected, stated they could not be expected "to suffer Conspirators to control their destinies." It endorsed the Clark resolution but opposed the Gilmer resolution, declaring it could not have been of greater aid to Sherman if it had come "from the darkest Abolition hole in New England."[13]

The regular Democratic congressmen echoed the theme that the work was incendiary. Shelton F. Leake (Virginia) demanded to know whether the representatives were asked to elect a man who was "stimulating my negroes at home to apply the torch to my dwelling and the knife to the throats of my wife and helpless children." Roger A. Pryor (Virginia) contended that, for the first time in the history of the country, a well-known writer had invoked the Southern slaves to rebel against their masters. Senator James Mason (Virginia), one of the few congressmen to read *The Impending Crisis*, thought its purpose was "to array man against man in our own States." John D. Ashmore (South Carolina) endeavored to show that there was an incendiary purpose in the work's distribution in South Carolina by Harrold Wyllis. Wyllis had been extremely secretive, waiting until the honest men of the country were asleep before "prowling through the highways and byways of the land," distributing his incendiary material.[14]

Holding the view that *The Impending Crisis* was conceived to promote revolution, many Democratic congressmen and their sympathizers charged that John Brown's raid was the direct outgrowth of its philosophy. In addition, the central theme of the Democratic argument came to be that *the Helper philosophy was that of William H. Seward and the other Republican leaders, and the speakership contest was a prelude to the election of Seward to the Presidency and the destruction of Southern rights.*

By the second day of debate Lawrence M. Keitt (North Carolina) projected Seward and the Brown raid into the focal positions they were to retain. In 1848, he charged, Seward made a speech holding that the systems of government in the North and the South were different and conflict must come between them. He said, "The party of freedom seeks complete and universal emancipation." Expressing these views, he was elected to the Senate and became "the head of the Republican party." In 1858 he delivered his renowned Rochester speech in which he envisioned an "irrepressible conflict." The Republican Party, faithfully following its most famous leader, endorsed the Helper book and aided in its dissemination. As a natural consequence came "the bloody raid" into Virginia. John H. W. Underwood (Georgia) concurred, stating that the raid was "the legitimate result" of Seward's "higher law" philosophy.

Thomas G. Davidson (Louisiana) conceived Seward's Rochester speech to be the Republican creed. "As a party, you are here to strike down the sovereign rights of [the] Southern states," he told the Republican members. They added insult to injury by insisting on the election of Sherman, a man whose "garments are dyed with the blood of its victims."

Another Democratic representative contended that Brown's raid was less frightening than its reception in the North. After the conviction of the traitor, the South heard stories of the tolling of Northern church bells, the firing of minute guns, and the holding of protest meetings. Men of superior intelligence even declared that Brown occupied "a position higher than that of the Savior of mankind."[15]

Such a radical position did not come into being overnight but was the result, in the opinion of William W. Boyce (South Carolina), of Seward's evolving philosophy, the basis of which was that "slavery is a crime." William Smith (Virginia) proclaimed that the essence of modern Republicanism was a fusion of Seward's "higher law" and Helper's abolitionist theories. This sanctioned the violation of any law the individual did not like.

David Clopton (Alabama) opposed Sherman's selection as a step toward the choice of a Republican President. John A. McClernand (Illinois) agreed that Sherman's election was the prelude to that of Seward and contended that there were other qualified Republicans not identified with "higher law" doctrines and "Helperism." In the opinion of Virginia representative Daniel C. DeJarnette, Seward stood before the country as a "perjured traitor," yet the American people were asked to elect him President.[16]

A number of Southern Democrats apparently concluded that, should the national government fall into the hands of men who subscribed to the concept of the "higher law" and to the doctrines of

*The Impending Crisis,* even the loyalty of the Southern people would not insure safety. Therefore, the debates brought a number of secession threats. Milledge L. Bonham (South Carolina) stated that "upon the election of Mr. Seward, or any other man who indorses and proclaims the doctrines held by him and his party . . . I am in favor of an immediate dissolution of the Union." Henry C. Burnett (Kentucky) shared this view, while William C. Anderson (Kentucky) urged the Southern states to wait for secession until Seward had "committed some overt act."[17]

Few congressmen felt Sherman's election would bring immediate disunion. The New York *Courier and Enquirer* quoted speeches made by Representatives Keitt, Lucius J. Gartrell, and Leake which seemed to indicate this view was their personal opinion, but only Georgia's Alfred Iverson joined the Washington *States and Union* in publicly avowing it.[18]

Privately, Robert Barnwell Rhett, Jr., held that the Southern representatives should withdraw if any Republican were elected Speaker. Moreover, the governor of South Carolina, William H. Gist, wrote the Charleston district congressman, William P. Miles, that the state would sustain her representatives if they withdrew upon Sherman's election, but he could make no commitments if a more moderate Republican, "who had not committed such an overt act" were chosen. " 'If . . . you upon consultation decide to make the issue of force in Washington write or telegraph me, and I will have a regiment in or near Washington in the shortest possible time.' "[19]

Alabama's James L. Pugh was a solitary congressional figure in demanding immediate secession regardless of developments. The speakership contest only afforded him a tense atmosphere in which to project his theories. He recalled that it was at the insistence of Stephen A. Douglas that the Congress abandoned the practice of legislating slavery in and out of territories. The power of a territorial legislature on the subject was left to the Supreme Court, but its decision was spurned by Douglas and his followers. With the unity of the Democratic Party broken, Pugh stated that the "truest conservatism and wisest statesmanship demand a speedy termination of all association with such confederates" and the formation of a new union.[20]

Although not this extreme, a large section of the Southern and the national Democratic press reflected the arguments of the regular Democrats. For them, as for the members of Congress, Brown's raid awakened a sense of immediate danger, and "for the first time the race question was thrust, stark naked, into the struggle of sections." The average Southern white man was convinced that, as the Southern radicals had said, Northerners were determined to free the slaves, regardless of the consequences.[21] A political tragedy occurred when Southern Democrats, like Alabama's Pugh, lost confidence in their Northern allies, many of whom were equally opposed to Republican principles.

From the time of the Brown raid until the climax of the speakership contest a metamorphosis in anti-Republican opinion was taking place. "The excitement throughout the whole country that followed the invasion of one of the slave States was such as has seldom been witnessed," wrote an Alabama journal. "The eulogy with which treason and insurrection was greeted by large classes of citizens in the free States, could not fail to make a deep impression upon the people of the South." Soon it became generally known that leading Republicans had endorsed *The Impending Crisis*. As a Richmond newspaper saw it, they were urging that "our food and wells of water shall be poisoned by our slaves. Hell itself cannot cap that climax."[22]

The horror which molded the latent public opinion was not confined to the South. A Pennsylvania newspaper charged that, in trying to place a Helper endorser in the Speaker's chair, the Republicans "were guilty not only of a *'studied design,'* but of a 'deliberate overt attempt' to produce secession." The *Cheshire Republican* (Keene, New Hampshire) did not wonder that the South should threaten secession unless it could be assured its constitutional rights. If this were disunionism, it wrote, "It is disunion resulting entirely from their [the Republicans'] own fanaticism, and disposition to infringe upon the rights of others." The same sentiments were expressed in the editorials of the Pottsville (Pennsylvania) *Demo-*

*cratic Standard.*[23] The *States and Union* felt that Seward's friends were guilty of a great mistake in not seeing that the larger question was union or disunion rather than the promotion of Seward as a presidential candidate.[24]

Once war came, a Southern newspaper, one of the abolitionists' most vocal opponents, ascribed the conflict to the endorsement of *The Impending Crisis.* By approving Helper's abolition scheme, the Republicans gave the South the alternative only of submission or separation, once they captured the executive department. Some might say the Republican endorsements were only threats, but "they convinced . . . the South that they did intend to carry them out." The endorsers became wartime leaders of the Republican Party. "Look over the names and see whether nearly all are not high priests at present in the party now engaged in carrying out *the very programme to which they pledged themselves,*" readers were urged. Helper became consul at Buenos Aires; Seward, Secretary of State; Lewis Clephane, postmaster of Washington, D.C.; C. A. Peabody, a "Judge of Mr. Lincoln's Courts in New Orleans"; and Abram Wakeman, postmaster of New York City. Some endorsers, including Francis P. Blair, Jr., and S. R. Curtis, were "really *fighting* to carry out their principles as they said they would." Almost all were, in some manner, making good their assertion, " 'WE HAVE DETERMINED TO ABOLISH SLAVERY, AND SO HELP US GOD, ABOLISH IT WE WILL.' "[25]

During the speakership contest, there were more moderate publications which proposed a conciliatory policy; notable among these was the pro-Douglas *Harper's Weekly.* It deplored the idleness and rancor produced by the contest and urged the Republicans to drop Sherman and concentrate their strength on some nonendorser of the Helper book to whose election the Democrats would tacitly agree. Then it cautioned the Southern Democrats against hasty action. Although the publication asserted Brown deserved hanging, it urged Virginia to pardon him and confound "the Northern Abolitionist party." The South was assured that only a handful of radical abolitionists regarded Brown as a martyr, and the North was told that "whatever the politicians and political newspapers may say, the Southern people, as a body, are decidedly opposed to disunion."[26]

Republican representatives replied infrequently to the severe indictments of the Democratic lawmakers and their allies. Few joined William Kellogg (Illinois) in repudiating *The Impending Crisis.*[27] Many Republicans defended their party by contending that it was the champion of intellectual freedom. Benjamin Wade (Ohio) and Senator Henry Wilson (Massachusetts) agreed their endorsements did not mean they approved of all the sentiments in *The Impending Crisis.* "I think some of them are intolerant," Wade said, "but I do not see why they are not proper to be submitted to the consideration of freemen."

John Cochrane (New York) defended his friend, Seward, claiming his language at Rochester was "but a figure of rhetoric." "The collison alluded to, the irrepressible conflict asserted, was but the harmless conflict of ideas." Surely no one should hold Seward responsible for "natural violence" when he had only "counseled intellectual war."

A bolder defense was made by John F. Farnsworth (Illinois). After disavowing any intention of arousing slave rebellion by his endorsement, he observed that the Democratic Party had been guilty of just as provocative action. Many of its members had approved E. A. Pollard's *Black Diamonds,* which advocated the smuggling of slaves into the United States, and viewed William Walker's invasion of Nicaragua with delight. Moreover, the influential Democratic newspaper *States and Union* reported, with approval, that Virginia was ready to secede from the Union should Sherman be elected Speaker.

Even more shocking were the contentions of Thaddeus Stevens that President Buchanan and the administration were behind the speakership dispute. He alleged that the President had long believed the best way to increase the strength of the Democratic Party among Northerners was "for the South to frighten them into the belief if they venture to elect a northern man with northern principles, this Union is to be dissolved." The Democrats were spreading the propaganda that, if the Republicans did not yield, the

House would remain disorganized until 1861. "We have fixed on an honorable and worthy standard-bearer," Stevens proclaimed, "and we shall stand by him if this House were not organized till the crack of doom."[28]

This was an extreme viewpoint, and Luther C. Carter (New York) expressed the opinion of more moderate Republicans when he explained that he was voting for Sherman in the belief that the plurality group should organize the House. "In thus voting," he said, "I do not indorse the Helper book any more than does a national man of the administration party indorse the inflammatory disunion speeches which have been made upon their side of the House."[29]

This moderation was not shown by the New York *Tribune,* the most vigorous defender of Helper and his endorsers. It was amazed that *The Impending Crisis* was considered incendiary and commented that the work was "an unimpeachable array of facts and figures." Greeley was flabbergasted when some Republicans recanted, or explained away, their loyalty to *The Impending Crisis.* He charged the New York *Herald* as being the author of the Clark resolution, although the paper knew "perfectly well that Mr. Helper never dreamed of exciting insurrection or civil war at the South. . . . To do so would be the height of absurdity; for the non-slaveholding Whites, to whom Mr. Helper appeals, constitute a large majority of the Southern voters; and whenever they shall say that Slavery must vanish, it will have to go."[30]

The *Tribune* deplored the waste of time and money in the congressional debates, especially when not one representative in ten had read the work or knew what he was debating. In an effort to correct this situation, the *Tribune* sought both to explain and distribute *The Impending Crisis.* It averred that Helper was making an appeal to "real democracy" in the South and was "addressing those who have long been under the financial, political, social and educational ban of their haughty neighbors." The effectiveness of Helper's plea was demonstrated in the fear it aroused among the Southern upper classes. "Helper is more dangerous than a 1,000 John Browns," it wrote, since he advocated an "insurrection of the mind and conscience." His work was "as impregnable as the Multiplication Table" and far more dramatic. After 100,000 copies of *The Compendium* were distributed by mid-January, 1860, the *Tribune* concurred with a reader in the belief that, if the Republicans remained constant in the book's distribution, the election of 1860 would be a party triumph.[31]

Throughout the fall and winter of 1859 and 1860 Helper devoted all his time to the distribution of *The Compendium* and the full edition of *The Impending Crisis*. Despite the numerous attacks made on him, in the Congress and the press, he held his peace amazingly well. Finally in January, 1860, in a letter to the editor of the New York *Times,* he flatly refuted the alleged charges of misconduct and inconsistency levied against him, with the exception of the theft from Michael Brown, which had been resurrected within a week after copies of *The Impending Crisis* reached Salisbury. At once "it was taken up by the so-called Democratic newspapers . . . with all the misrepresentations and distortions that the evil spirit of slavery could suggest." Not only did they castigate Helper as a persistent thief, but they falsely charged that he was expelled from the Salisbury Presbyterian Church. Helper marveled that men could sink so low. It was true that he had submitted his resignation to the church; however, it had been refused since there was no provision for this action in the Presbyterian book of discipline. At last, he had written the church that, despite its action, he no longer regarded himself as a member. If any doubted these facts, Helper offered to open his correspondence to them; by this action he hoped his critics would be persuaded to concentrate on his writings, not his character.

The newspaper which published Helper's letter of defense, the New York *Times,* gave one of the most nonpartisan evaluations of his works. It noted that *The Impending Crisis* caused little controversy until the New York *Herald,* "with its accustomed zeal and industry," set about "the pleasant and patriotic task of proving that the whole North" was "a vast hive of Abolition conspirators— that John Brown's crusade was prompted, aided and endorsed by thousands and tens of thousands of our most prominent and active business and public men, and that the South must be expected to be speedily overrun by armed hordes from the Northern states."

The *Times* recognized that the endorsers of Helper's work were in an awkward position because they had signed without ever having read *The Impending Crisis,* a common but dangerous political practice. By endorsing and distributing *The Compendium,* Republicans "abandoned the conservative ground on which they had hitherto vindicated their claim to respect as a national party, and entered upon the intermeddling, illegal and unconstitutional aggressions which have hitherto been confined to the Abolitionists." Helper's work was legitimate when it was used in the South for the self-reformation of Southerners; however, when it was chosen as a campaign document for general Northern use, the *Times* believed that it became the instrument for "an aggressive movement." Sherman and most of the endorsers were not abolitionists, but the *Times* condemned their actions in branding themselves as such.[32]

The regular Democrats understood the political advantage to be obtained from the endorsers' dilemma. They lost no opportunity to emphasize the sectional nature of the Republican Party and to identify it with irresponsible action. John A. McClernand (Illinois) condensed much of this argument in one sentence, stating, "The question before us at this time is, whether we shall select a Speaker standing upon a national platform or upon a sectional platform." The Democratic Party was the only national party, William H. English (Indiana) contended, and in it the American people had the organization which could bring justice to all its regions. He warned, "We must guard against sectionalism and extreme views in our own household." The Democratic Party "must not degenerate into a mere southern sectional party, or a party that tolerates sentiments of disunion; if it does so its days are numbered and its mission ended." A number of Northern Democrats directly addressed their Southern colleagues. Philip B. Fouke (Illinois) declared that his Southern friends did not realize the conditions under which Northern Democrats had to fight. "We stand constantly trembling for fear that by some indiscretion of our friends we may be swept away—swept into political non-entity." In return for

Southern propriety he pledged, "We are willing to stand by you to the last. We are willing to carry the flag of the Democratic party into the thickest of the fight."[33]

In the immediate matter of selecting the Speaker, it was not the Southern but the anti-Lecompton Democrats who caused the party the most difficulty. The eight anti-Lecomptonites from outside Illinois refused to caucus with the party, although Douglas urged them to do so, and they did not vote for the regular Democratic nominees. In fact, three consistently voted for Sherman.[34] During the debates they were thorns in the side of the regular Democratic forces. One described the administration forces in the House as being "perfectly disorganized, perfectly demoralized, without cohesion, without unanimity of any kind." As a result, the House "is to be kept inorganic, and the country is to be tortured from one end to the other."[35]

The anti-Lecomptonites did not fail to explain their independent course. Horace F. Clark (New York) felt the administration's territorial policy was "almost as dangerous to the peace and harmony of this Republic" as was "the interminable wrangle about the question of slavery." Garnett B. Adrian (New Jersey) observed that the failure of the Democrats to unite on the speakership question was a barometer of what lay ahead. If the entire party would only agree to nominate Douglas and accept the Kansas-Nebraska Act, he declared, "no Republican will ever be elevated to the presidential chair in opposition to that great and distinguished man."

Division greatly hurt the Democratic cause throughout the speakership contest. In balloting through January 7 the maximum votes received by Democratic candidates were 88, while Sherman's maximum number was 112.[36] It was obvious that the only way in which a Republican could be defeated was by a union of the non-Republican forces on a single candidate. The pressure placed on the Southern Americans, in particular, was intense. No Southerner would dare support any man who had endorsed *The Impending Crisis,* but by their independent policy, so the Democrats charged, the Americans were aiding the South's worst enemy.

To pleas for coalescence, a number of Americans replied that the Democrats were responsible for the division in conservative strength. Thomas A. R. Nelson (Tennessee) charged that the biased policy pursued by the Democrats was responsible for the growth of Republican power in the North. Various factors made union with the Democrats difficult. William C. Anderson (Kentucky) contended that American support of a Democratic candidate would be a confession that their indictment of the Democrats had been false. If union took place, the Americans would forfeit their plans to obtain protection for American labor, since a Democratic speaker "could stifle every investigation, and oppose everything we promised to our constituents in the South."

Despite the difficulties, as early as January 13 William Smith (Democrat, Virginia) proposed a common candidate to the Americans, but this overture was not received with warmth. Joshua Hill (American, Georgia) insisted that the Democrats should become harmonized among themselves before they sought American support. This retort amazed John H. W. Underwood (Democrat, Georgia), who could not see how any Southerner would disrupt plans upon which the nation's future depended. He observed, however, that an effort should be made to obtain American support for a Democrat since many Northern Democrats simply could not sanction an antiforeign, anti-Roman Catholic American. To this confession Hill replied that the intolerance Underwood described was not general in his party and was not true of the Georgia Americans.

On January 26 a majority of Democrats gave their support to the American, William N. H. Smith (North Carolina), but in doing so with misgivings, a number felt they had to explain their action. As a result of this co-operation, for the first time in the contest Sherman was not the plurality candidate. The votes stood 112 to 106.

Faced with the formidable Democratic-American coalition and the rejection since late December of a motion for a plurality rule, the Republicans realized that no endorser of *The Impending Crisis* could be chosen Speaker, and on January 30, 1860, Sherman withdrew his name. Principle, he stated, led him to retire, since he felt it would be a tragedy if, by any means, a supporter of the administration or an advocate of disunion should be elected. His policy had always been that, if any one of his associates could receive more votes, he would retire, and now that time had come.

As their new candidate the Republicans chose the American, William R. Pennington (New Jersey), a Sherman supporter who had introduced a motion for a plurality rule in an attempt to obtain his election.[37] To the majority of Democrats he was completely unacceptable. "The endorser of an endorser is just as accountable, in the eyes of the law, as the principle," wrote a Democratic journal.[38]

In three ballots Pennington polled 115 votes to Smith's 113. Realizing that victory was beyond him, Smith withdrew as the coalition candidate. The Democrats were then unable to obtain substantial American support, and on February 1 Pennington was elected, ending the longest speakership battle in the nation's history. His victory came by obtaining the votes of George Briggs (American, New Jersey), Henry W. Davis (American, New York), and Garnett B. Adrian, (anti-Lecompton Democrat, New Jersey), which had been withheld from Sherman.[39]

Never before in the country's history had greater personal bitterness been demonstrated on the House floor than during the contest. L. O. B. Branch (North Carolina) challenged Galusha Grow (Pennsylvania) to a duel, which was stopped only when both were arrested and placed under heavy bond. On the basis of an alleged insult to Senator Stephen A. Douglas, William Kellogg and John A. Logan became involved in a violent argument which was consummated when Logan drew a pistol and said, " 'By God, if I can't talk, I can do something else.' " Pandemonium broke loose when John B. Haskin (anti-Lecompton Democrat, New York) dropped his pistol while making derogatory remarks about a regular Democratic colleague.[40] Most of the members came armed with deadly weapons, and each side had armed supporters in the galleries.

Many individuals and forces in the country hoped the termination of the contest would bring a new harmony to the sections. Thurlow Weed, one of this number, stated that had he known *The Impending Crisis* counseled "a severance of the business, social and religious relations existing between slaveholding and non-slaveholding citizens" or even countenanced "servile insurrection" he would not have endorsed or contributed to its publication.[41]

*Harper's Weekly* gave a sigh of relief at the ending of the contest. It felt the security of the nation had been threatened by the long dispute which had aroused sectional feeling, retarded the country's commerce, and led to the accumulation of useless millions in the subtreasuries of the United States. As Senator William Bigler (Pennsylvania) observed, "Nothing has made so much bad blood as the endorsement of the Helper book and attempt now making to promote a man who did this to the responsible station of speaker of the House. The next most offensive thing is the sympathy manifested for old Brown."[42]

Many of the Southern states took official positions reflecting their extreme concern with the danger to the union in the Republican surge to power. Tennessee charged her representatives in Congress "to look on all who [are] in any way affiliated with Black Republicans as enemies," and that any action on their part "tending to elect a Black Republican Speaker would be an insult to their constituents." Florida solemnly resolved that the election of a Republican President would be adequate cause for secession. South Carolina requested that the slave states meet and take united action. It appointed commissioners to convey the resolution to Virginia and express sympathy for the Brown raid. Mississippi accepted South Carolina's invitation and sent a commissioner to Virginia expressing her desire to aid the state in repelling any invasion.[43] Shortly after the contest the Alabama legislature resolved that the state would not submit to the domination of a sectional party. In response to the resolution of South Carolina, that body declared its belief in a state's right to secede and held that the increasing "assaults upon the institution of slavery and upon the rights and equality of the Southern States" might lead her reluctantly to exercise that prerogative.[44]

During the contest many of the Southern people attempted to bring personal pressure into the sectional struggle, and nonintercourse meetings were held in many places. The citizens of Westmoreland County, Virginia, resolved not to travel or visit the North nor to trade with anyone who handled Northern products. In Berkeley County, Virginia, the young men and women agreed to wear homespun clothing, while in Alexandria $150,000 was raised to purchase a ship for direct trade with Europe. Thirty-two agents of New York and Boston houses returned to Washington stating that they had to abandon their Southern businesses. The New York *Tribune* reported that eleven others were met at Virginia railroad stations by vigilance committees and were en route to the North. Southern students in Northern colleges returned to study in Southern institutions. The whole body of Southern medical students in Philadelphia, between three and four hundred, departed in the last week of December, 1859, many going to the University of Virginia.[45]

Southerners were told of union meetings being held in the North, but many were skeptical of their effectiveness. No Massachusetts officials were present in Boston's Fanueil Hall to hear Edward Everett's and Caleb Cushing's conciliatory speeches, observed the Richmond *Semi-Weekly Examiner*. It reasoned that the governing cliques saved their sympathies "for the felon Brown, and endorse nothing that is not like Helper's infamous book—full of hatred of the South." It held that action spoke louder than words and there could be no excuse for anyone endorsing "Helper's incendiary publication."[46]

A Southerner observed that the legislative action of many Northern states was in conformity with the dogmas expressed in *The Impending Crisis*. "Their statute-books are filled with enactments, conceived in a spirit of hostility to the institutions of the South." As long as these remained, there could be no peace between the sections.[47]

The New York *Herald* was hopeful that Pennington's victory was the first step toward conservative triumph over "the abolitionized Republican party." It knew that Sherman was the strongest Republican candidate for Speaker and that the "fanatics strained every nerve to save his endorsement of Helper's book" and obtain his election, which could not be done. The *Herald* trusted this failure meant the overthrow of the Seward program and "the brutal and bloody philosophy of the Rochester manifesto."[48]

Despite the *Herald's* optimism Pennington's election was not considered a victory or even a draw by Southerners. The *Daily Richmond Enquirer*[49] reported his election with black death trimming. The Richmond *Semi-Weekly Examiner* did not see how any Southerner could trust Pennington because of his "union with the Black Republicans—his continued, zealous and unhesitating service in their ranks—his nomination and election by that party—his refusal to vote for a South American or a Southern old line Whig." Furthermore, as Speaker, he filled the House with "Freesoil subordinate officers." "The most noted leader of the strictest sectional party—the endorser of Helper," John Sherman, was placed at the head of the crucial Ways and Means Committee, along with a Northern majority. Also Pennington gave the North majorities on the important Commerce and Judiciary committees.[50]

Although displeased with Pennington's election, the New Orleans *Bee* felt that the dispute arising over *The Impending Crisis* had made Seward a less desirable candidate for the Presidency and that the Republicans would be forced to pass over him for "a more eligible person." This could be one positive national gain from the bitter contest.[51]

Even if it be conceded that the dispute played a great part in keeping Seward from the Presidency, there is no doubt that the speakership contest contributed immeasurably to the sectional hatred from which secession sprang. Like other such affairs, it was an unexpected development arising on an unpremeditated issue. To the average Southerner in Congress Helper became a dangerous figure who symbolized an attack on all he held most dear. Those who endorsed Helper's work had committed the unpardonable sin of aiding and abetting the destruction of Southern homes and society. Little did the Southerner stop to realize that the average Northern endorser was no more familiar with the work than was the average Southerner who attacked it.

Alone, *The Impending Crisis* did not produce the speakership crisis. Its endorsement came at a convenient time to serve as the most dramatic symbol for the contest of sections. Following the Brown raid, no better instrument could have been found to increase sectional bitterness. Today one can see the Southern error in attacking the endorsers. This action gave *The Impending Crisis,* and especially *The Compendium,* a large circulation in the North and imbued it with a status of dogma to many who otherwise would never have heard of it.[52] In the expression of opinions which the lengthy and violent dispute drew from the Congress and the people of both sections, the forces of moderation found it difficult to obtain a hearing.

It is impossible to state the number of copies of *The Impending Crisis,* in regular editions or as *The Compendium,* sold or given away, but a conservative estimate would be 75,000 copies. As Helper personally aided in the shipment of these volumes, he was pleased with the prominence his labor at last was receiving. While unable to predict the exact results, he was confident that his books were making major contributions to the destruction of slavery.

After Lincoln's election the New York *Herald* ascribed much of Republican success to Helper's work. "For weeks and months," it wrote, "express loads of the vile production were forwarded into every nook and locality of the Union, disseminating views which soon became deeply rooted in the rural districts, and against which the anti-constitutional newspapers did not pretend to utter a protest."[53]

Certainly the use of *The Impending Crisis* contributed greatly to the spirit of fear and hatred out of which secession and war erupted. Helper was not surprised that the Southern oligarchy would resist to the end in an effort to retain its favored position. However, he was grieved at the outcome since, as a Southern yeoman, he had hoped to see his people freed from the curse of slavery without further suffering. The last thing he wished was to place Southern people in arms and have them overrun by Negro troops and subjected to Negro political domination.

*Chapter Five*

# Contemporary Criticism

WHEN THE SPEAKERSHIP contest made *The Impending Crisis* a well-known book, the Democratic and proslavery forces were stunned and quickly marshaled their intellectual strength in self-defense. Helper's work, based on apparently undeniable facts, was a keen challenge to their existence and must be refuted if they were to survive. If his conclusions were correct, slavery would be destroyed and, with it, the successful Democratic coalition.

To prevent this development, four major works were written as thorough refutations of Helper's study, the most lucid and complete Northern rebuttal being Gilbert J. Beebe's *A Review and Refutation of Helper's "Impending Crisis."* Beebe, editor of *The Banner of Liberty* (Middleton, New York), which in 1856 attained the largest circulation of any Democratic publication, was one of the most forceful party journalists in the nation. He perceived that *The Impending Crisis* constituted a major challenge to the Democratic Party and in his extremely compact, 64-page work undertook the monumental task of disproving Helper's statistical arguments. Once informed of the "apocryphal, delusive and damning heresies" in *The Impending Crisis,* Beebe felt thousands would desert the Republican Party, which used it as a "text-book."[1]

*The National Democratic Quarterly Review* in Washington sponsored the second retort, that of Louis Shade, entitled *A Book* for the "*Impending Crisis!*" *Appeal to the Common Sense and Patriotism of the People of the United States.* "*Helperism*" *Annihilated! The "Irrepressible Conflict" and Its Consequences.* It contended *The Impending Crisis* was written "to destroy the happiness and prosperity of this country, and introduce discord, civil war, and bloodshed into our midst." Shade was surprised by Helper's "ridiculous, and in some respects even childish, application of statistics." He sought to promote Democratic victory by demonstrating that *The Impending Crisis* was primarily directed "against *the free white laborers,* mechanics, and merchants of the North" rather than against the South.[2]

Samuel M. Wolfe, a Virginian, produced a third and elaborate Southern answer in *Helper's Impending Crisis Dissected,*[3] published in Philadelphia in 1860. He substituted a fervent Southern nationalism for the loyalty to the Democratic Party, which had characterized the works of Beebe and Shade, dedicating his 220-page volume to a number of congressmen[4] and all patriots who wished the "defeat of Helper*ism* and Sherman*ism.*" After the speakership contest he concluded that some notice must be taken "of the *many* lies contained in the work" of the "vile wretch."[5]

Professor Elias Peissner of Union College, Schenectady, New York, produced the moderate and, at times, humorous fourth work of refutation, entitled *The American Question in Its National Aspect. Being Also an Incidental Reply to Mr. H. R. Helper's "Compendium of the Impending Crisis of the South.*[6] He indicted Helper for placing excessive confidence in the new science of statistics and for misjudgment rather than deliberate perpetration of falsehoods. "All sciences, in their infancy, are somewhat presumptuous," he wrote, and so it was with statistics. The superintendent of the New York Census of 1855 stated that his tabulations presented a labyrinth of the state's wealth and production almost impossible to survey. However, Helper, seemingly unaware of statistical limitations, took intricate national figures and arrived at definite conclusions, creating many false impressions.[7]

Another widely read work of the 1860's, *Southern Wealth and Northern Profits,*[8] probably owed its inception to *The Impending*

*Crisis.* Its author was Thomas Prentice Kettell, a former editor of *The Democratic Review* and financial writer for the New York *Herald,* who answered a number of Helper's arguments while maintaining that the prosperity and happiness of both sections depended on their continued peaceful trade.

Numerous other rebuttals were made to one or more of the concepts found in *The Impending Crisis.* In the South particularly the authors attempted to do so without mentioning the hated work. The critics were quick to attack the weakest argument of *The Impending Crisis,* that the Northern hay crop was worth many times the value of all the products of Southern agriculture.[9] Ironically, because of its dramatic nature, this argument became the most powerful single weapon in Helper's antislavery arsenal.

In his calculations Helper valued hay at $11.20 per ton, while the census used $7.00. In his comparisons of individual Southern crops and hay, Helper often contrasted a Southern nonstaple and the Northern staple. He falsely compared the Southern cotton crop and Northern hay crop and calculated the value of "the uncut western prairie grass" as if it were baled and ready to be sold for cash when, unlike cotton, not a single ton of it was exported. If the free states had sold their hay crop, they would have had to abandon their cattle, sheep, and horses. The Northern need for hay was a weakness rather than a strength, because its animals had to be fed on hay approximately six months of the year, while the Southern animals could graze on live pasturage.[10]

Although the 1850 returns did not show a single pound of hay to be produced in the districts of Darlington, Georgetown, Marlboro and Union, South Carolina, it reported 7,291 horses, 3,999 mules, 2,105 milk cows and 2,023 work oxen in the area. The proponents of the hay argument failed to realize that, when the pastures "were down," Southern animals fed on fodder, the stripped, cured blades of Indian corn, which the census did not consider as hay. Georgia produced only 23,449 tons of hay, or one-third that of Rhode Island, yet the Southern state had many times the number of cattle, horses, and sheep of the New England state because, in 1850, she produced 30,080,099 bushels of Indian corn.[11]

Beebe felt that, instead of developing the hay argument, Helper might as well have estimated at the Eastern price the value of Western timber and contended that the "wilderness forests" were worth several thousand dollars an acre. Helper "could not have selected a better article [than hay] with which to cram the Abolition asses of the North."[12]

Helper's contemporary critics were more successful in challenging the invalid hay argument than any other aspect of *The Impending Crisis,* although they were equally zealous in criticizing the whole work. Their contentions usually fell into two categories, both often expressed simultaneously by the same writers. One was an irrational reply which pictured the weaknesses of the South as strengths; the other was the presentation of a variety of explanations for the South's failure to keep pace with the North.

The iconoclastic Beebe presented a point-by-point refutation, although at times he fell into the irrational group. He found comfort in the fact that the North had more public schools than the South and prayed that the "abominable system" would never spread to the South. When compensation was commensurate with merits, the best Northern teachers accepted positions as private instructors in the slave states. Properly, the South left education to parents, and the large number of superior men produced by the system was evidence of its success. One could search the two houses of Congress and not find a dozen "respectable, gentlemanly, well educated or refined members" from the North. If native white illiteracy was greater in the South, this was because it was a sparsely settled, agricultural region affording fewer educational opportunities. Considering this limitation, her showing was grand and was achieved without the plundering of millions of dollars from the public pocketbook.

The number of books in Northern public libraries was more than those in similar Southern institutions, but three-quarters of those in the North were "the mere wishy-washy, namby-pamby, nonsensical novels and cheap nullities imposed upon school districts by rascally legislators." The books of true value were purchased by the people; furthermore, the South had its per capita proportion of newspapers, while it gave extensive support to Northern publications.

Undeniably, the South had fewer representatives and senators than the free states, but this fact only indicated the absurdity of Helper's claims that the South was dominating the Union. If the property of Southern churches was of less value than that of the North, this shortcoming could be attributed to the spiritual nature of the Southern people, who had not "gone so far in imitating heathen pagodas . . . [as] to insult their Maker, while pretending to worship Him . . ." Also the Bible and colonization causes were not lavishly supported in the South because they were simply designed to "gull the simple-minded, 'and lead captive silly women.' " Moreover, everyone in America could obtain a Bible and religious literature.

The North patented more new inventions than the South, but many of these were "jimcracks that Southerners would not deem worthy of notice," especially while their land was "teeming with such wonderous wealth as the tables" of exports exhibited. Much of Northern affluence depended on Southern raw materials and consumption of Northern manufactures, as withholding patronage would display. Southern reservoirs of population, filtering to cities, purified the cosmopolitan areas. The rural centers of the nation were morally superior, and if Helper had truly venerated Jefferson, he would have seen the cities of both sections only as necessary evils, recognizing "the smaller, fewer and farther off" they were, the better "for the morals, peace and happiness" of the people.[13]

The percentage of deaths, the amount of imprisonment, and the incidence of insanity among the people were used by more than one writer as evidence of Southern superiority, but uniformly they failed to consider the milder police power present in a rural society. It was conceded that the North was increasing faster in population, but "Which is better . . .? To produce fast and die fast, or to produce slower and live longer?" (Kettell alone attributed the North's rate of growth to immigrants' following "the parallels of latitude to which they have become accustomed.")[14]

It would appear that the view of Helper's contemporary critics toward slavery was equally irrational. To them it was a positive good and the "wave of the future" which offered a permanent solution to both the race and labor problems. They protested Helper's description of the slave's lot at the hands of "cruel, merciless" masters. The slave mart and the whipping post engendered horrors which existed only in the imagination. Instead of a slaveowner "stalking around 'with fire and frenzy' among the 'shrilling' cries of slaves," throughout the South, the most cordial relations existed between planter and slave. Innumerable masters listened patiently to requests for new clothes, shoes and other personal favors. Servants, both young and old, played with white children and joined their young masters in all sorts of recreations, constituting a "large and peculiar source of enjoyment" in their lives and distinguishing them "so happily from that of the free laborer[s]" who had nothing but "menial intercourse" with their employers. Slavery did not drag the Negro down from "the condition of a nomad, a heathen, a brute," but raised him "to that of a civilized and comfortable creature."[15]

According to *The Southern Literary Messenger,* the proper object of society is "the greatest happiness of the greatest number." A comparison of slavery with the wage system in a "modern industrial society" would indicate a greater prevalence of wretchedness and suffering in the nonslave areas, where the free laborer was forced to offer his services at the same price the peon received. Ultimately he was compelled to seek relief and sink into the pauper class. The result was the production of a small number of millionaires and a vast group of near indigents. In the South such "prodigious inequalities" did not exist, and the slaves were superior in physical comforts and "moral and mental condition" to their corresponding classes in free society.[16]

If anyone had compared the food, clothing and nursing of the slaves with that of the Northern industrial workers, he would agree that the bond servants received the greater reward for their labors. The average wage of free Northern workers was estimated at four dollars a week, hardly enough to keep soul and body together, much less support a family. With these facts considered, could it be that those in the North who were most vigorously attacking the slave system were lip-servers of freedom and not truly humanitarian? Despite the Declaration of Independence, so often quoted by slavery's opponents, many Northern states had passed laws indicating a belief in Negro inferiority, e.g., a Massachusetts law forbade intermarriage and a Connecticut law of 1833 restricted the education of "Africans."[17]

A Northerner contended that Helper's failure to indict Southerners for their treatment of slaves was evidence that he could not build a humanitarian or religious case for emancipation; however, in his "city of refuge," Helper envisioned free Negroes freezing and starving! He could have assumed no more absurd position than his belief in a diverse origin of the races. This was anti-Biblical and would leave unexplained the amiable relations which existed between the races.[18]

The history of slavery in America indicated that, generally, the slaves were content with their lot. For example, when the British invaded the Southern states during the Revolution, the great majority of slaves refused offers of freedom and gold as a reward for deserting their masters. In the War of 1812 no one fought more loyally at New Orleans than did groups of Negroes.[19]

Among Helper's critics the author of *The Union* was unique in contending slavery was an unsatisfactory permanent arrangement for meeting Southern labor needs. Even if slavery were a tender relationship from which the Negro received many advantages, "there is nevertheless that restless and inherent desire of freedom implanted in the breast of every one" which would prevent any slave from ever knowing contentment. It would also lead to frustration for every master who considered the Biblical injunction: "Do unto others as you would have them do unto you."[20]

In the midst of harsh criticism there were some authors who were not at all critical of Helper and were greatly influenced by his major theory that the aristocracy dominated Southern life. The slaveholding class had been influential enough in the South, wrote W. W. Handlin in 1862, to "control and direct all nonslaveholders and bind them to their policy"; this domination was the direct cause of the war. "Could one conceive of any powerful oligarch existing in any state without attempting to control its operations?" E. W. Reynolds asked. "Besides the slave-capitalists are not simply one class [in the South]. . . . They are the Dominant Class, having positive *control* of the social, religious and political power of those States." Since the slave power was virtually absolute and it considered free society its natural enemy, the law of self-preservation led it to instigate war to overthrow its rival.[21]

Such kind words from Helper's critics were very rare, for most made vigorous indictments of his treatment of the slaveholding class. Many writers refused to recognize that there was a basis for Southern discontent. They maintained that over half the white population had a connection with slavery and that every white man profited from the lower position in which the Negro was held. What would happen to the masses of Southern whites if three to four million Negroes were turned loose "to wander & prowl"?[22] Because of the common interest of all Southerners in slavery, it appeared to many that there could be no antagonism. When Edmund Ruffin read *The Impending Crisis,* he marveled that anyone could be so deluded as to believe hostility over the Negro existed between slaveholders and nonslaveholders. A Northern traveler-critic observed that anyone who had visited the slave states would realize the charges of a class struggle were false. It was often repeated that the contention was prepared exclusively to appeal to Northern readers, since all Southerners would recognize its falsity. Indeed, a work of such "fabrications . . . so intemperate and ferocious" in tone, could have owed its preparation only to "one of the craziest of the . . . fanatics, assisted by other persons, who designed to use it for party purposes."[23]

A Virginian held that John Brown labored under the Helper delusion. The failure of his raid was positive proof not only of white cohesion but of the unity of all Southern society. Slaveholders held the majority of Southern offices, and every Southern President had been a slaveholder, but plebeian confidence in patrician neighbors did not indicate vassalage to them. Which of the slaveholding Presidents were incompetent or dishonest? Which of them could the country have spared? Was their election not an indication that free people would choose the best man regardless of his social and economic condition? Was it not false reasoning which led Helper to indict slavery for the election of every Southerner to positions of consequence and hold that every Northerner reached the bureaucracy because of talent? Could Helper not see that Southern people of all classes were aware of many benefits conferred on everyone by their slave society? Even after the depression of 1857 "the prosperity and self-respect of the Southern people" seemed to be "unequalled in the world." The Southern poorhouses and jails were comparatively empty. Its cities were undisturbed by mobs and "unpunished violence." Its pulpits were not the platform of "fanaticism and political passions," and its legislation was "untainted by the thousand isms which have found their congenial soil in free society." Happily, "Maine-laws, Sunday laws" and other outmoded manifestations of New England Puritanism were conspicuous by their absence.[24]

*The Southern Literary Messenger* traced most of the undesirable social developments taking place in Western Europe and in the North to the perpetual struggle between capital and labor, nonexistent in the South. This struggle would never end while the basic source of labor was free. From Southern slavery flowed the stability which produced a contented society; therefore, it was the greatest of blessings. In agreement, another defender of the system contended that the interests of the working classes and the yeomanry would be aided by reopening the slave trade, thereby affording them opportunities for advancement into the planter class.[25]

*Russell's Magazine* concurred in these beliefs but urged its readers to remember that the South and its standards were different from the rest of the nation. Climate alone forced Southern inhabitants to become "a thrifty agricultural people," while the North followed agriculture only as an aid to other endeavors. As a result, a stable Southern economy emerged which made slow but sure the increase in production and consumption. Southerners could not expect to enter into the "race of progress" which occupied much of the civilized world, for avenues of great, sudden wealth were closed to them. Observing this inability, Northerners were apt to say that the South was retrogressing and decaying, but such was not the case. The South, continuing to advance in accordance with her best traditions, was advised to cherish its conservatism, "be content to advance cautiously and safely in wealth, and gracefully . . . like moral and intellectual creatures, enjoy the life which God has allotted." [26]

From a concern with slavery as an internal institution, a number of Helper's critics turned to an attack on his abolition scheme. They indicted *The Impending Crisis* by analyzing the motives for its publication and considering its practical effects. Few questioned the fact that it was an "incendiary work" which abounded "with incentives to treason, massacre, and bloody revolution." Inspired by "Numbers and Testimonies," Helper had concocted a fiendish plan for "war, blood and death," and under its tutelage the frenzy against slavery was reaching a climax.[27] The people of the North were being taught to hate slaveholders deeply, and a formula had been developed to arouse masses of Southern people against the "Lords of the lash . . . the slave-driving oligarchy."

"Apt scholars," the most conspicuous of whom was John Brown, were found to carry Helper's ideas into action. Stimulated by the "kindred insanity" of Helper and Brown, Northern public excitement logically produced Harpers Ferry. Brown and his associates forfeited their lives "for their folly" in believing *The Impending Crisis*. Their inability to provoke rebellion demonstrated "the fidelity, happiness, and contentment of the negroes of the South." The Republican Party espoused *The Impending Crisis,* the instrument of Brown's downfall, and while it disseminated the work, the South could expect nothing but a succession of "traitorous attempts to subvert its institutions and to incite its slaves to rapine and murder."[28]

Cognizant of the influence abolition literature had on the minds of the people, *The Southern Literary Messenger* urged that action be taken to keep "incendiary publications" out of the South. In spirit, the Northern states were violating the domestic tranquillity on which the Union was founded by exporting abolitionist literature.[29] A Northern critic found consolation in those statistics of Helper which revealed the extensive illiteracy of nonslaveholding whites, to say nothing of the slaves. Helper could not hope to reach the subjects for whom his book was written, since they could neither read nor understand *The Impending Crisis.* What he should have written was a spelling book to teach Southerners to read![30]

Whether or not Helper's work could reach the audience for whom it was originally designed, he had marshaled an impressive array of evidence, and to a historically minded people his hundred pages of testimony were disturbing. They had not thought of their great leaders as abolitionists, and the picture of Washington and Jefferson as enemies of slavery had to be eradicated.[31]

W. G. Brownlow flatly denied that the "Founding Fathers" were opposed to slavery. They wrote a fugitive slave law into the Constitution, and members of the Constitutional Convention insured the continuance of the foreign slave trade until 1808. They divided the Union into a free area north of the Ohio, while permitting slavery in the South. Washington and Adams signed acts admitting slave states when a veto denying their admission would have been sustained. The Constitutional Convention sanctioned slavery by adopting the three-fifth clause, and Jefferson in the purchase of Louisiana guaranteed the protection and preservation of slave property. To Brownlow these illustrations were proof that Helper and like-minded thinkers were misinterpreting the nation's most venerable statesmen.[32]

The journalist Beebe observed that Washington, Jefferson and Madison owned slaves all their lives. The contention that they felt slavery to be evil charged them with "base hypocrisy in practicing so differently from their pretended preaching." Jefferson and other young patriots disliked the British practice of dumping slaves into America as revenue-raising measures and included a protest against it in the first draft of the Declaration of Independence, which was removed, largely at the insistence of New England. During his administration, however, Jefferson acquired more territory suitable to slavery than any other President.

The numerous excerpts Helper gave proving the Fathers' opposition to slavery were merely "mangled Bones, torn with sacrilegious hand from venerable bodies." They only revealed how the Fathers agreed with Helper, not how they disagreed. "By garbling men's letters or speeches," they may be made to say anything; even "the Bible itself may be made to seemingly sustain atheism." At the most, a Northern professor wrote, the Fathers sought to harmonize union and reform through manumission as an ultimate goal. They would have been horrified at Helper's attempt to use "the organs of an excited populace" for freeing the slaves.

The critics were equally skeptical of Helper's foreign testimony. They wondered how England, whose policies had "starved to death millions of generous-hearted Irishmen and simple-minded Hindoos," as well as thousands of her own toiling masses, could dare raise her voice against Negro slavery.[33] They reminded their readers that, only a few years before, humanitarian France had attempted to introduce "voluntary Negro labor" into her tropical colonies. A Northern scholar wondered if a "constitutional" Montesquieu would have acted differently from a "constitutional" Madison in a comparable situation. He noted that eighteenth century France was a gloomy age for the peasant and artisan; during this period, "Rousseau wrote his *Contrat Social* to starving millions, and Montesquieu's *Esprit des Lois* was but a futile remedy for a dying generation." Such philosophy would not be pertinent to America. Helper's greatest inconsistency, however, was his quotation from modern Russian and classical writers. With all but a small fraction of the Russian people living in serfdom, subject to the cruelest tyranny, what could their writers say to the free, prosperous American people? The very example of Greece and Rome proved that a slaveholding people could "rise to the highest excellence in literature and the arts."[34]

For many readers the "Living Witnesses," cited by Helper, were such a "motley crowd" that their philosophy seemed to fly apart. Some of them, Peissner observed, appeared to continue in the tradition of moderation exemplified by Washington and Jefferson, but there were those who wished to "furnish pikes and money for others to battle and to die in the cause of human liberty." The prominence of Northern clergymen in the group drew the ire of the Yankee Beebe who believed that "incendiary abolitionism" first came from the pulpits of New England. Having succeeded in dividing their communions into Northern and Southern branches, the abolitionist ministers aspired to dismember the Union and, ultimately, to unite church and state. Now, as in other ages, "the most infernal villains that have ever cursed our earth have 'Stolen the livery of the Court of Heaven To Serve the devil in.' "

Helper's Biblical argument was deeply resented, and his opponents stated there was not a word in the Bible condemning slavery or indicating that it received only a temporary blessing. Slavery was protected by both the Mosaic Law and Gospel teachings; any other statement would be blasphemy. Helper perverted the liberty in Christ to mean freedom from the condition of servants and lowered the spiritual admonition to "call no man master" to the level of human relationships. The very status of the Negro would lend weight to the traditional interpretation that Ham, cursed and degraded by God, was the head of the African race, while Shem was the head of the copper-colored race and Japheth of the Caucasian race.

The injunctions given Christians to be content with their earthly situations and serve their masters led some writers to believe that New Testament teachings were as proslavery as those of the Old Testament. In not recognizing this interpretation, Helper was prejudiced and had committed the horrible sin of perverting "the Holy Scriptures to evil," even making the inspired writers contradict themselves.[35]

Most of the arguments presented against the philosophical portion of *The Impending Crisis* were based on wishful thinking, but rationalization of Helper's statistics proved far more difficult. The only possible rebuttal to major evaluations of the free and slave states was a per capita comparison which greatly improved percentages in the South's favor. The contemporary critics of *The Impending Crisis* used this technique continuously. If one would consider the population of states and per capita development, "our wonder and surprise would be reduced at least fifty per cent," a writer observed.[36]

Another defense was to arrange spot comparisons which revealed slave regions in a favorable light. Using Helper's reasoning, one might compare New York and Philadelphia, finding the latter degenerate since its exports were less than those of the former.[37] Beebe felt that the strategic geographical location of New York explained its having twice the population of Virginia, in 1850. Possessing the finest port on the Atlantic coast, New York had almost monopolized commercial communications with Europe, and most of the immigrants had entered her gates, many remaining in the state. In numbers, New York City had surged ahead of all other cities, even Boston, "the most fanatical, puritanic, abolition city in the Union." This fact, alone, demonstrated that absence of slavery and faith in a free society did not insure predominance. The differences in manufacturing and the value of real and personal property could be explained in terms of population and specialization. "A densely settled State, which does not produce half the agricultural staples consumed by its population" should certainly manufacture many times more than an agrarian state, and its property, centered in urban areas, should be evaluated much higher.

In the comparisons of populations, no cognizance was taken of the mid- and lower-South. Percentage-wise the great, dynamic increase in Southern population had come in the new states of the Southwest, but Helper, selecting his areas to prove his preconceived premises, had not chosen to contrast the increase in any Northern state with that in Alabama, Mississippi, Louisiana, Texas, Kentucky, Missouri or Arkansas. If Massachusetts and Tennessee were compared, it would be seen that the New England state increased in population from 378,717 to 994,514 between 1790 and 1850; at the same time the Southern state increased from 35,791 to 1,022,717.[38]

In addition to population, Helper discussed industry, contrasting the predominance of the North in manufacturing with the meager production of the South. His contemporary critics replied by resorting to the per capita argument and by noting Northern dependence on raw materials. They retorted that the South deliberately chose an agrarian existence because of its advantages and that, at any time, it could obtain manufactured articles from Europe rather than the North; however, the world could not dispense with Southern products. Peissner felt that Helper overlooked the relationship of manufacturing and population. He failed to realize that, as numbers increase, manufacturing multiplies in a geometric ratio. Therefore, if one hundred people produce only one-fourth as much as two hundred, it does not mean that they are decadent but that they are the victim of numbers. About one-half the value of Northern manufactured goods consisted of raw materials furnished by the South. When this factor was taken into consideration, a large portion of the Northern triumph was seen to be myth.[39]

Wolfe noted that the mills of Georgia were supplying most of the coarse plantation goods used there and that they were of comparable quality and price with those of New England. Should the South establish nonimportation, he felt that Georgia could furnish plantation textiles to half of the Southern states. Moreover, there was nothing which the North supplied that could not be obtained elsewhere, should economic warfare come, but where could the North obtain the products received from the South? The very thought of nonintercourse would make the fanatics of New England turn pale![40]

In his running debate with Abram Pryne, Brownlow held that fanaticism was forcing the South to develop her resources. Her coal, iron and copper appeared inexhaustible, and her extended shoreline insured that trade with Europe could continue even in war. Only when the South cut off the cotton, which turned most Northern spindles, would the North begin to appreciate her.[41]

If Helper's program were carried out, the Northern Democrat Louis Shade advised, it would result in "the destruction and ruin of the Northern factories, who are now employing thousands of men and women in the Southern trade." The Northern workman might well bless the institution of slavery if it were responsible for the heavy Southern purchases in the Northern market. Should slavery be destroyed, laborers might well have "to work day and night

for a pittance hardly sufficient to satisfy the most necessary wants."
Occasionally they might be slaughtered by the dictators of management, as a number of workmen recently were at the Pemberton
Mills, "sacrificed at the altar of Mammon" in "pious, Republican
Massachusetts." The Northern workingman should ponder these
facts when his best customers were called criminals and base characters because they bought from him and encouraged his industry.

This critic wondered, however, why the South was singled out
for special treatment. The Northwest and the Pacific Coast were
also dependent on the North for manufactures, yet they were not
called decadent. The South could remove this stigma by following Helper's program; then the "barbarous" Negroes would destroy
the land, and at last the South would be free of Northern manufactures.

Beebe agreed that Helper's manufacturing argument was an
attack upon the North and wondered if this fact would be perceived
before its manufacturing and commerce were transferred irrevo-
cably to the South. The compendium of the 1850 Census reported,
on the basis of an inquiry sent out by the Commissioner of Patents
in 1848, that the wages paid agricultural labor were lowest in the
Northwest, highest in the Southwest, and approximately the same
in the North and South. Thus the South could easily obtain the
labor force necessary to develop her industry and destroy much
of the Northern economy.

Kettell did not understand why Northerners would attack an
economic system which had functioned to their advantage. More
than one-half of the whole American export trade was based on
products exclusively of Southern origin, and many Northern exports were based on Southern raw materials. By the 1850's the
Northern fleet annually earned much of the free states' commercial
wealth through transporting Southern goods. Aided by import
duties, bearing heavily on the South and West, and by the fishing
bounty, the North was able to accumulate an economic surplus
which was invested in stocks, bonds and notes of insurance com-
panies. Then, by extending credit to other sections, the North used

its surplus to make more wealth. The result was that "a portion of every artisan's work is paid for by Southern means."[42]

The editor of the Richmond *Examiner,* E. A. Pollard, concurred with Kettell in the belief that slavery had nothing to do with the industrial and commercial predominance of the North. He contended that slavery, existing in the South from the colonial period, had been compatible with her early commercial prosperity. Also, the Helper argument was refuted by conditions in Jamaica; abolition had taken place and prosperity had vanished.

The inequities of national legislation were blamed for most of Southern failure to equal Northern material progress. The Louisiana Purchase "opened the Mississippi River" and "turned the tide of emigration to its upper branches." The new empire of the Northwest drew much of the wealth and numbers that otherwise would have gone to the South and Southwest. Statistically, Helper was greatly aided by the new states and territories.[43]

Perhaps the most disturbing of Helper's statistics to the average Southerner were those proving the North's superiority in agriculture; these figures were carefully considered by the Southern apologists. As a result, they found that the fertility and price of land, as well as the density of population, in the marketing area determined production. Yet despite the denser Northern population, Helper's tables revealed that, in quantity of wheat per acre, Texas and Florida equaled Pennsylvania and excelled every other Northern state except Massachusetts. Delaware, Maryland, Florida, Missouri, and Texas exceeded Maine and Michigan in wheat productivity per acre, while Delaware and Missouri equaled New Hampshire, New Jersey, and Illinois. Similar results were obtained in comparing state production of such typically Northern crops as Indian corn, Irish potatoes, oats, and rye. Helper carefully chose these products to "rig" his findings, and this was comparable to a Southerner selecting sweet or Carolina potatoes, which could hardly be grown in many Northern states, to prove Northern agricultural inferiority.[44]

*The Southern Presbyterian Review* held that smaller production in many of the older Southern states was due to the availability of cheap, fertile Western lands which encouraged wasteful agricultural methods and soil exhaustion. "Had there not been a boundless continent before us the results would have been far different," and if Helper had compared the returns from the newer Southern states with the older Northern states, there would have been no similarity to his earlier statistics. Helper, and those who thought like him, held that slavery was producing careless cultivation, but such was not the case. Soil conservation was not a national practice, and all Americans, "Slave States and Free, North and South—are exhausting our land and our hands." Staple agriculture might lend itself more readily to rapid expansion, but the slave system should not be blamed for the American phenomenon of wastefulness.[45]

The aroused defenders of slavery were equally fluent in countering *The Impending Crisis'* "proof" of the superior value of Northern farms and domestic animals. "The live stock of the South *per capita* [obviously meaning whites only] is more than double that of the North," wrote the *Southern Presbyterian Review,* "while the population of the South, bond and free, is but as 9 to 13 to that of the North." When population was considered, the North was $100,000,000 inferior to the South in its number of animals slaughtered; thus, in accordance with Helper's reasoning, these figures would show that the South was much thriftier than its Northern neighbors. Surprisingly, the value of Northern farms and implements lacked "$134,931,929 of equalling the same proportion to population of Southern Farms and Farming Implements and Machinery."[46]

Helper turned from his comparison of farming wealth to that of landed property, stating that slavery tremendously reduced the value of every acre of land in the South and that emancipation would bring an immediate increase in its value. Beebe challenged these figures, contending the census Helper used did not classify lands in Northern, Northwestern, Southern and Southwestern categories. Instead, it gave the average price of occupied lands in New England, the Middle States, the South, the Southwest and the

Northwest. The highest average price for a Northern area, New England, was $20.27, not $28.07 as Helper contended. Considering the occupation of the land, the average value of all free states' land was only eight dollars an acre, scarcely over two dollars more than that of the Southern average. Beebe conceded that the average land prices of some specific Southern states were less than those of specific Northern states, North Carolina and New York, for example. Property values, however, will always be higher in a densely settled state with few waste lands than in a sparsely settled state with a great deal of waste lands, and the totality of the situation must be considered, not "rigged" comparisons.[47]

Neither could one say, as Helper did, that because one city, New York, was wealthy enough to buy an entire Southern state Southern society was decadent, due to slavery. Frequently the wealth of a kingdom is concentrated in one city. There was no Negro slavery in nineteenth-century England, but London "could easily buy one or two provinces of its own—New York and a few European kingdoms included."

The idea that abolition would quickly increase the value of Southern lands was branded as absurd. "We need say nothing to expose the folly and stupidity of such a representation." The experience of Jamaica following abolition indicated that it would take a hundred years for the Southern lands to reach the value Helper had predicted, during which time the nation would lose twenty billion dollars in cotton exports. However, the writer Beebe foresaw freedom diminishing the value of Southern lands by only one-fifth.

One of Helper's general critics accepted his argument at this point. Only in slavery could he find an explanation for the lower land values of the naturally richer South; consequently, he thought that Southerners should welcome any feasible plan for compensated emancipation.[48]

Helper's contemporary critics left no phase of his arguments unanswered. They performed an essential task in defense of the South and the Democratic Party when they offered alternatives to Helper's theories, shrewdly revealing his essential weaknesses.

On the other hand, at times they were guilty of the same illogical reasoning which they felt to be characteristic of Helper. In their fine-spun analysis they often conceded the points they were trying to refute. They could not deny that, in sixty years, the South had fallen badly behind in population, industry, and agricultural production. The most they could do was attempt to soften the impact of this fact and try to exonerate slavery as a contributing factor.

*Chapter Six*

# Modern Criticism

THE QUESTION OF slavery's effect on American life has remained unanswered in the twentieth century. Historians of the South have devoted much scholarly attention to the profitability of slavery to the slaveholder, and in the course of the last few decades the prevailing opinion has changed from a belief that slavery was generally unprofitable to the opposite view.

In determining the profitableness of slavery, Ulrich B. Phillips and his followers contended that an allowance must be made for interest and depreciation of capital invested in land and slaves. Studies would indicate, Phillips held, that by the 1850's only those slaveholders "whose plantations lay in the most advantageous parts of the cotton and sugar districts and whose managerial ability was exceptionally great were earning anything beyond what would cover their maintenance and carrying charge."[1]

Following Phillips' concepts, Charles S. Sydnor demonstrated that profits from slave labor were low, even on the relatively new, fertile lands of Mississippi. Lewis C. Gray held slave prices, by the 1850's, were such that slaves could not be employed profitably on the lower fertility lands, which characterized most of the area of the older states. The returns "could not produce a surplus sufficiently large to pay interest on the high capital values made possible by competition of regions where slave labor was employed to better advantage." He believed this was responsible for the mistaken notion that slavery could "thrive only by expansion." Gray even doubted the profitability of raising Negroes for sale to the Southwest, since their increase brought only moderate interest on the capital invested and provided no maintenance allowance. The greatest weakness of the slave system, Ralph Flanders found, lay in the protection that had to be given its capital, and the major expense of slave labor lay in its management. Disease, death, accidents, runaways, and theft all posed a constant menace.[2]

Thomas P. Govan successfully challenged the older concept of interest and demonstrated that it was not "an actual expense of the planter" but that profit was "a combination of this interest on investment and wages for management." Furthermore, most of the slaves and land in the South were not purchased after 1849, and market prices did not furnish a just basis for calculating profits.[3] In the light of these contentions, the profitableness of slavery has been re-examined.

As a result, Alfred H. Conrad and John R. Meyer have presented the most convincing argument for the over-all profitableness of slavery to the planter. Comparing the returns of slaves with those of other capital assets, they discovered prime field hands returned a yearly profit of 2.2 to 13 per cent, slave mothers of ten children, 8.1 per cent and those of five, 7.1 per cent. (This was an over-all average, higher for the female, explained by the need to attract capital for breeding purposes.) Sale of slaves from the seaboard states westward furnished a major item in the feasibility of the system and made possible a profitable economic function for the exhausted lands of the East.

After 1845 the rise in slave prices was "solidly based on the increase in the value of the crop per hand, owing to the concentration of production in more fertile areas, the greater efficiency of the American-born slaves, lowered transportation costs, and the development of new high-yield varieties of cotton from the fourth decade of the century on." Between 1843-45 and 1860 slave prices on the New Orleans market rose about 150 per cent, but during the same period, the value of cotton production per hand rose 300 per cent. Abnormal situations at the turn of the century had given a wrong impression of what the relationship between cotton and slave prices should be.[4]

Kenneth Stampp was amazed that the apologists for slavery rarely used the "most obvious and most practical argument of all," that slavery was profitable. Slavery flourished and slave prices rose in the 1850's because slavery was "justifying itself economically." The risks in slave ownership and the cost of maintenance were discounted before the price of slaves was determined. Most owners had a natural increase in their number of slaves; this was a clear gain, not a new need for added interest as earlier accounting tabulations would have it. Rising hiring prices indicated that "the slave was earning for his owner a substantial, though varying, surplus above the cost of maintenance."

In Arkansas, where lands were so new that soil exhaustion was not a factor and where slaves were purchased at the high prices of the 1850's, slavery has been shown to be generally profitable, even among the small owners. The number of owners of four slaves or less increased from 3,334 in 1850 to 5,806 in 1860. Many of this group probably were unconcerned "with whether or not their slaves produced a measurable net profit each year"; yet the increase in their number indicates that the farmers "did not consider the ownership of slaves economically burdensome."[5]

The sugar industry was one requiring large outlays of capital in expensive equipment and slaves. Largely due to varying weather conditions, it suffered greater uncertainties than the cotton industry. Through the years the tendency of sugar prices was downward, but despite this trend, enough information is available "to indicate that the Louisiana sugar industry as a whole was profitable," and well run ante bellum plantations made profits in all but the few years of very low prices.

Paul W. Gates summarized the reasons earlier historians felt slavery to be unprofitable. They neglected "the capital gains from the rising value of slaves and land in newly opened areas, the profits from rearing slave children, and the high return cotton planters received from selling into the Deep South the surplus slaves of older communities or from rearing their own slaves in the newer areas."[6]

Those who believe in the unprofitableness of slavery to the slave-holder must prove their contention. Although modern scholarship indicates that, at least in the short run, it was generally profitable for individual owners, more work needs to be done in the field. In particular, a detailed study of the debt structure of slaveholders would be valuable. It is possible that the paper capital gains earned by planters, with the rise in slave prices, were offset by increased debts. It is certain that profits were made, or slavery would not have expanded and prices of land and slaves increased. The question is, "Who earned the profits?" Was it the slaveholder or his Northern creditor? Was it literally true that the individual slaveholder and slavery as an institution had to expand to survive? Was rapid expansion the only way the planter could gain respite from his debts? Much of the evidence marshaled by the revisionists consider only part of this economic picture, and until more research is done, a definitive answer can not be given.

Even if it be conceded that slavery was profitable for the average slaveholder, Helper's indictment remains. Did slavery adversely affect the masses of Southern whites who were nonslaveholders, and was it to blame for the failure of the South to keep pace with the North? There is much evidence to indicate that the answers to these questions are a qualified *yes*.

Some of the earlier historians accept most of Helper's arguments. Phillips succinctly reflected many of them in his statement that "the slaveholding regime kept money scarce, population sparse and land values accordingly low; it restricted the opportunities of many men of both races, and it kept many of the natural resources of the Southern country neglected." Flanders wrote that, custom and tradition had led to slavery's use primarily for single-crop, non-scientific farming and that "habitual neglect in training the Negroes had engendered the idea that the latter were incapable of learning." He found that few owners made fortunes from the use of slave labor, but that the mere ownership of Negroes conferred status in a stratified society.

It was Helper's contention that slavery was a means to maintain oligarchical control in the South. In his view, slavery solved the race problem by uniting the inferior, exploited Negroes and the slaveholders against the masses of whites. Phillips and his followers, while rejecting Helper's oligarchical contention, saw slavery primarily as a solution to the race problem. Surprisingly, some of the revisionists accept the same view. Govan wrote, "Slavery appears to have been not so much an economic system as a social order to permit two unlike peoples to live together." Stanley M. Elkins placed great emphasis on the noneconomic aspects of slavery, agreeing with Govan that one must rule out the question of whether free labor would have been more profitable.[7] It is interesting that any who contend slavery was profitable find the major reason for its existence to be noneconomic.

Helper's study demands a comparison of the achievements of free and slave labor. Although he compared many aspects of Northern and Southern life, the basis of Helper's argument was economic. If the South had not fallen behind in material development, the rest of his contentions would have collapsed like a house of cards. The study of the validity of his work is therefore confined to this all-important area.

It is not adequate, because of changes induced by the war, to contrast the Southern economy of the 1850's with that of the post-Reconstruction years for a picture of the comparative results of slave and free labor. Helper's work, based on usually accurate statistics, give a truer picture.[8] Clearly the South fell behind the North in most fields of economic endeavor in the ante bellum period. As Robert R. Russell has noted, before 1860 Southerners generally had come to recognize the Northern superiority in many areas.[9] The most that contemporary critics could do with Helper's statistical indictment was to reduce the South's percentage of inferiority by calculating per capita instead of over-all development.

On the purely agricultural level it is logical to assume slavery inhibited over-all economic progress. One may concede that much of the unfrugal care of Southern land can be traced to the nature of the soil, heavy rains, and failure of management to plow and fertilize properly. It is also true that the leading Southern experiments with crop improvement and land conservation were made by slaveholders and that much of ante bellum American agriculture generally was unscientific and exploitive. Yet the fact remains that the plantation system, based on slavery, largely relied on the exhaustion of the soil for its survival. It may be true, as Conrad and Meyer believe, that exhaustion resulted from the scarcity of labor, but slavery closed much of the South to free labor and helped create conditions which made exhaustion, in the short run, more profitable than conservation. (Exhaustion, of course, violated a basic business theory that provision must be made for conservation of plant before profits are considered.)

Slavery was closely related to the prevalent one-crop system, which was chosen because it seemed to offer the most secure and immediate profits. With the South's labor factor being what it was, its creditors were interested only in staples and dictated economic policy to many of the slaveholders. Creditor control continued with a vengeance in the post bellum period, the heritage of both the pre-war years and the 1860's. Because of creditor influence, it is incorrect to point to the South's reliance on one-crop agriculture until the 1930's as evidence that slavery was not a major factor in preventing diversification.

Much of the original motivation for one-crop agriculture lay not in the Negro's stupidity but in the failure of a caste society to develop his capacities for being an efficient, reliable worker. One need only read of the overseers' and masters' woes to be convinced that slave labor was inferior to free labor. Could it ever be otherwise? What incentives were present for the slave workers? As Paul Gates has written, those who relied on slaves, "who were forced to do their work under the threat of the lash," found it inadvisable to use expensive machinery. The hoe manned by a poor Negro living at the very margin of subsistence was the pace of Southern agriculture before 1865. Such a system could not compete with the farms of the North and Northwest which were being rapidly mechanized and whose workers had a vested interest in their progress.

Slave labor overcame the advantages of free labor, Stampp be-

lieved, by paying less, better exploiting women and children, having
longer working hours and more rigid discipline and by permitting
less agitation and bargaining.[10] This list is amazingly like the
arguments early twentieth-century conservatives presented showing
that unionized factories could never compete with management-
dominated organizations. Not only does it fail to consider the
workers' incentive, but it also neglects the workers' role as con-
sumers. Here may have been the South's greatest weakness.

By 1854, as Eugene Genovese has shown, Eastern manufacturers
were dependent on the rural market for their economic survival,
but the purchasing power of the Southern white masses and the
almost nonexistent purchasing power of the slave was so small that
the South could not sustain industry. Production costs, even with
slave labor, were too high to compete with Northern firms servicing
a wider market. Without industries and cities, of course, diversification of agriculture for large producers was very difficult.[11]

Slave labor was the author of agrarianism. Those planters who
defended the rural way of life were in the grand tradition of ra-
tionalizing a necessity. With slavery as the basis of the Southern
economy, no other way of life was possible.

Southerners contended that, under the plantation system, there
was no real stratification of white society and the poorer whites of
ability could move into the planter class. Of course, some were
able to make this transition, but the mobility of Southern life has
been exaggerated.

Frank L. Owsley and his students did a monumental service in
modifying the myth of the Southern "poor whites." They demonstrated that the majority of small Southern farmers owned "family
sized farms" and that complete segregation of planters and small
farmers never occurred. Yet the very statistics in *Plain Folk of
the Old South* which prove these facts also reveal the stratification of
Southern society. A study of the Owsley statistics reveals that a
large percentage of nonslaveholders owned less than two hundred
acres of land, while a majority of slaveholders owned more than
two hundred. The richer the soil, the higher the concentration became at opposite ends of the scale. During the 1850's the percentage
of slaveholders in the surveyed Black Belt areas and those holding

over five hundred acres of land increased.[12] The Owsley statistics seem to prove that to be a large land owner in the 1850's one had to be a slaveholder. For a nonslaveholder to break into this category, in an era of high prices for slaves and fertile lands, required too large an initial investment for all but the very ingenious.

This thesis is borne out by increasing planter control of the Black Belt regions, a development closing opportunities for advancement to the masses of white farmers.[13] It was the slave who was the basis of Southern nonsubsistent agriculture. "The great majority of the staple crops was produced on plantations employing slave labor," but fully three-quarters of the Southern whites had no direct slave interest. In 1860, 3,500,000 of the year's 5,387,000 bales of cotton were produced in Alabama, Mississippi, Louisiana, and Georgia. "It is no mere accident that these same states were also at the top of the list in the number of large slaveholders." The large owners dominated their states' economy and had a political and social "influence all out of proportion to their numbers."[14] One could be certain that, as a class, they would not institute reforms to aid the white commonality.

With regard to industry, Stampp, among others, has even questioned the ability of an affluent agricultural society to return profits comparable to those of an industrial and commercial society. But what of the direct influence of slavery on Southern white industrial workers? Slave labor was used in cotton mills, coal mines, and in the lumber and iron industries. Some seem to think it aided economic progress; however, this is questionable. "The competition of slaves injured the dignity and lowered the self-respect of the white manual laborer." Whenever they could, white workers wished to work apart from slaves and usually sought a clear division in their labor. White workers were violently opposed to the teaching of trades to slaves, believing they constituted a major threat because they worked at cheaper wages. If pay and services for slave labor had been equal, slave workers would have been no menace, but it was the lower pay, longer hours and less favorable working conditions that furnished a motivation for the introduction of slaves into industry.[15]

Results of the pressure of slave labor were unfortunate on white

workers and the South generally. It retarded the development of a
large class of free laborers who could have aided in the support of
a vigorous economy. A remarkable study has revealed "that the
position of white labor in the South showed little if any improvement in the ante-bellum period" and attributed much of this fact
to the squeeze of slave competition. Many Southern white workers
actually lost "their freedom of occupational choice and mobility."
Apprenticeship of children was often a means to obtain cheap
labor, and poor or delinquent adults were literally sold into labor
in a number of states. Troops quickly broke a number of strikes
in the South, especially those among Irish railway workers. Generally, the courts were unfavorable to strikers, much more so than
in the North. In Virginia, South Carolina, and Louisiana, "white
laborers as compared with slaves held an unfavorable and even
degraded position." They enjoyed few returns for hard labor and
even lacked the security of the slave.[16] Living in a North Carolina
town and seeing such conditions, one can understand how Helper
would develop his extreme bitterness. Conversely, it is easy to realize
why contemporary apologists for slavery regarded it as a condition
much better for the worker than freedom.

Slavery clearly promoted the concentration of wealth in a few
hands and served to keep the South an agrarian society. Robert R.
Russell rightly contended that the lack of economic opportunity
was the greatest factor in the failure of the South to attract thousands of immigrants and experience economic growth. Slavery was
a major cause of this failure and should not have been excused as
Russell did.[17]

Helper's conclusions in *The Impending Crisis* were generally
correct. Slavery was a retarding factor in Southern development
and contributed to the South's dependence on the North. But slavery was not the whole story!

*The Impending Crisis* was an abolitionist document which, like
all works of propaganda, overstated its case in an effort to obtain
converts. Moreover, Helper's limited education and experience
did not equip him for a judicious appraisal of the North and the
South. Like passionate leaders of every age, he limited historical

causation to one factor—obviously an oversimplification. As a Southerner, there is no excuse for his failure to make allowances for the differences in an agrarian and industrial society. There is more reason for his ignorance of the North, however. If Helper could have lived in the East for a few years before writing *The Impending Crisis*, there is the possibility he would have come to appreciate the influence of unique factors other than freedom in Northern development. Perhaps, among others, he would have allotted some role to the significance of natural resources, the nature of European immigration into the North, and to the continued effects of the Puritan spirit. Failure to do so reflected his own limitations.

A more equitable evaluation of North and South would have done much to make Helper's work acceptable to a larger number of contemporary and present-day intellectuals. It should be remembered, however, that Helper wrote to arouse the unschooled masses. His lack of objectivity was welcomed by semiliterates in the North, and it is doubtful that he could have modified his work sufficiently for the South to have permitted its circulation.

*Chapter Seven*

# Consul at Buenos Aires

HINTON ROWAN HELPER, in 1861, was one of the best known men in the United States as a result of the prominence which *The Impending Crisis* had received in the speakership contest. However, most of the circulation of his work had been at or near cost, and he was forced to devise some means of support. When private endeavors failed, he turned to the Republican Party, in whose victory he had played no minor role, and demanded a government post. Its response, with a second-class position in Argentina, determined Helper's subsequent career.

When Helper began to seek employment, he found he was not prepared for a profession or trade and first turned to an avenue which offered hope of financial reward without physical labor, the speaker's platform. Twice in the winter of 1861 he scheduled addresses based on *The Impending Crisis,* both times without success. On January 9 he scheduled a lecture, entitled "Two Systems of Labor," for Clinton Hall, Astor Place, New York, the admission being but twenty-five cents. When only forty-two people purchased tickets, the lecture was canceled. Unrebuffed by his reception in sophisticated New York, the indefatigable Helper continued plans for a tour beginning February 19. For his initial engagement, in Dayton, Ohio, he purchased newspaper advertisements and had handbills distributed throughout the city. When only twenty-three tickets were sold, he concluded that the American people were apathetic to his subject and canceled his engagement and tour, never to lecture again; instead he looked to the Lincoln administration for an appointment.[1]

In applying to the President for a third-class consulate position at Antwerp, Glasgow, or Southampton, Helper stated that his stand, in favor of free labor, prevented him from obtaining profitable employment. He also included letters from three members of *The Compendium* committee corroborating his opinion. William H. Anthon, the chairman, declared, "Contrary to general opinion the publication of the work has produced but little pecuniary profit" to Helper, "while it has closed to him most of the sources of profitable employment in this city and vicinity." Edgar Ketchum testified that Helper "has done nobly and has suffered for it"; while W. C. Noyes assured the President that Helper "has done and suffered much in the cause of freedom."

In a consular appointment Helper saw an opportunity to write another book of major importance. In it he hoped to persuade the American people to expel the Negro from their national life. He was confident the President would see the value of the endeavor and would weigh it heavily as he considered the application.[2]

The first weeks of the Lincoln administration were too full to devote much time to consulships, and Helper's request remained unanswered. He could not understand such ingratitude. Only the necessity for money led him to relinquish his pride and appeal directly to Republican patronage-mongers, chief of whom was Hiram Barney, collector of the Port of New York. David Dudley Field and a number of other prominent New Yorkers called on Barney in Helper's behalf, but with little success. Barney conceded to Helper that he had received a letter from President Lincoln regarding him but would not disclose its details, whereupon Helper resolved to spare himself "the humiliating necessity" of another interview. He, then, appealed to his friend, Treasury Secretary Salmon P. Chase, to obtain an appointment as consul at Leeds, England. Not only would it "be gratifying to both myself and [my] friends," he wrote, "it could hardly prove otherwise than agreeable to my enemies inasmuch as the business of the office would take me from them—out of the country." If this could not be arranged, Helper, now desperate for money, urged Chase to obtain a position for him in New York or Washington which would enable him to support himself "decently" while working "in the interests of free labor throughout the Continent."[3]

From July to November, 1861, Helper anxiously awaited action which did not come. His money and patience gone, he moved to Washington and, with politeness but firmness, called his condition to Lincoln's attention. "Month after month has elapsed," he wrote, "since I first had the honor of applying to you with numerous and highly respectable recommendations for some position in the public service which it was hoped and believed would be granted graciously and without delay." In the interim he had received only assurances and expressions of approbation and had "been enticed on from one point of time to another" until he had come to "a most awkward and unhappy quandary." He earnestly appealed to Lincoln, "as the President and as a Man," for an immediate appointment.[4]

Helper wrote much more frankly to Chase who, in September, had suggested that Secretary of War Simon Cameron appoint him to a paymastership. After two months Cameron stated that there were no vacancies, and he did not know when one would occur. This was too much for the anxious candidate who lamented to Chase, "I have so long been the victim of fruitless promises, delays, and disappointments that I have at last become embarrassed and miserable beyond expression. A change of some sort is now absolutely necessary for me." He suggested to Chase that the President give "an *absolute* order for my appointment, without additional or unnecessary delay, to some other respectable position either at home or abroad." Cameron had twice virtually promised him a paymastership, and Helper was willing to accept such an appointment or even a measureship in the Boston or Philadelphia customhouse. "Though I do think I ought to have a better position than this," he wrote, "yet I would rather accept *it* than wait longer."

When Helper heard that the consul at Buenos Aires was an

appointee of Franklin Pierce and was "unfriendly to Mr. Lincoln's administration," almost incidentally he suggested to Chase that he would take the position.[5] To his surprise, the administration acted promptly and, on November 13, 1861, offered him the job. He was so pleased to obtain it that his bitterness quickly evaporated and, in a gracious letter of acceptance, promised, "by strict attention to the duties of the office, . . . to promote the interests of American Commerce and Navigation and such other interests as may come within my province." Seldom has any promise been better kept.[6]

Fortunately Helper's appointment did not create an unpleasant situation at the consulate in Buenos Aires for, at the same time, the incumbent consul, William H. Hudson, asked for a leave of absence. A short time previously, the salary of the Buenos Aires post had been reduced to $2,000 a year, a much smaller stipend than when Hudson accepted the appointment, and experiencing financial difficulties, he was happy to leave. He had managed to survive only by retaining some of the fees which normally would have been remitted to Washington and by borrowing heavily from Buenos Aires businessmen. As late as May 25, 1866, the government paid Hudson $1,666.67 "extra salary" to aid him in closing his accounts.[7]

No time was lost by Helper in making preparation to assume his new position. He executed his bond December 7 and, while waiting for his passport, called on a number of merchants and the Argentine consul in New York City in an attempt to acclimate himself to his new position. It was at this time that he first heard of the fluctuating nature of Buenos Aires currency, which was the bane of importers' existence.

On December 14 the consul-designate's passport arrived, and he planned to sail immediately but waited until January 5 in order to take the "Ophelia," an American vessel. Although advised to go via Liverpool or Southampton on a British ship, he felt it his duty to sail "American," but only his militant patriotism compensated him for the constant sea-sickness of the long, ninety-eight day cruise.

En route, an incident occurred off Cape St. Rouge which Helper dutifully recounted to the State Department, the first of his meticulous and lengthy reports from Latin America. As the "Ophelia" passed the Baltimore-owned "Banshee," its captain, James Kean, gave "three cheers for Jeff Davis"! Helper realized that the offense was not "one of the most grievous sort," but he thought the government might well consider "whether a man who basely insults the flag which protects him on the ocean may not be actuated by the instincts of a traitor on land."

In an era when many American vessels in Latin American waters were seeking protection from Confederate raiders by changing registry, the conduct of the "Banshee's" captain concerned the State Department, and the collector of the Port of Baltimore was asked to investigate. When the incident was called to the ship company's attention, it suspended Kean for over a year, and he was restored only when he pledged never again to commit similar indiscretions.[8]

The new consul arrived at Buenos Aires April 12, as the American minister to Argentina, Robert M. Palmer, departed. For a short while Helper was the leading American official in the city, which led him to form the habit of conducting himself more as a minister than a consul. Within two weeks he had assumed the full duites of his office, completing the transfer of all responsibilities from his predecessor.

The first dilemma to confront Helper was the confiscation of Argentine goods by the New York Customhouse on the grounds that the Buenos Aires consular certificates defrauded the United States government of tariff revenue. Helper continued his predecessor's practice of expressing the value of Buenos Aires paper money, which differed from that of other Argentine provinces, in terms of United States dollars. A wide variation in evaluation took place, since the Buenos Aires currency fluctuated as much as fifty per cent in one day. What the New York collector actually desired was a statement that the certificates were based on "the patriot doubloon," which had a technical, but not real, value of $15.58.

Helper continually wrote Secretaries Seward and Chase in an attempt to resolve the situation. Careful tables were prepared to show the semiannual fluctuation in the currency's value since 1826, and samples of the money were sent the secretaries in the hope that seeing the money would aid them "in arriving at a speedy and just decision." Protesting that he could not spend much of each day listening to the rightful complaints of Argentine merchants, Helper informed Chase that the unreasonable New York action "must cease at once and forever, or someone else must be sent here, in my stead, to hear" them. Helper was a determined man, and when aroused, his nuisance value alone made him impossible to ignore. After sixteen months of chronic persistence he probed to the depths of the matter and corrected it, something his predecessor had not been able to do.[9]

Partially because of extenuating circumstances, Helper did not confine himself, as consul, to matters dealing primarily with trade and travel. The new American minister, Robert C. Kirk, who arrived in Argentina two months after Helper, was not a zealous man and was only mildly concerned with promoting inter-American relations. However, Helper, while seeing Latin American weaknesses, was enchanted with the new world he discovered and, true to his romantic nature, envisioned the potentiality in the cultivation of United States interests. He did not hesitate to report fully on all conditions attracting his attention and to make appropriate recommendations.

Helper's tenure came during the Civil War era, and as an ardent patriot, he investigated any suspicion of treason. In September, 1862, he obtained twenty-seven pages of letters from the male members of the Thomas J. Page family in Richmond to their exiled women and children in Florence, Italy. (Page was a former lieutenant in the United States Navy who had surveyed the La Plata waters in the 1850's.) He read them, marked the treasonous passages and forwarded them to Seward, who approved his action in the matter; this spurred Helper to great zealousness in the protection of United States interests.

Helper was particularly impatient with those who, he believed, were attempting to use their United States citizenship in an abusive way. In 1863, as Argentina began preparation for the Paraguayan

War, many children of United States citizens, seeking immunity
from military service, asked for issuance of certificates of protection.
Helper was convinced that most of those applying had no intention
of ever living outside Argentina and were "of no more worth to
the United States than the home-born, permanent residents of
Australia." Therefore, with the approval of Kirk, he resolutely refused to issue certificates to anyone failing to prove his intention of
returning to the United States. When a number of United States-
born Negroes also applied for certificates, Helper's wrath was fully
kindled, and he promptly denied their request. Although he had
ample ground for his decision in their long Argentine residence,
his racial hatred was a primary motive. "I could not, of my own
accord, do anything whatever to increase or enlarge, even in the
smallest degree, the colored population of America," he wrote.

After issuance of their certificates, six or seven United States
citizens succumbed to the influence of the Argentine capital and
became openly disloyal. The large British colony in Buenos Aires
was openly pro-Confederate, and the success enjoyed by Confederate raiders in 1863 and 1864 was appealing. Helper understood
these pressures, but his extreme loyalty prevented any tolerance of
participation in Confederate activities. He urged the State Department to require all holders of United States passports and certificates of protection to take an oath of loyalty by July, 1864; those
who refused should have their papers canceled.

Reports for the State Department on the activities of the openly
treasonous were prepared by Helper in the belief that the "hostile
and rebellious" should have their foreign travel restricted. In March,
1864, he relayed his suspicions of Baltimore's Joseph Sterrett, a
regular visitor to Buenos Aires. Locally known as an "intense and
undisguised" rebel and "decidedly obnoxious to all Union men,"
Sterrett delighted in haranguing groups with the "keenest shafts of
denunciation and abuse" of the United States. Helper urged Sterrett be required to take the oath of allegiance before again being
allowed to leave the United States.[10]

In September, 1865, Helper's patience with Daniel Deshan, Jr., of Boston came to an end. Earlier, Deshan had taken the oath of allegiance under protest and had defiantly flown the Confederate flag on his vessel. Then, while Helper was away, he joined a pro-Confederate demonstration before the consulate. The consulate's neighbors, all Argentines, hearing the refrains of "Dixie" in the early morning, believed "the actors were friends, overflowing with patriotism." Helper suggested Deshan be admonished and required to give bond before going abroad again.[11]

Helper's intolerance of Confederate sympathizers was influenced by his position, through which he saw the toll the war was taking on the United States' economy. Federal law stipulated that he keep a record of the transfer of ownership of American vessels sold in Buenos Aires and required him to see that sailors in the United States Merchant Marines received three months' severance pay when American ships were sold there. Thus he knew the terrific loss the American fleet was sustaining, as the owners sought to protect their crafts from Confederate raiders by selling or transferring their ownership. Nine American vessels changed hands in Buenos Aires from January to April, 1862, and by October, 1864, the number placed under the Argentine flag reached seventeen.

As a result, a new situation arose, unforeseen by American law. In most cases the crews much preferred to remain with their ships under new ownership, rather than receive three months' extra pay and be stranded in Buenos Aires. While fully informing Seward, Helper, to permit continued employment of the sailors, followed a policy originally pursued by former Consul Hudson of collecting only one or two months' severance pay.[12]

Because he did not have specific authority for his action, Helper cautiously applied his lenient "extra-pay" policy. When the "Talisman" was sold in September, 1863, all of its crew was retained, and the consul collected only one month's extra wages, to be used to aid destitute mariners. To secure himself, he took separate receipts for two months' extra wages from every sailor aboard. They were happy to give such protection to Helper, since had they not sailed with the "Talisman," now under the Argentine flag, they would

have been left jobless in Buenos Aires. Between September and
November, 1863, not a single United States' vessel arrived or cleared
for any American port.

In the case of the "Zone" in December, 1863, Helper felt additional security was needed, since unlike the "Talisman," it prepared
to clear for a non-American port. Before allowing the sale to be
recorded, he required a bond from the new owner, stipulating that
it was his intention to put the vessel under the United States flag
again, "so soon as the sea shall have been sufficiently cleared of
pirates and privateers."[13]

American vessels were not driven from Southern waters through
empty fears. In June, 1863, Helper was distraught upon hearing
that the "Alabama," the "Georgia," and the "Florida" had been
"prowling along the Brazilian Coast" and that one of them, off the
mouth of the La Plata, was ready to capture any United States vessels. Even if the rumors were exaggerated, he knew that grave
damage was being done to American commerce by fear of Confederate cruisers in the Argentine area. American vessels in Buenos
Aires found it impossible to obtain freight, and foreign merchant
fleets were making serious inroads in former American territory.
As the only remedy, he urged the dispatching of a United States
steamer to the La Plata.

Helper's plea was answered following the "Conrad's" capture by
a Confederate cruiser in June, 1863. (It was converted into the
"C.S.S. Tuscaloosa.") Consequently, the U.S. steamer "Mohican"
was sent to Argentine waters in early 1864. By that time, however,
American vessels were enjoying greater freedom of movement and
the "Mohican" remained only a short time in Buenos Aires.[14]

A concern for the rights of ship owners and sailors characterized Helper's actions. He was a stickler for enforcing the spirit
as well as the letter of the law when he agreed with its intentions.
When, in October, 1862, Captain William H. Gooding proposed to
sell the "Kossuth," the vessel he commanded, on the grounds of
unseaworthiness, Helper protested. He felt Gooding was prejudic-
ing the rights of the American owner and urged Kirk to appoint
a commission of "three highly respected and disinterested mer-

chants" to pass on the action, but Kirk overruled Helper and authorized the sale. Helper solemnly protested, both to Kirk and Seward, that his rights had been invaded and refused to have any connection with the sale, placing all the responsibility on the minister.

Another incident concerned the discharge of two seamen at Montevideo by the master of "Spark the Ocean." Refusing to pay any extra wages, he warned them not to tell their story to an American consul. Helper was furious when an ill member of the crew came to him for help and revealed the episode. After placing the sick man in a hospital at the consulate's expense, he made an investigation and sent details of the occurrence to Seward, recommending the captain be restrained from such acts in the future.[15]

In spite of his detailed responsibilities, Helper kept well informed on matters affecting Americans in his region. In October, 1865, the new American steamer "La Portêna" arrived to inaugurate regular service to Montevideo. Before leaving the United States the crew signed a year's contract, which included a provision that they would serve under an American captain. Once the vessel was in Argentine waters, it was decided that an Italian officer would actually run the ship. When this action occurred, Helper was upset and warned the company's agent that, when a foreign shipmaster boarded the "La Portêna," it forfeited the right to claim the assistance and protection of the United States. Helper knew that there was much smuggling between Montevideo and Buenos Aires and was afraid this American vessel would become involved. More immediately, he feared the crew would be discontent or abused. American captains, he wrote, "are, as a rule, but little addicted to dancing, chatting, and card-playing in the cabin, and are apt to be on deck" tending their ship when not asleep. This policy could not be expected from an Italian master. In December Helper began to suspect that the "La Portêna" might be chartered to the Brazilian government, which was then at war. This suspicion was basically correct, since the ship was sold to Brazil in the summer of 1866. The crew was paid its back and two months' extra wages, but to avoid a third month's payment, they were forced to "desert." A number of American seamen were left in a position where they were likely to become government charges, and Helper had begun negotiations to obtain an extra month's pay for each when his tenure closed.[16]

Helper's sense of responsibility did not end with his official duties. He felt an obligation to lead his fellow Americans in Buenos Aires and set an example of how an American citizen abroad should behave. In doing so, he came nearer being the spokesman for United States citizens in Argentina than did anyone else.

When the American community received news of the preliminary Emancipation Proclamation, Helper felt the predictions of *The Impending Crisis* were at last fulfilled. Overjoyed, he addressed a letter to the masters of all American vessels in the harbor asking them to honor the President as they hoisted their flags and clipped Lincoln's address from the columns of the Buenos Aires *Standard,* to be framed in gold. He proclaimed the message to be second in importance only to the Declaration of Independence. He understood it to favor "the deportation of all the Negroes from the United States" and conceived this proposal to be "full of good sound common sense" and "worthy of being earnestly, fully, and speedily acted upon."[17] Upon Lincoln's death, Helper drew up the resolutions accepted by the American colony to express its grief and sense of loss. In the clear and beautiful style which he could use, Helper deplored "the dastardly and fiendish assassination" of Lincoln. He eulogized his "unswerving honesty and patriotism" which exalted him to a position occupied by Washington, Adams, Franklin, Madison, Jefferson, and Jackson. Among these, Helper wrote, "we know of but one name that will shine with more dazzling lustre on the impartial page of history. . . . We would solemnly proclaim and consecrate [Lincoln] to posterity as the second Father of his country."

Within a month after the adoption of this resolution, a large group of United States citizens chose Helper to frame an address conveying their felicity to President Andrew Johnson. In so doing, Helper revealed his personal admiration for a man of his own background who shared many of his racial and social views. While expressing grief over Lincoln's death, the address declared, "There is brightening in our hearts an ever-present gleam of joy," the knowledge that Johnson was President. "We entertain the most steadfast confidence in you as an eminently able and worthy representative of the free people of America and we pray God, that he may still strengthen you, and, in strengthening you, strengthen us and every inhabitant of our land, in all that is good, noble and true."[18]

The governor of Buenos Aires province declared July 4, 1865, a day of celebration in honor of Americans. In the evening the leading American citizens gathered for a dinner at the Hotel Provence, at which Helper was the principal speaker. His address disclosed his continued concern for the South's well-being and his loathing for any punitive federal policy for it. His theme was the need for "manly kindness and conciliation" in dealing with the defeated South. Considering "the complete suppression of the rebellion" and "the perfect indication of the great principles upon which our Government was founded," Helper advocated the national government "continue the practice of moderation" to the fallen foe. This policy was not only simple justice to the Southern masses but also the wisest means to attain a "happy readjustment." The majority of Southerners had never desired disunion but had been forced into it by a "small and mischievous minority," seeking to extend and expand slavery. To Helper, conclusive proof of this theory was demonstrated by the percentage of Union general officers coming from the Southern and border states. Their number came to 73, each of whom he named to receive the approbation of his audience. On the other hand, study as he might, he could find only nine general officers of Northern birth who served in the Confederate armies. Turning to the United States Navy, Helper mentioned four Southerners whose names "will be famous in history so long as floating batteries or men-of-war shall be found upon the water." These were Farragut, Porter, Goldsborough, and Winslow, "that brave and dauntless Old Coon, who captured the pirate Alabama."

Not the least of Southerners to serve the nation nobly, Helper proclaimed, was Andrew Johnson, a man "in many particulars, more like Andrew Jackson than any man in America." Both were born in the Carolinas, migrated to Tennessee, received appointments as generals of militia, served in the House and Senate and came to the Presidency in times of peril. "Both were Southern men, and it became the duty of both to deal stringently, and both did deal stringently, with the dissaffection and treason of their slaveholding neighbors." Now, through moderation, Johnson had the opportunity to recognize the essential loyalty of the majority of Southerners.[19]

Helper was never backward in expressing his views, as his addresses to fellow Americans demonstrated, but where his country's welfare was concerned, he did not confine his words to Americans, a notable example coming in October, 1864, when much of British opinion was offended by the seizure of the Confederate cruiser, "Florida," in the Bay of Bahia by the United States steamer, "Wachusetts." Helper felt that the Buenos Aires *Standard,* an influential English journal, had editorially misrepresented the case, and he sought to set the record straight. While doing so, he managed to retain his sense of humor. Reminding his readers that the British attitude toward seizure had changed since the War of 1812, he dealt at length with the capture of the "Essex" near Valparaíso in March, 1814, by the "Phoebe" and "Cherub." "It is, I submit, tolerable apparent," he wrote, "that the English, as the first stoopers, in the Pacific, and the Americans, as the second stoopers, in the Atlantic, have both 'stooped to conquer!'"

While the pro-Confederate attitude of many Britishers disturbed Helper, there were many other aspects of life in Buenos Aires which were attractive to him. He made this revelation in the fall of 1864, when a report prepared for the State Department presented a series of tables picturing the commercial life of Argentina. Much of the report, however, dealt with the flourishing city of Buenos Aires. Throughout Argentina, Helper reported, agriculture was undeveloped and farming implements, primitive. For example, the English Cotton Supply Association sponsored the cultivation of cotton, but with very little success. He also saw tremendous possibilities for improvements in the economy and was much concerned that the United States orient its commercial policy so as to profit from Argentine development. Wool, hides, and jerked beef constituted the main exports, but Helper predicted that a means would soon be discovered for exporting "mess beef" to Europe and the country would prosper; this trade opened in the 1870's with the advent of the refrigerator ship.

Much of Helper's faith in the Argentine economy was based upon an affinity for the racial nature of the people. He believed that a relatively large proportion of Caucasian blood made Argentina, with the possible exception of Chile, the most enlightened nation in Latin America. As a first step for closer relations with Argentina, he urged, in 1864, that a regular United States steamship line be established between the two countries. Already large quantities of agricultural tools, sewing machines, and books were imported into Argentina from the United States. He felt that better transportation was all that was needed to open a large market for clothing, pianos, engines, railway iron, and similar products from the United States. If the sum of $150,000 per year the United States had proposed to subsidize a line was not sufficient, then it should be increased to $500,000.

When a route was instituted only to Rio de Janeiro, Helper was greatly disappointed. The initiative for Argentine development, in Helper's view, rested with the United States. With a superior culture, "untrammelled by the clogs of Monarchy and Catholicism," the United States could spread republicanism and enrich its commercial area of development, if it would awaken to the opportunity.[20]

Much of Helper's hope for the economic growth of Argentina came from his faith in Don Bartolomé Mitre, a leading creole, who had recently become president of the Argentine confederation and governor of Buenos Aires. He liked his racial background, approved of his republicanism, and believed him to be a man of honor and efficiency who was building a great nation. He was so appreciative of him and his friendly attitude toward the United States that he sent miniature portraits of Mitre to Seward and Chase.

When the confederation of thirteen provinces opened its new sessions in Buenos Aires, May 25, 1862, Helper and a number of

other consuls were much impressed by the "sights, sounds and cere-
monies of the occasion." Upon Kirk's arrival, in June, 1862, the
Mitre government extended every possible courtesy. Helper felt
honored to be "a representative of our country among a people so
appreciative of our efforts to establish a positive and lasting comity
among nations." He was even more pleased to receive a special
invitation to attend Mitre's inauguration, October 12, 1862, and in
attending, believed he had witnessed a "truly important event."[21]

As the foreign affairs of the Argentine area rushed toward a climax in 1864, Helper was in full accord with the Mitre government.
His knowledge and evaluation of conditions were highly accurate,
and he kept Seward fully informed of developments. In December,
1864, Helper realized that the Mitre government was trying to remain neutral, but he questioned its ability to do so. "Eighteen
months ago, three or four Uruguayan refugees and adventurers in
this city," led by Venancio Flores, "sailed hence in an ordinary
whale boat," Helper wrote, and landed in Uruguay. Then began a
dreadful civil war.

The difficulty sprang from the determination of Paraguay, then
under its third great dictator, Francisco Solano López, to prevent
Brazilian domination of the unstable Uruguay. Repeatedly during
the nineteenth century Argentina and Brazil had intervened, but
López was determined that this should not happen again. Brazil,
"from motives of self-aggrandizement" and "sympathizing with
the revolutionists," did not see fit to observe "the common laws of
neutrality," Helper wrote. He was not sympathetic with the Flores
revolution and attributed its victory to the aid it had received from
Brazil.

For over a year, after denying Paraguay passage through its territory to carry on hostilities against Brazil and Uruguay, the Mitre
government tried to remain completely neutral. In the latter part of
this period Helper became convinced that Paraguay was an ag-
gressor, deliberately provoking war. In February, 1865, he had an
interview with Senôr Lima, the Brazilian minister expelled from
Asunción, who stated that his country would not permit a stabiliza-
tion to take place under which López would remain head of the
Paraguayan government.[22]

In response to the continued aggression of Paraguay, the Mitre government declared war, May 1, 1865, signing a secret alliance with Brazil and Uruguay. In one day mobilization began in Buenos Aires, and Helper was shocked to see the people rush "with gleeful grimace" into a death-bearing conflict. Forgetting the American Civil War, he attributed this response to the racial impurity of the people. The only solution, he believed, lay in the domination of all Latin America by "Germanic, Anglo-Saxon, and Anglo-American peoples."

Helper early foresaw that the allies would have difficulty attaining victory. In August, 1865, he observed that many of the Argentine troops lacked discipline and that one division had become completely disorganized. Few men were volunteering in Buenos Aires, and to fill the need for manpower, even the emaciated were being inducted. After the bloody battle at Estero Bellaco, Helper correctly predicted that the conflict would be a long one and cessation would come only through exhaustion. It was not until 1869 that Paraguay was forced to capitulate.

Helper's pro-Mitre attitude was well known among the Argentine ruling clique, and it fostered cordial personal relations with government leaders. Therefore, in the absence of Kirk, Helper did not hesitate to open a discussion concerning allied prevention of the seating of a United States minister in Paraguay. In requesting an interview, he stated that many in the United States were surprised and disappointed in the interference with Charles A. Washburn's position. In a meeting with Rufino de Elizalde, Minister of Foreign Affairs, Helper reviewed Washburn's six-month endeavor to obtain passage to Asunción. Elizalde was courteous and explained that Argentina had never refused nor granted permission to Washburn. When the minister volunteered to see Washburn and give personal attention to his case, Helper withdrew.[23]

Helper enjoyed his relationship with leaders of the Argentine government, but, true to his nature, he gave equally careful attention to less imposing duties. Time and again, his routine was complicated by the failure of the State Department to supply proper forms, and he had to dispatch urgent pleas to Washington for them. Frequently he obtained hospitalization for ill seamen and, for those who died, took possession of their fina! effects and saw they obtained Christian burial.[24]

Helper's interests were extremely diverse, and he sought to familiarize United States leaders with Argentine life and culture. For example, he gathered seeds of the leading trees and plants "peculiar" to Argentina and sent them to Commissioner of Agriculture Isaac Newton. (He also convinced Newton that the United States should import 100 alpacas from Bolivia, but before the purchase could be made his consulate ended.)[25] Through friendship with the learned German director of the Buenos Aires Museum, Professor Herman Burmeister, Helper obtained drawings and descriptions of the leading birds for the Smithsonian Institute, and as a result, the American Geographical and Statistical Society extended membership to him in 1863. He also furnished fifteen pages for the volume *Commercial Relations* (1865) describing life in Argentina and even went to the trouble to obtain for Seward a copy of the contract between the Argentine government and Don Estevan Ram y Rubert for the improvement of the navigation of the Salado River.[26]

Although a hard-working and effective official, Helper was susceptible to feminine charms and fell in love with a lovely Argentine woman. When he married Marie Louisa Rodriquez, March 13, 1863, he reported the event to the Department of State in order that it might know "he had married advisedly, and in keeping with the honor and dignity of his position." His wife was a native of Buenos Aires and a lady "of pure Spanish descent," who had spent five years in New York City with her parents, where she attained much of her education. Helper believed that, during her sojourn in the United States, "she became, in hand and heart, as thoroughly American as if she had been born in the capitol at Washington." To her American patriotism she added a cosmopolitan quality, as she was able to speak English, Spanish, and French, with great fluency, and Italian, to some degree. Altogether, Helper wrote of his wife, she "is, in every respect, an estimable and accomplished lady." He was very proud of her and, in order to furnish "a moment's innocent amusement" to Seward, forwarded him an editorial from the Buenos Aires *Standard,* commenting on the fact that over one-half of the consuls in Buenos Aires married there. It listed nineteen consuls who had taken mates in the city and noted that six vice-consuls had followed the example of their superiors. The article proclaimed that both "have made themselves equally happy in the arms and affections of Buenos Aires angels—the most graceful, amiable and accomplished ladies of the Southern hemisphere." Helper found the editorial's remarks to be "no less true than strange."[27]

The only question that arose to mar Helper's happiness was his grossly inadequate salary of $2,000 yearly, from which he had to pay several hundred dollars for clerical help. When he began to think of the money he needed to support a wife, he made in February, 1863, the first of his many requests for a salary increase and noted that the fees collected by the consul were greater than his salary. Certainly his services to the government were worth at least $3,000 a year! Helper lived as frugally as anyone could, attending the theatre as infrequently as once a year, but in spite of his efforts, he could not live within his income.

After much consideration Helper frequently wrote the State Department, asking for raises and suggesting various means to finance them. Though he met with little success, his persistence spurred him to continue his efforts. First, he urged that he be given a new position of consul-general in Montevideo, with a $4,000 salary.[28] Failing in this endeavor, he found a new excuse for a raise when Congress decreed that, after July 1, 1863, all exports to the United States must be accompanied by three, instead of one, consular certificates. He sought to increase the revenue of the consulate and improve his basis for a salary increase by charging for each certificate issued. However, the Treasury Department halted this scale of fees before it could have an influence.[29]

Next, Helper invoked the aid of the ministers to Argentina and Paraguay, who petitioned the State Department in his behalf. When these requests produced no result, he suggested to Senators Charles Sumner and Henry Wilson that chargé d'affaires or subconsuls be appointed, at salaries not to exceed $5,000, instead of ministers, who received $7,500, in minor countries like Nicaragua, Costa Rica, and Honduras, and thereby the consuls' salaries could be increased.

In something of the same approach Helper suggested to Seward that a yearly poll tax be levied on Americans living abroad and the funds used for salary increases. With every endeavor leading to defeat, he took matters in his own hands and petitioned Congress for relief, requesting Seward to recall him if it were not approved. He again proposed that he be paid $3,000 annually from 1862 and, asking Congress' indulgence, for the first time stated he had not remitted all the fees collected. "I only ask," he wrote, "that I may not be required to refund to the Government, at any time, moneys which under a studiously economical and self-denying management of affairs generally, my position as Consul here has literally compelled me to spend, and which should in justice and fairness, constitute a part of my regular salary." When he submitted his accounts for 1863 and 1864, Helper informed Seward that he had used some of the fees he had collected. "I am," he wrote, "in a literal sense at least, indebted for an excess of fees received here over and above the amount of my very inadequate salary."[30]

Despite all his efforts, Helper's petition arrived after Congress adjourned. Since his expenses were running about a $1,000 a year more than his salary, he was greatly disappointed but decided to remain at his post until the lawmakers had a chance to act. In order to remind Seward of his plight, however, Helper wrote him a convincing thirteen-page letter in October, 1866, reviewing fully his economic status. He believed his salary, only a portion of that given consuls of other nations, was a "disgrace"! The prestige of the United States was suffering due to the miserliness of its government. His sense of decorum had led him to spend income that was not his; he asked relief for his country more than himself.

When no word regarding action on his salary arrived by March, 1866, Helper, in a brief letter, asked Seward to relieve him "without delay," stating he liked Buenos Aires and his position, but he could not *afford* to stay. "It is ruining my pocket and producing no good effect upon my general nature."[31]

Finally, in October, 1866, after Congress had failed to approve his desperate pleas, Helper gave his resignation to Alexander Asboth, the new American minister to Argentina, and he and his family sailed from Buenos Aires, November 25, 1866, aboard the "Hosea Rich."[32] After a sixty-nine day passage, they arrived in New York City, February 2, 1867.

While recovering "from the very unwelcome effects of much seasickness," Helper stayed at the home of Julian Allen. The prominent New Yorker was glad to intervene in his guest's behalf and wrote Seward stating that, in his opinion, it was only justice to relieve Helper of his obligation.[33]

Within a week Helper arrived in Washington to plead his cause personally, and he succeeded in convincing Seward of the justness of his contentions. The remedy, however, lay with the Congress, not the State Department, and Helper took his case to N. P. Banks, chairman of the House Foreign Affairs Committee. Helper's argument was appealing to Banks, particularly the portion demonstrating that the consul's salary was only half the current fees. When he wrote Seward expressing a willingness to initiate legislation covering Helper's shortage, tabulated at $5,000, the secretary concurred, writing his approval across Banks's letter. Unfortunately, in the congressional rush, no action was taken.

Helper was most conscious of his reputation because of the earlier attacks which had been levied on him, and for the next three years he unsuccessfully sought congressional action to remove the blight from his name. Grant's Secretary of State, Hamilton Fish, seems to have been responsible, in 1870, for the final failure of Congress to act. Fish advised the lawmakers to comply with Helper's request only if they were willing to make good all deficiencies in foreign appointees' accounts.[34]

Fortunately for Helper, the government never sought to collect his shortage. Yet he was grieved, not only by the stigma to his character, but also by the ingratitude of Congress. He had served faithfully and with ability at a major consular post during a trying period, and surely he deserved a living wage. He realized that most who knew of his service would recall only that his accounts were short. For a man of Helper's temperament this was a heavy cross to bear, but at least he had the satisfaction of knowing he had performed his duties well. Moreover, he had acquired a gifted, obedient wife, who never impeded his work, and his horizons were broadened by almost five years residence as the second most important American official in one of Latin America's more cosmopolitan cities.

*Chapter Eight*

# Militant Racist

FOLLOWING HIS RETURN from Buenos Aires, Helper devoted himself to the work he had temporarily abandoned in 1861. He had hoped *The Impending Crisis,* by the destruction of slavery, would free the Southern white masses from the grinding poverty he felt came from Negro-aristocratic control. Much to his distress, "liberation" of the whites did not follow emancipation. As a result of it, the freed Negro, instead of being completely removed, had come to enjoy a new form of tyranny over white workers, since he received the suffrage and, in many cases, jobs coveted by whites. Helper turned to the one weapon he knew, the pen, in an effort to crush the Negro competitor, who he felt was more dangerous to the Southern masses than ever. In three years he produced three books setting forth his diagnosis of the nation's ills and drawing a blueprint to alleviate them.

While writing the first of these works, *Nojoque, A Question for A Continent,* Helper and his family lived in Asheville, North Carolina, boarding with Captain William Polk, son of the Confederate bishop-general. Among their closest friends was the prominent railway promoter, Colonel John A. Fagg, from whom Helper received many ideas he was later to use. An Asheville resident recalled often seeing the "tall, strongly built" Helper as he walked about the city; he was always alone because his abolitionist work had made him *persona non grata* to most of the people.[1]

Helper's racism was so unpremeditated and so dominated all his thought that he did not prepare his readers for the militant anti-Negroism in *Nojoque,* published in 1867. Many who knew him only as an abolitionist were shocked at his writing such a work. For the next two years, as he expanded his attack on the Negro, he also sought to correct the impression that he was abandoning his earlier views. Some had said that *The Impending Crisis* was written "in the interest of the negroes, and in a spirit of hostility to the whites," which was "simply untrue." Helper had dedicated it to the Southern nonslaveholding whites and in it had repudiated the concept of the unity of races, urging Negro colonization. Not a single line would justify the assumption that he "ever regarded the negro otherwise than as a very inferior and almost worthless sort of man, . . . to be freed, colonized, justly and liberally provided for, and then put wholly upon his own resources, and left to himself."

*The Impending Crisis* had been written, intentionally, as preparation for *Nojoque.* It urged the abolition of slavery as "only a necessary step, a *sine qua non,* towards the accomplishment of a still nobler work," the removal of the Negro from American life.[2] A. B. Burdick, the publisher, knew Helper had "always been zealously in favor of both emancipation and colonization, on the plan of Jefferson, Lincoln, and other eminent statesmen of the old Republican school." Helper's "greatest objections to slavery" were that "it kept the two races in juxtaposition, and was, as he believed, while generally disadvantageous to the country, far more detrimental to the whites than to the blacks."[3]

Unfortunately, upon his return from Buenos Aires, Helper did not correctly assess the political situation. He felt that Negro segregation and removal could be accomplished within a few years, if the people were adequately informed. *Nojoque* was an attempt to arouse the people to the Negro menace and was dedicated to the "Enlightened and Progressive Portion of the People of the New World" who could, by their votes in 1868 and 1874, remove all non-whites by 1876. After the centennial year he was sure Americans would allow "No Slave nor Would-be Slave, No Negro nor Mulatto, No Chinaman nor unnative Indian, No Black nor Bi-colored Individual of whatever Name or Nationality" again to "find Domicile anywhere within the Boundaries of the United States."[4]

*Nojoque*'s theme was succinctly expressed in the title of its first chapter, "The Negro Anthropologically Considered—An Inferior Fellow Done For." To Helper, the Negro was the result of a separate, distinct creation and infinitely inferior, in every respect, to the white man. Since there was no statistical information on which he could draw to prove this assumption, he devoted much of *Nojoque*'s 474 pages to a presentation of expert testimony in an effort to prove his contention.

The writings of eminent scientists were prominently used in Helper's work. Summarizing papers in the *Transactions of the London Ethnological Society* and Dr. William B. Carpenter's *Principles of Human Physiology,* he concluded that "from the hair of his head to the extremities of his hands and feet," every part of the Negro, "however large, or however small, whether internal or external, whether physical or mental, or moral, loses in comparison with the white, much in the same ratio or proportion as darkness loses in comparison with light, or as evil loses in comparison with good."

Additional testimony, concurring with this belief, was marshaled from the most diverse sources. Although one may well question Helper's use, nevertheless, it must be conceded that the selections were a tribute to his knowledge of literature and his catholic taste.

Helper believed black to be "A Thing of Ugliness, Disease, and Death . . . a most hateable thing" which it was as natural for white men to loath as to "abhor hideous Satan." Had not Pinamonti pictured the outer walls of hell as being ebony in color? Shakespeare (Sonnet CXLVIII) wrote, "I have sworn thee fair, and thought thee bright, Who art as black as hell, as dark as night."

In more than one hundred pages of *Nojoque,* Helper sought to prove the white man's innate love for white as opposed to black, not only in pigmentation but in every physical object. Traditionally white was regarded as "A thing of Life, Health, and Beauty." Daniel the Prophet (XII, 10) wrote, "Many shall be purified and made white." Lord Bacon proclaimed, "God's first creature was light." John Dryden wrote, "At the cheerful light The groaning ghosts and birds obscene take flight." Who "indeed on this side of the infernal regions would ever think of having a black carpet, a black-window curtain, a black tablecloth, a black napkin, or a black handkerchief"? The good health of the Quakers could possibly be attributed to their being as averse to dark clothes as they were to the devil. Helper had long respected the antislavery Quakers and felt divinity must be guiding them in their selection of apparel.

It seemed to Helper that almost every person, real or imaginary, who had received divine honors "and most of our pre-eminently distinguished fellow-men" were represented as fair and "white-haired or golden-haired," a fact that could not be explained by mere chance. Charles Darwin, in writing *Origin of the Species,* attributed man's evolution to natural selection and stated, "Nor ought we to think that the occasional destruction of an animal of any particular color would produce little effect; we should remember how essential it is, in a flock of white sheep, to destroy every lamb with the faintest trace of black."[5]

Even the lowest animals, the creatures of instinct, "the beasts, the birds, and the fishes—many distinct species of which are apparently quite similar, set up daily and hourly examples of the eminent propriety of each kind forming and maintaining separate communities of their own." They were always found in herds, flocks and shoals of their type, and a stray animal would be removed if he tried to intrude. The white man could not be expected to do less than the lower animals. Surely any white man would have felt as Helper did when, passing through the galleries of the two houses of Congress, he "beheld there, uncouthly lounging and dozing upon the seats, a horde of vile, ignorant, and foul-scented negroes." For once he wished he had been a Hercules in order to clean the Augean stables.[6]

Helper believed "To be a slave of the white man, yet, if possible to be a slave exempt from the necessity of labor, has always been the ruling ambition of the negro." The slave came to the South "hatless, and coatless, and trouserless, and shoeless, and shirtless—in brief, he was utterly resourceless, naked and filthy." He was retained only because white planters, "unnaturally submitting to a wrongful relation," were depraved enough to protect and sustain him.

In his residence in Latin America Helper became convinced that its relative poverty and insignificance, compared to North America, could be traced to the large proportion of its people who were "black and bi-colored—negroes, Indians and hybrids." Not only were many of them hopelessly ignorant and superstitious, they were frequently morally depraved as well. Their Roman Catholic religion served only to reinforce the worst aspects of their racial deformities, Helper found. "The Catholic religion, in every place where it exists, operates as a powerful barrier to the progress of general knowledge and good morals, and . . . it is particularly inimical to civil liberty and republican government." He prayed the day was near when its "nonsensical and ridiculous ceremonials" would be renounced in Latin America and Catholicism would find "exclusive companionship with the superstitious and heathenish Hindoos, who gave it birth." He advised Latin Americans, "Turn half of your churches into school-houses, libraries and lecture-rooms; and the other half into foundries and machine shops."[7]

Helper's purpose in writing two later anti-Negro works was not to demonstrate the inferiority of the Negro, but both dealt with the subject. This was particularly true of *The Negroes in Negroland*, published in 1868, much of which was quotations from a wide variety of sources. Helper was most pleased with excerpts from David Livingstone, Thomas Jefferson and Abraham Lincoln.

After observing the Negroes in their homeland, Dr. Livingstone wrote, "Among the negroes, no science has been developed, and few questions are ever discussed, except those which have an intimate connection with the wants of the stomach." In all of eastern and western Africa the noted missionary found not one single bookshop or other evidence of an intellectual vitality among the people.[8]

In his *Notes on Virginia,* Jefferson gave what one of his modern biographers has characterized as "the tentative judgements of a kindly and scientifically minded man" on the Negro.[9] He wrote:

Deep-rooted prejudices entertained by the whites; ten thousand recollections, by the blacks, of the injuries they have sustained; new provocations; the real distinctions which nature has made; and many other circumstances, will divide us into parties, and produce convulsions, which will probably never end but in the extermination of the one or the other race. To these objections, which are political, may be added others, which are physical and moral. The first difference which strikes us is that of color. Whether the black of the negro resides in the reticular membrane between the skin and scarf-skin, or in the scarf-skin itself; whether it proceeds from the color of the blood, the color of the bile, or from that of some other secretion, the difference is fixed in nature, and is as real as if its seat of cause were better known to us. And is this difference of no importance? Is it not the foundation of a greater or less share of beauty in the two races? Are not the fine mixtures of red and white, the expressions of every passion by greater or less suffusions of color in the one, preferable to that external monotony, which reigns in the countenances, that immovable veil of black which covers the emotions of the other race? . . . The circumstance of superior beauty is thought worthy of attention in the propagation of our horses, dogs, and other domestic animals; why not in that of man? Besides those of color, figures, and hair, there are other physical distinctions proving a difference of race. They have less hair on the face and body. They secrete less by the kidneys, and more by the glands of the skin, which gives them a very strong and disagreeable odor. This greater degree of transpiration renders them more tolerant of heat, and less so of cold than the whites. . . . They are more ardent after their female; but love seems with them to be more an eager desire, than a tender, delicate mixture of sentiment and sensation. Their griefs are transient. These numberless afflictions, which render it doubtful whether Heaven has given life to us in mercy or in wrath, are less felt, and soon forgotten, with him. In general, their existence appears to participate more of sensation than reflection. To this must be ascribed their disposition to sleep when abstracted from their diversions and unemployed in labor. An animal whose body is at rest, and who does not reflect, must be disposed to sleep, of course. Comparing them by their faculties of memory, reason, and imagination, it appears to me that in memory they are equal to the whites; in reason much inferior; as I think one could scarcely be found capable of tracing and comprehending the investigations of Euclid; and that in imagination they are dull, tasteless and anomalous.[10]

Helper could not have agreed more with anyone. Yet he drew equal satisfaction in quoting Abraham Lincoln, whose racial views Helper believed he shared. In the Lincoln-Douglas debates Lincoln had stated, "I am not, and never have been, in favor of making voters or jurors of negroes, nor of qualifying them to hold office, nor to intermarry with whites; and I will say further, in addition to this, that there is a physical difference between the black and white races, which I believe will forever forbid the two races living together in terms of social and political equality." "You and we are a different race," he told a group of Negro visitors in 1862. "We have between us a broader difference than exists between any other two races." "As I think your race suffers greatly . . . by living with us," Lincoln stated, "ours suffers from your presence."[11]

Helper was much devoted to Lincoln and mourned his assassination as a major national tragedy. Certainly this would not have been true had he felt Lincoln wished to protect and preserve the Negro. Richard Hofstadter has substantiated Helper's views of Lincoln's anti-Negro feelings, which were an emotion quite common to the white masses of the Old Northwest, attributing Lincoln's rise in national power to his "bridging the gap" between the small but politically potent abolitionist group and the Negrophobe masses of the Northwest.[12]

After much reflection Helper prepared a list summarizing the more than trivial differences which separated the Negro and the white man. Points of Negro inferiority included:

His low and compressed Forehead;
His hard, thick Skull;
His small, backward-thrown Brain;
His short, crisp Hair;
His flat Nose;

His thick Lips;
His projecting, snout-like Mouth;
His strange, Eunuch-toned Voice;
His scantiness of Beard on his Face;
The Toughness and Unsensitiveness of his Skin;
The Thinness and Shrunkenness of his Thighs;
His Curved Knees;
His calfless Legs;
His low, short Ankles;
His long, flat Heels;
His glut-shaped Feet;
The general angularity and Oddity of his Frame;
The Malodorous Exhalations from his Person;
His Puerility of Mind;
His Inertia and Sleepy-headness;
His proverbial Dishonesty;
His predisposition to fabricate Falsehoods; and
His Apathetic Indifference to all Propositions and
   Enterprises of Solid Merit.[13]

In 1877 Helper, en route to South America, stopped at Dakar
where, seeing the Negro in his homeland, his earlier views were
confirmed. His vessel arrived at 1:00 A.M., but he was so anxious
to see "the Africans in Africa" that he went ashore at once and
made an inspection trip lasting until 7:00 A.M. His tour began in
the native quarter where one thousand people lived in about two
hundred huts. Never did he have such "weird impressions" as those
he experienced standing under a gigantic baobab tree, as the
"savages about him" grunted and stared, and two vampires flitted
about. Helper was impressed with the complete absence of the
simplest machines. Women and girls were conspicuously carrying
water back and forth in gourds on their heads, but the men did
nothing "except to loll and loiter about, beg, grin, giggle and guf-
faw." With dawn, the most conspicuous sight was that of women
pounding millet; while working, the flabby breasts of the older
ones flopped and those of the younger ones quivered like "globules
of calves-foot jelly on a dish in transit."

For breakfast Helper moved into the French section where, at a cafe, he saw three Negro women spend thirty minutes trying to capture and kill a pullet. Although sorry for the chicken, "many a circus has afforded me much less amusement," he wrote. During the meal "swarms of the nasty Negroes" gathered around him, begging for food. Upon complaint, the landlord chased them away with a plank from a dry goods box, but they always returned. Helper longed for a "full-loaded Gatling gun" and a "well-charged blunderbus." More than ever he saw it was "utterly impossible for clean-natured and clear-sighted white men ever to disdain the Negro in a manner at all commensurate with his manifold and measureless demerits."

After breakfast Helper and a friend paid twenty francs to meet a tribal king and his eight wives, "all, like himself, blacker, if possible, than the ace of spades." With them were thirty-four "princes and princesses." The king's house was inferior to the meanest North Carolina Negro kitchen, and all his property could not have been worth more than two hundred dollars.

Helper saw no potential in the native people, an extremism unshared by the average Southern white churchman who gladly contributed money to African missionaries. Looking at the seven by eight foot huts in which the natives lived, he concluded it was senseless to work with such a "God-forsaken race." A Jesuit, "a queer and questionable prig of piety," stationed at Dakar might as well "be sustained in a community of gorillas or baboons." The Negroes' depravity at home completely disgusted Helper, and he regretted that he had no "Orsini bombs" with which to destroy them utterly!

Since the dawn of history, Helper contended, white Africa had offered civilization to the Negro. No continent had enjoyed such contacts with superior cultures on its margin, but civilization was repulsed. Lower-class white men sold the Negro into slavery, and mistaken philanthropy preserved the Negro race.[14] Helper believed that the Negro, through the centuries, had formed an "effete race" and that it should be removed from contact with white society. "The negroes, like the poodles and the pointers, will always be the dependents and the parasites of white men," he wrote, "just so long as white men, unnaturally submitting to a wrongful relation, are disposed to tolerate the black man's infamously base and beggarly presence."

Helper did not advocate the killing of Negroes but their segregation from white society. He did not wish to deal with them "in such summary and sanguinary manner as the Lord God of Israel is . . . represented as having dealt with the Cannanites," yet he believed the white man ought to deal with them in such a way "that the will of Heaven . . . may meet no opposition." He urged that a "well-defined landmark (or ocean-mark)" be chosen as a boundary for a segregated Negro state. They should be left there "to be the recipients of such future care and protection as Providence may be pleased to extend to them." Set apart from the white man, God and nature would destroy a race that proved incapable of taking care of itself. As a first step, all Negroes should be expelled from the cities where contact between persons was much more intimate than in rural areas. Moreover, the Negro in the city deprived white workers of their jobs, and Helper believed his "obnoxious filth" produced yellow fever and other epidemics.

The Indians east of the Mississippi River had received the type treatment Helper proposed for the Negro, and he believed the result would be the same—the Negro would perish and the United States would be the beneficiary. A state of universal refinement and amiability would prevail only after the "country shall have been thoroughly cleansed of the vulgar and disgusting negroes and their next of kin, who must themselves be required to be the unreturnable bearers hence of their own worse than worthles [sic] bodies."[15]

Helper conceded that association with whites brought partial elevation to the Negro, but he felt that the gain, unfortunately, was offset by a corresponding degradation of the whites. The presence of large numbers of Negroes in the South explained the Northern superiority in many fields. "While we here are cursed with the black imps of Africa," he wrote, "you there are blessed with the white genii of Europe."[16]

Another outspoken opponent of slavery, Maine's James Pike,

shared Helper's contempt for the Negro and urged his segregation from white society. In the mid-1850's Pike joined the Republican Party because of his "sincere belief that the Negro could not and should not be incorporated into the American democratic system." At that time, as well as later, he advocated the Gulf States be set aside as a Negro receptacle. In 1873 Pike went South, at the instigation of Whitelaw Reid, to report for the New York *Tribune* the true condition of South Carolina under Reconstruction. The result was a series of essentially racist articles later published as *The Prostrate State: South Carolina Under Negro Government*. Like Helper, Pike's work closely identified "ignorance and corruption, on the one hand, and Negro blood on the other." However, Helper disagreed with Pike's immediate postwar views on Negro suffrage. As early as 1865 Pike advocated the Negro be enfranchised. He felt that the freedman was unfit to vote but that it was essential he be allowed to do so to afford protection and to test the truth of his theory that the races could not live together.[17]

As a challenge to the Radical program, which depended on Negro suffrage, Helper wrote *Negroes in Negroland*. He believed the Radical endeavors were a violation of "the divine plan" for the black race and were a profound disservice to the masses of Southern whites.

Before the war Helper knew that, because of their association with slaveholders, many Negroes had a better opportunity for education and easy living than most Southern whites. It had been hard for a white man to obtain work in the better Southern homes or as barbers, valets, waiters or other personal servants. After 250 years of economic displacement the majority of the Southern people reasonably could have hoped for justice through Northern victory, but because of the "unnatural bond of sympathy" between the freedman and their former masters, this was not to be. "Hordes of blacks" offered their services for nominal wages, and their old owners hired them. As if this were not bad enough, Helper incorrectly believed the Radicals took away the votes of most Southern whites and left them at the mercy of grasping politicians and the Southern aristocrat-Negro coalition. With little political power and no economic leverage, the yeoman class seemed helpless. In such circumstances Helper knew many families in various Southern states who were leaving for Illinois, Indiana, and even Brazil. Poverty was so extreme that some departed barefooted and had no garments other than the clothes they wore.

In an 1868 tour of North and South Carolina, Helper found destitution beyond description. When an appeal was made from Marion, North Carolina, to wealthy Baltimore men, they gave cotton thread to be distributed to the near starving, but many had to be turned away. In Columbia, South Carolina, Helper was met by emaciated, unemployed white women and girls who tearfully asked him for bread. At the same time he saw "multitudes of sleek, stupid, foul-smelling, filthy, greasy, and grinning negroes . . . laxingly occupying places which would have been infinitely better occupied by whites."

Without a change in the political status of Southern whites, Helper saw no means to improve the lot of the masses. Disfranchisement and the threats of unlimited confiscation had led to an almost complete suspension of public and private works. Crime was rampant among the Negroes, and white men had learned it was better to suffer in silence rather than to protest needlessly. Six of the eight stores in a town near Salisbury were robbed shortly after the coming of "the Radical negro bureau." "Terrorism reigns supreme among the white females of every family, and sleep is banished," Helper wrote.

Only a few dozen Southern traitors misled their people into war. For them, Helper held the greatest contempt and felt they should have been hanged when the Union armies came into their regions. It was a tragedy that millions of white Southerners, who had no responsibility for the war, were being punished. There were no true Union men in the South except white men, but despite this fact, Radicals developed a pro-Negro program which struck a terrific blow at white Republicans and their attempts to gain political power. "Because of its gross excesses, its shortcomings, and its corruptions," Helper wrote, the first thing right-thinking Americans must do was to destroy the Radical Party. "We were, and are still,

Republicans," he wrote, "not black Republicans but white Republicans."

As a Southern Republican, Helper realized Radical Reconstruction was a farce. It was totally unneeded, and Helper could swear that there were not two hundred white men in North Carolina who would re-establish slavery if they could; there were not over five thousand in the entire South. The only large class who would were the Negroes themselves, who preferred the security of slavery to their new condition.

Helper addressed *Negroes in Negroland* to the North, without whose fraternal co-operation he believed the South was doomed. In its introduction he protested the practice of stigmatizing as a traitor everyone "who, in the exercise of his constitutional rights and honest convictions, raises his voice in opposition to the destructive measures" of the Radicals. If the Radical program could be defeated, the South would begin the process of imitating Northern economic, social and intellectual development. Freed of the great burden of slavery, it could begin the achievements Helper had envisioned in *The Impending Crisis*.

Helper felt the Radical program was destroying what it supposedly was creating—a united, loyal South. The Southern governments, overturned by congressional action, were legitimate and loyal, and the vast majority of Southerners only wished an opportunity for their states to resume their rightful places in the Union. The Radical threat to impeach Andrew Johnson was another attempt to throw the whole country into a state of disorder. Helper knew Johnson was "at times somewhat stubborn and imprudent," yet the President had "always been rigidly faithful in the performance of his constitutional duties, inflexibly honest, thoroughly patriotic, and eminently solicitous to promote, in all proper ways, the public good." The white Union men of the South believed Johnson to be "a truly able and patriotic President," a far more competent man than anyone the Radicals suggested to succeed him. The North had not enfranchised the Negro; why should it be demanded of the South? Therefore, Helper appealed for Northerners of all shades of opinion to support Johnson and overturn the

Radical wrongs perpetrated on the South. They constituted "a consummate outrage, an unmitigated despotism, an unparalleled infamy, and atrocious crime."[18]

For a dozen years Helper had felt that the South must be opened to immigration from the North and Europe, if it were to rise economically and successfully compete with other areas. This progress could be accomplished only through industrialization and the provision of attractive working conditions for white laborers. With the complete triumph of Radical policy and the election of Grant in 1868, Helper lost faith in the old parties as instruments to achieve this objective, and his political views took a decided turn to the left. He became convinced that only a new political party, devoted to the interests of the American working man, could ameliorate the worsening condition of the white working class, both North and South. He spent much of 1869 projecting this idea and much of 1870 setting it forth in a new work, entitled *Noonday Exigencies in America,* which was published in 1871.

In the summer of 1869 Helper conferred in New York with William J. Jessup, president of the New York State Workingmen's Association. Jessup was so impressed with Helper's ideas that he asked they be condensed in letter form for presentation to the August, 1869, meeting of the National Labor Convention in Philadelphia. Helper complied with Jessup's request and presented a stinging indictment of both the Republican and Democratic parties.

It seemed that "almost all financial and political power" in the country was "being rapidly and surreptitiously concentrated into the hands of a very small number of our people," which would give "mastership to the few and entail galling and grovelling vassalage on the many." When the Radicals, motivated by plutocratic interests, began to gain control of the Republican Party in 1866, the masses lost their last instrument of political power in either North or South. Helper feared that, unless some change was made, in ten years seven-eighths of the American people would be crushed.

"The irrational and fanatical leaders of the Radical party and their black and barbarous minions have erected ... Ethiopian walls" between the North and the South, Helper declared. Working for

the Negro, the Radicals had the same effect on Southern development as the proslavery Democratic Party. Basing his figures primarily on 1870 immigration reports, he demonstrated that an agricultural society whose labor was dependent on the Negro could not
compete for immigration with a free, industrial society. From 1855
to 1870, 1,789,530 immigrants landed at Castle Garden, New York,
bound for five free states—New York, Pennsylvania, Ohio, Illinois,
and Wisconsin. During the same period only 22,511 arrived who
were destined for ten Southern states—Virginia, Florida, Alabama,
Mississippi, Arkansas, Louisiana, Georgia, North Carolina, South
Carolina, and Texas. While the war had produced unfavorable conditions for Southern migrants, the Southern lack of appeal was
also due to its concentration of Negro labor. With the coming of
Radical Reconstruction, "agitated, chaotic, and uninviting conditions" were prevalent everywhere, and the South became less attractive than ever. As a Southerner who desired to see his section
progress, Helper urged the National Labor Convention to aid in
the formation of a new party to overthrow the Radicals. Both the
Southern and Northern masses had much to gain by such action.

Jessup referred Helper's recommendation to a convention committee composed of James C. Sylvis of Pennsylvania, James Carr of
New York, W. J. McLaughlin of Massachusetts, Sigfried Meyer of
New York, and Halliburton T. Walker of Alabama. They were impressed with Helper's ideas but asked for additional time to study
the situation. For their information Helper enlarged his ideas in
his work *Noonday Exigencies in America* and sent each member a
complimentary copy.[19]

Helper sought to convince his readers of the need for the creation
of a nonsectional labor party. He knew many old Whigs and Republicans who, while they had opposed secession and slavery, also
opposed Negro equality. In 1868 many of these had voted the Demo-
cratic-Conservative ticket, but the past blunders of the party were
so numerous that it had no chance of victory. The free trade tradition of the Democratic Party made it unavailable to the workers as
a tool for their advancement, and Radical control of the Republican Party made it unacceptable.

Ironically, this situation arose at a time when the American white laborer needed political intervention more than ever. The New York *Times* reported that three-fifths of the skilled laborers of the city were working "for less than a sum sufficient to sustain an average family in decent condition." The New York *Tribune* declared "not less than 200,000 persons are now within sight of our city steeples who have no work, no real homes, and no means which insure them a livelihood." The New York *Herald* reported, "A large number of our people inhabit cellars and some of the filthiest, dirtiest holes, where one would suppose not even a dog could stand the miasmatic effluvia for fifteen minutes."[20]

Helper realized that the purchasing power of the dollar was less than before the war and that money was drifting into the hands of a small group of people. David A. Wells, former Commissioner of Internal Revenue, had written "while the aggregate wealth of the country is increasing as rapidly as at any former period," yet its distribution "is most unequal among the people; . . . under the system of inflated currency, and indiscriminate taxation, *the rich are becoming richer, and the poor poorer."* Helper felt that the public policy of the Radicals was directly responsible and urged their defeat.

If the condition of Northern working men was bad, that of the Southern laborers was even worse. Helper believed that in the cities not less than one-fourth of the Southern freedmen were employed in hotels and homes of white people; they did "in a most imperfect and slovenly way, the light work which, by the laws of right, honor, fitness and decency, should be given to white females only." The plight of innumerable "fallen" white women could be traced to Negro employment. When their economic condition became bad enough, they chose to pursue the one occupation still open. As if this were not bad enough, many chaste white women were ravished by the blacks. "The very negroes we have taken within, are, in effect, encouraged to pursue and outrage the same unfortunate white females whom we have turned without," Helper wrote. This was particularly true in the rural areas where more and more white women were forced to seek outdoor work in order to survive. However, the great majority of Southern rapes were not generally known, since pride led many to conceal attacks, and the Radical press often would not carry stories of outrage.

As a first step toward the relief of white workers in the South, Helper placed his hope in an improved taste of the traveling public. When travelers "shall have attained that high degree of respectability and refinement" which would keep them from patronizing "negro-waiting hotels or other negro-waiting establishments," then conditions would begin to improve. Next, it could be hoped that Northern philanthropists would see their error in subscribing liberally to Negro schools but offering "nothing for the education of the much larger number of always worse-treated poor Southern whites."

In Helper's mind it was possible for treason to be committed against a race as well as a nation, and treason against the white race was a greater crime than against the state. Any employer who engaged a nonwhite man was "a vile traitor to his race, and a sower of the seeds of immorality, dissention, strife, demoralization and ruin." To get rid of nonwhite workers and "polluters of society," Helper conceived a plan for forcing them to immigrate from the United States. Not later than July 4, 1876, he held, all jobs should be "rigidly and scrupulously" withheld "from the black and brown races . . . as an effectual reminder to them of the momentus propriety of their emigrating from among us." The implementation of this plan should be one of the first achievements of a new political party. Helper felt that only with its triumph would the American people have "a public policy which shall be in harmony, and not in conflict, with the laws of nature and nature's God."[21]

As a platform for a new political party, Helper submitted eighteen points for consideration:

> 1. Fidelity to the principles of republican government. As these could not be put into practice where slavery existed, he felt they could not be in a community "made up of any Considerable Number of Negroes, Mulattoes, Indians, Mongolians, or other Black or Brown Representatives of the Naturally or Grossly Inferior Races of Mankind."

2. "The Perpetual Maintenance of the Union, under the Administration of Just and Propitious Laws."

3. No further patronage of British vessels.

4. The acquisition of all of British America in payment for the "Alabama Outrages."

5. "The Gradual Absorption into our Great American Nationality of both Mexico and Central America, down to the Isthmus of Darien."

6. Immediate purchase of San Domingo, Haiti or Cuba, to be used as "a sort of Waste-Basket Receptacle of our American Negroes and Mulattoes and for All of our other Black and Brown Rubbish of the Genus Homo."

7. Development of a policy to overflow "the Semi-Africanized States of the South with Northern and European Emigrants, who will Americanize those States" and make possible the ideal of "a Peaceful, Prosperous and Powerful Continental Republic."

8. A stricter subordination of the military to civil authority. Recognition that promotion of military men to high office is an incentive to war and at variance with the principles of republican government.

9. Payment of every dollar of the national debt, but not at a higher rate than stipulated.

10. A more just equalization of salaries of those in the civil service.

11. A law regulating appointments in the civil service to prevent "such Disgraceful and Demoralizing Scrambles for Office" as was recently seen in Washington.

12. "Recognition by Law of the Obvious Distinctions which Nature has been Pleased to Make in the Several Races of Mankind; and no more Tyrannical Forcing of White People into Intimate Association or Relations with Negroes." No denying white men justice by having Negro jurors. "No Degradation of White Children by Sending them to Negro Schools." No fraternization with Negroes in the community.

13. No encouragement to Chinese or other Asiastics to become coolies in the United States.

14. Liberal inducements to all Negroes, Mulattoes and Mongolians

to emigrate beyond the prospective limits of the United States.

15. A national convention to meet in Philadelphia on July 4, 1876, composed of at least 5 representatives from each state and 2 from each territory to remain in session until they submit a new constitution or revise the old one. They must correct the relations of the central government and the states in such a manner that the states will "be Put on an Absolutely Just and Equal Footing; with Correlative Prerogatives and Obligations so Specifically and Unmistakably Defined as to leave Thenceforth not an Iota of Good Ground for Complaint or Dissatisfaction in any Place Whatever."

16. Statutes stigmatizing drunkeness as a crime with penalties severe enough to make America sober. Yet there should be "No Whetting of the Appetite for Spirituous Liquors, by Laws which Forbid the Use of them."

17. "No more sending of Negroes Abroad as Representative Americans. . . . The White Man only is the Representative American; and Wherever it is not Proper for the White Man to go in that Capacity, no one Else should be Sent."

18. Justice to the country's females. "No further Patronage to Hotels, Boarding-Houses, Refectories, nor other Places, where the Employment of Negroes Within, forces White Women Without; and no further Direct or Indirect Responsibility on our Part for such Base and Brutal Outrages as Negro Men are now so Frequently Perpetuating against White Women."[22]

Helper's proposed platform was unique. Half of its planks were concerned with racial matters and reflected his belief that the Negro question was a national problem requiring national action. Segregation and removal of the Negro from the South were essential for its prosperity and for that of all America.

The remainder of Helper's platform indicated his devotion to the Union, his militant nationalism, and his progressive attitude toward civil service reform. He loathed those who led the South out of the Union, but he was politically realistic enough to work with anyone in ending Reconstruction and elevating the position of white workers. His advocacy of imperialism to the south came from both pride in America and racist contempt for the Indian and Negro blood so prominent in Latin America.[23] His desire for a civil service law, equalization of government salaries, complete fiscal responsibility and control of government by the civilian authority reflected the enlightened public opinion of the times. In fact, the desire to attain these things gave birth to the Liberal Republican movement.

The organization to which Helper presented his recommendations, the National Labor Union, was substantially influenced by them. The following year, 1870, it divested itself of its Negro members, voted to urge the government to exclude Chinese laborers, and prepared to undertake a third party movement. Although Helper could not claim exclusive responsibility for this action, he was pleased at the union's acceptance of the most pressing portion of his pleas. (The Negro members themselves were not excluded from the union but chose to go, largely for political reasons. The use of Chinese coolies, transported from California as strike-breakers in Massachusetts in June, 1870, had its influence. Also, as early as 1868 the union had urged the necessity of the formation of a labor party, although it had cautioned against the selection of presidential electors in the states. Even allowing for these factors, it is striking that the year after a committee was appointed by the National Labor Union to consider the ideas contained in *Noonday Exigencies in America,* its major demands were acted upon, and others appeared to be on the way to being endorsed.)

Unfortunately for the success of the party launched by the National Labor Union, all of its representatives from national trade unions withdrew in 1871. Many were not opposed to the political ideals of the new venture, but they were primarily unionists and did not wish to get into politics. Delegates to the conventions of 1871, mainly representatives of local unions and intellectuals, voted to hold separate political and industrial conventions in 1872. At the political convention Associate Supreme Court Justice David Davis of Illinois was nominated for the Presidency but withdrew his candidacy after the Democratic convention, and by that time, it was too late to nominate another candidate. Consequently, with its political hopes blighted and its national trade unions lost, the National Labor Union quickly declined and was completely interred by the depression of 1873; many of its ideals later found expression in the planks of the Greenback, Greenback-Labor, and Populist parties.[24] That Helper could interest such an organization in his diagnosis of the ills of American society illustrates the degree of liberalism in his thought. Although it sprang from a racist basis, its presence cannot be denied.

By 1872, when the National Labor Union tried to establish a labor party to overthrow the Radicals and Reconstruction, Helper was in Latin America and had turned his attention from racial conditions in the United States to those in the countries to the south. Had he been in the United States, he would have been disappointed at the abortive labor party movement, but it would not have been his first experience with political failure.

In 1868 one of Helper's racist works, *Negroes in Negroland,* was used as a party textbook by the Democratic Executive Committee. Unfortunately it met with little success, and only 1,000 copies were distributed. Unlike *The Impending Crisis,* none of Helper's racist works presented a ready-made, politically acceptable argument for either major party. While the Democrats could warmly approve his indictment of Reconstruction, they could not accept his castigation of their prewar position and the Southern upper classes. The Republicans, of course, could not admit any validity in his bitter attack on the Radicals, nor could a majority of either group publicly accept all of his racial arguments.

Among Southerners it is hard to say which of the indicted groups, the aristocracy or the Negroes, was most offended by Helper's works. The opinionated editor of *The Southern Review,* Albert Taylor Bledsoe, felt that Helper was not the exclusive author of *Nojoque.* "His wild ravings are there, and his disgusting coarseness of style, showing a total want of literary taste and intellectual refinement"; however, he felt that the quotations were so extensive and varied that they indicated Helper had received much aid. Portions of the writing also were in "strange contrast with the low vulgarity of Mr. Helper's conceptions and language." When James Wood Davidson devoted six pages of his *Living Writers of the South* to lauding Helper's works, *The Southern Review* tore into Davidson. Bledsoe asserted that Helper was "one of the most miserable renegades, and mendacious miscreants, the world has ever seen," and that he had written his own encomiums for the Davidson book.[25]

Probably many upper-class Southerners who knew of Helper's works agreed with John H. Gilmer that he had "made avowals and developed a *policy* which should mark him as the Intellectual Blackguard and Literary Infidel of the century." Helper and his friends had prepared "a doom 'for the colored people' far worse than slavery." Every Christian man, no matter what his color, would be overcome with disgust and indignation when he read Helper's works. He was not content to extinguish the Negro, but also "the *Catholic* must accompany him into the 'regions of darkness and deep despair and oblivion prepared for them from the foundation of the world.' A war between races is not enough to satisfy the morbid appetite of this world revolutionizing innovator," wrote Gilmer, "but there must at the same time, and as a part of the same policy, be inaugurated a war of religions."[26]

Some Negroes were severely hurt by Helper's attacks. Reverend E. R. Carter felt he must refute Helper's argument that only "the fair Caucasian race can [produce] statesmen, orators, poets, philosophers, historians . . . etc." After citing numerous Negroes who had excelled in these fields, he concluded, "Greatness has no color; learning is neither white nor black. There is no such thing as colored intelligence, white intelligence or black intelligence. There is no such thing as a white God."[27]

It would be easy to shrug off Helper's racism as an eccentric aspect of a mad mind, but it would be absurd to deal in such a fashion with the one unifying theme of his career. He wrote *The Impending Crisis* with the explicit purpose of freeing the Negro in order that he could be removed from the United States. In all his contacts with Latin America he sought to understand and explain its life in terms of the racial composition of its people. He devoted the latter years of his life in an effort to improve transportation and commerce with Latin America in order to bring it the benefits of a whiter and, what he assumed to be, a superior civilization.

Helper felt, in his attempt to segregate and remove the Negro from American life, that he was striving for the same principles that had actuated the nation's great leaders. From Jefferson to Lincoln, he held, every wise statesman had acknowledged the divergence of races and had not advocated that the white man be degraded to the level of the Negro. In Helper's view the "greatest of our American forefathers—those who were foremost in the formation of our Government, Washington, Adams, Jefferson and others—were entirely right in their views of both slavery and the negro; they hated the one, and cherished no undue love for the other."[28]

Lincoln's humanitarianism and his sense of political sagacity were too great to permit him to develop a racial program such as Helper's. Yet they shared a basic Negrophobia! As a Westerner, Lincoln argued that the territories must be free in order that white labor would not have to compete with Negro labor. The bitter contempt of the Northwest was expressed in the severe laws its states erected against the entry of free Negroes.

Frank Blair, Jr.'s *Daily Missouri Democrat* expressed the opinion of Lincoln and many of his followers in its motto, "White Men for Missouri and Missouri for White Men."

At first Lincoln, like Helper, saw colonization following emancipation as the ultimate solution to the Negro problem. As late as 1862 he tried to persuade a group of Negro callers to set up a colony in South America. "Lincoln was, as always, thinking primarily of the free white worker: the Negro was secondary." In this action he reflected fear of competition of free, black labor by both the "submerged whites of the South and wage workers of the North."[29] This outlook was precisely Helper's also. His difference from Lincoln came in the logic with which he carried his views to their conclusion, to the biting invective with which he expressed his contempt for the Negro and the tenacity with which he held his position. Of course, Helper did not have the sobering effect of running for office nor seeking to implement a policy once he was in office. As a theorist he could afford the luxury of dealing only with the ideal. Also, Helper had served an apprenticeship in a town and thought more in terms of the artisan and industrial worker than did Lincoln. Helper's bitter anti-Negroism was common among Southern workers, even in the ante bellum period. Significantly he wished to expel the Negro first from the cities and towns, the centers of civilization, and allow more time for his removal from the countryside.[30]

It would be hard to say whether Helper's primary motive in Negro removal was to take a social, cultural, and economic drag from society or to insure jobs and prosperity for white workers. Certainly in his mind there was no separation of these two factors. He saw economic progress as a concurrent achievement of a unified society and felt that it would come with the advance of every aspect of Southern life, once the Negro was removed.

Helper did not shrink from fully expressing his militant racist opinions, even though they found no substantial groups ready to accept and utilize them. He sincerely believed his theories offered a solution to the most urgent problem in national life, and it was not his nature to withhold his views to curry popular favor.

*Chapter Nine*

# Personal Envoy

DESPITE HIS DEVOTION to the ideal of "racial purity," circumstances forced Helper to become a practical man. Research for his books, written and published only after much investigation, was apparently subsidized by his wife. When they returned no royalties, Helper was keenly disappointed and began to plan some means to support his family, now including an infant son. Again confronted by his lack of professional training, he searched desperately for a position of dignity which would afford a livable income. Typically, from his few years residence in Argentina, he assumed that he was an expert on all things relating to Latin America. By 1870 he had conceived the idea of becoming a personal agent for those who had unsettled claims and, in the fall of the year, became the representative of Joseph H. Colton, an elderly New York map publisher with a long-standing claim against Bolivia.

In 1858 the Bolivian government contracted for Colton to produce 10,000 wall maps of the country for $25,000. Only $2,000 of this was paid, although Colton's expenses amounted to $22,300 and the Bolivian Congress, in 1864, had authorized payment of the original claim with interest.[1] Little did Helper realize when he became Colton's agent that he was channeling the remaining years of his life into activities connected with Latin America. Had he foreseen the thousands of miles of travel, the endless labor and frustrations, and the all too frequent failures that were to occupy the next 39 years, he possibly would not have begun this new endeavor.

Throughout his career Helper was often rash, but no one can ever accuse him of failing to be thorough nor of lacking perseverance. Upon investigating the Colton claim, he found that the Bolivian government had promised, in May, 1869, to give it serious consideration. Although Secretary of State Hamilton Fish had prevented Congress from acting on his accounts, Helper did not hesitate to confer with him, and Fish agreed to instruct the United States' Bolivian minister to use his good offices in an attempt to reach a settlement.[2]

Knowing something of United States diplomacy in Latin America, Helper concluded that only by going to Bolivia could he expect results. In the summer of 1871, leaving his family behind, he sailed to Buenos Aires and, late in October, made the journey through upper Argentina and the difficult crossing of the Andes on muleback. Upon arrival at the Bolivian capital, his worst fears were realized. The American minister, Leopold Markbreit, was 150 miles away vacationing in the mountains at Cachabamba. For several months Helper had to carry his struggle alone, unaided by any United States official.

At once Helper carefully prepared his case and began negotiations with the Bolivian government, submitting vouchers and other evidence as it required. With the instinct of a detective he located the two engineers who signed the 1858 contract, obtaining their affidavits. Both warmly urged payment of the just debt but explained that the successful rebellion of Melgarego had led to the "trampling out and ignoring of all the preeminent rights and duties of the nation."[3]

When his case was fully presented, Helper found the government would not consider the claim until the United States minister was in residence. Realizing dispatch was needed if action were to be obtained at the current session of Congress, he hounded Markbreit until his return to La Paz and saw him daily thereafter. "He pursued me like my shadow so that my colleagues wondered at my patience," the minister wrote. He and Helper attended a number of conferences with President Morales, at which little was accomplished. When Helper pressed for action, everyone was offended. At one meeting Markbreit wrote, "Mr. Helper conducted himself in such a manner that the President afterwards said to me that if it had not been for my presence he would have ordered him out of the Palace." But Helper's stern tone produced results. On February 1, 1872, the Congress set aside $51,985 in Bolivian money, or $41,585.54 in gold, from the first funds of a new foreign loan to settle the claim.[4]

With the passage of this act Helper felt that his Bolivian mission was a success and started for home immediately, journeying via Arequipa and Lima to Panama, across the isthmus and hence to New York. He wrote Markbreit from every convenient location along the route, urging him to use all possible speed in collection of the loan.

Once at home Helper could not close the case. Although both the Secretary of State and the Bolivian president had declared that settlement would be made by June, 1872, no payment was forthcoming. Markbreit urged patience, stating payment would be made before December, but Helper was skeptical and devised a strategy that was ultimately to prove successful—use of United States intimidation of Bolivia. If settlement were not made when the United States Congress convened, he proposed to appeal to it, suggesting that two war vessels be dispatched to Cobija or Mejillones and if Bolivia were stubborn, that the United States consider breaking diplomatic relations.[5]

In early 1873 Helper went to Washington to plead his case but found that no action could be taken in the few remaining weeks of the congressional session. He conferred with Fish, who promised to urge the newly appointed minister to Bolivia, John T. Croxton, to use greater vigor in an attempt to attain a settlement. Far more significantly, Helper concluded he must assume a more active role in dealing with the Bolivian government. Henceforth, he wrote directly to Bolivian officials, merely sending copies of his letters to the American Secretary of State and minister to Bolivia.

In February Helper delivered the first of his personal attacks, writing the Bolivian Secretary of State that he had been "deceived" by the "false promise" to pay by December, 1872. If payment were not made by August 15, 1873, no recourse was left but an appeal to the United States Congress. Moreover, Helper pledged to publish, in pamphlet form, all the papers relating to the loan, sending free copies of this exposé to the governments of Europe and South America.[6]

Leaders of the United States government gave Helper little encouragement in personal diplomacy. "In the case of a contract between a citizen of the United States and a foreign Government," Fish wrote, no Secretary of State had felt himself "authorized to regard any such contract as guaranteed by this Government." In signing a contract, Colton, he assumed, had considered Bolivia's "ability and disposition" to pay. He had done all that he could legitimately do in extending the use of the government's good offices.

Congressman Leonard Myers advised Helper of the difficulty in obtaining the intervention of Congress. When, as in the case of Venezuela, claims were made by a number of people, the United States had interposed, but there were few cases when this had been done for one person. Moreover, the Colton claim was an old one, which greatly decreased the chances for action.

Fortunately Helper was not a man to be easily discouraged, and his sense of justice, as well as his finances, were involved in the Colton claim. He felt that there was a defect in diplomacy, if the just debt of the citizen of one country could not be collected in another. Bolivia had promised to pay Colton from the first proceeds of a foreign loan, and this loan was successfully negotiated in the summer of 1872, but the promise was not kept. A country this unreliable was less fitted to be recognized as a republic than Buncombe County, North Carolina, deserved to be classed as an empire.[7]

As Colton's representative, Helper reminded President Thomas Frias of their meeting at Chuquioaca in 1871 and of his contemplated action. He predicted that, if the claim were not paid, Croxton would be "the last United States minister sent to Bolivia." Before

Frias could reply in April, 1873, that payments would "commence to be made" during that year, Helper was en route to Argentina. There he hoped to gain substantiation of his case against Bolivia and to allow his wife and son to visit her family.

To obtain the most expeditious passage, the Helpers took a British vessel sailing via Southampton to Buenos Aires. They broke their voyage, for pleasure and business, by stopping a few days in London. There Helper tried to see the Bolivian minister to Eupore and, failing to do so, mailed him a copy of his February ultimatum.[8]

Once in the Argentine, Helper obtained from the consul-general of Bolivia, in Buenos Aires, official acknowledgment of the Colton claim contained in the quarterly reports of the Bolivian Department of Finance and Industry. Armed with this document, he returned to the United States in the fall and began work on a memorial to Congress. With his usual care he prepared an extensive copyrighted pamphlet, entitled "Bolivia, as the Insidious Author and Persistent Perpetrator of a New International Crime," which was sent to press January 3, 1874.[9] He included in this complete resumé of the Colton claim many of the letters exchanged with the Bolivian government, asserting that six ministers and former ministers of the United States could verify the truth of its contents. Bolivia had "hood-winked" ministers and "audaciously trifled with all our illustrious Secretaries of State, from the days of the Hon. Lewis Cass to the Hon. Hamilton Fish, inclusive." Repeatedly it had promised to pay the Colton claim and then refused to do so. Helper, asserting that instability and dictatorship were the most notable features of Bolivian life, calculated that, since independence, the state had been troubled by forty-seven revolutions and many of the country's presidents had died by assassination. He urged the United States government to see that Colton received $41,588.54 in gold, plus $26,840 collection fee, and to suspend diplomatic relations with Bolivia as a nation unfit to be recognized as a civilized state.[10]

Helper sent copies of this strong document to Senator Simon Cameron, chairman of the Foreign Relations Committee, and other strategic government leaders. He informed the Bolivian Sec-

retary of State, Casimiro Corral, that the charges for collection of
the debt would be eliminated if the principal and interest were paid
through February 1, 1872; otherwise, he would ask the Congress to
act on the memorial.

Collection had become a matter of personal honor to Colton and
Helper. For two years President Morales and his cabinet, "with
pious hypocrisy," had promised payment with apparently no intention of doing so. In a letter singularly free of "smooth and mystical
and misleading phrases," Helper pleaded for justice. Because of
the racial nature of the government leaders, however, he had few
hopes of success.[11]

While waiting, Helper continued the search for additional materials to strengthen his case. He wrote to scores of the most influential Americans, sending them the memorial pamphlet and asking
they suggest a course of action. Henry A. Blythe replied that, if
Helper had figured his claim at $99,855.62 "and expended all above
$50,000 in carefully oiling the machinery of the Bolivian Govern-
ment," he would have had no difficulty. Frederick L. Olmstead
applauded the publication of the pamphlet and observed dishonest
people must be denied the fruits of civilization. Judge H. G.
Onderdonk wrote, "Were Mr. Colton a British subject, I doubt
not that a frigate would, long ago, have appeared off the coast of
Bolivia" and enforced payment. A former American minister to
Bolivia, John C. Smith, demonstrated that Helper was not alone
in his racist attitude. He recalled that during his ministry Bolivian
President José Maria Linares had agreed to make payment and
believed he would have fulfilled his promise had he not been over-
thrown. "Lonares was a lawyer by profession, of good family, and
of pure Caucasian descent." Smith observed, "The mixture of races
is the greatest curse of Bolivia; . . . hybrid Presidents there have no
regard either for personal character or public reputation."[12]

No such congenial reports came from Croxton or Markbreit.
Croxton suggested that Helper authorize him to use ten per cent of
the claim for the expenses of "an anonymous agent" to aid in collection. This infuriated Helper, who resolved to have no further
dealings with him. If possible, Markbreit exceeded Croxton "in

rapacity and audacity." For his expenses and twenty-two per cent of the claim, he proposed a trip to Bolivia for collecting it. Helper was "dumbfounded" that a man who had received thirty separate promises of payment without results would concoct such a scheme.[13]

May 6, 1874, Helper formally requested the House Foreign Affairs and Senate Foreign Relations committees to consider his memorial and, throughout the summer, fall and winter, worked consistently to obtain action from the Congress. From the letters he had received and from such diverse writers as Hugo Grotius, Samuel Pufendorf, John Marshall, and Andrew Jackson, he prepared a series of reports for the committees. His largest transmission to the Senate Foreign Relations Committee, over one hundred pages in length, was sent May 18, 1874. He urged the congressmen to see that, henceforth, in no country would an "American embassy ever be degraded" as had the one in Bolivia.

Helper's fame as the author of *The Impending Crisis* and benefactor of the Republican Party aided him in dealing with Republican leaders. He wrote frankly to Senators Simon Cameron, Hannibal Hamlin, A. S. Merriman, and T. O. Howe. Their aid obtained favorable action in the committee and on the floor, in spite of Fish's failure to lend support. When Cameron asked Fish's advice, he replied that the State Department considered the Colton claim a just one and had instructed its ministers to use their good offices in obtaining settlement. He maintained, however, that this action was as far as he could go, since the United States did not condone "diplomatic interposition" in private claims.[14]

Senator Howe's report, based on Helper's views, was passed by the Senate, January 19, 1875, and received unanimous House approval March 3. It reviewed the Colton claim, pronouncing it a just one, and observed, "No other American state could extinguish its debts with its revenues in so short a period of time" as Bolivia. If Bolivia would not pay the claim, the report recommended the United States "consider whether we can afford longer to maintain a diplomatic representative at the capital of that Republic." It requested the President of the United States to call on the Bolivian government to pay the claim, with interest, according to the agreement of February, 1872.[15]

Helper was immensely pleased with the action of Congress, but he warned Cameron that Bolivia "will not scruple to trifle also with our President, and even with Congress itself." His lack of confidence was, in part, due to the attitude of the newly appointed minister to Bolivia, Robert M. Reynolds, who, believing that Bolivia would pay the claim in 1875, advised against congressional action.

Afterward, Helper expressed his disdain to Reynolds, writing, "I suppose I might . . . refrain from all further correspondence with persons or places more distant than the White House, or the State Department." Yet, he assured the minister, he would appreciate his help.

Once the United States government intervened, Bolivia came to terms promptly. Reynolds signed a settlement and received drafts for five payments from President Frias on May 10, 1875. Under them, two payments were to be made from customs received at Bobija, Bolivia, and the remaining $41,588.54, in three payments from customs collected at Arica, under terms of a subvention treaty with Peru. By the treaty's terms over half the payments were to be made by the Peruvian government from sums collected for Bolivia. This feature introduced a new factor that was to cause serious trouble.

Helper was satisfied with the settlement but was dubious as to the manner in which the treaty would be fulfilled. In the summer and fall of 1875 he was anxious to leave New York City to visit North Carolina and the Northwest but hesitated to do so when told that Bolivia was proving hesitant in meeting her first note. Encouraging Reynolds to demand exact compliance with the settlement, Helper wondered if he would be "an accusant and litigant" against Bolivia from his place "in the Heavens."[16]

Bolivia paid the first two notes, but a major crisis arose when the first of the notes to be paid by Peru came due. Peru insisted on paying a $20,000 draft in paper money worth approximately one-half of the equivalent in gold or silver. Some such action had been feared by Helper, and he urged Reynolds to press the Bolivian government for a rectification before it made its annual move from La Paz to Chuquisca. He warned, "In all cases of this kind, where an ignorant and base-blooded Catholic nation is the delinquent, correspondence at a distance—even if the distance be no more than ten miles from the desks of the officials—will result in ˜nothing better than promises."

It soon became apparent that Bolivia was more the victim than the culprit in this case. Peru charged Bolivia as if the draft had been paid in gold. Upon learning of this situation, Helper protested to the Department of State, and Minister Richard Gibbs in Lima was asked to use his unofficial good offices. By this time, however, Helper had outmaneuvered himself in Bolivia. Following his advice, Congress had discontinued the American ministry in La Paz, after July 1, 1876, and Reynolds had been ordered home.[17]

When Reynolds arrived in New York City in November, 1876, accompanied by the body of his son who died en route, he brought a new draft for $19,609.40, payable in silver in Lima on March 1, 1878. Helper and Colton again had their patience tried before the matter was resolved. The June and December, 1876, notes were paid late and only upon the exactment of a higher collection fee. Then, suddenly, the Bolivian Minister of Foreign Affairs J. Oblitas, protested an error had been made in the payment of the claim and requested Colton to repay $16,683.40! Helper was chagrined, believing that this was a means to avoid paying the March note. He declared that never, in his forty-seven years, had he seen anything comparable to this demand. If interest rates had been calculated in South America, as they often were, Bolivia would be forced to pay an additional $64,000 to settle the claim. When hearing the demand, Helper was in Rio de Janeiro, and he resolved to be in Lima when the note came due. If it was not paid, he planned to sue all the nations involved in the highest available courts, demanding $70,000 as a settlement, plus an allowance of $6,000 a year after March 1.[18]

Helper's presence in South America at the time related to his representing the Ernest Fiedler estate in an effort to collect a twelve-year-old debt from Brazil. In 1867 Fiedler, the owner of the steamship "Circassin," signed an agreement with Domingo de Goicouria, a Brazilian immigration agent, to make a voyage from New Orleans to Rio de Janeiro with not over six hundred steerage passengers. For this transportation Fiedler was to receive 42,000 American gold dollars in addition to sixty dollars for each cabin passenger. Goicouria was to have ten days to load and unload the vessel and was to pay $350 for each day it was detained.

In anticipation of the voyage Fiedler invested $15,000 in supplies and repairs. When the "Circassin" arrived in New Orleans, no passengers presented themselves, and at the end of ten days, its captain began to ask demurrage. At this time Goicouria's successor ordered the empty vessel to sail to Rio de Janeiro, but the captain refused, and Fiedler contacted the Brazilian chargé d'affaires, asking him for instructions. He replied that the vessel should not sail and the contract should be considered null and void. Since Fiedler had suffered a loss of $20,000, however, he promised to seek indemnification for him.

Three years of negotiation proved completely fruitless, the Brazilian government holding that Goicouria and his associates had no authority to act in its behalf. It contended that Fiedler should have received and retained any powers of attorney they had. In addition, Brazilian authorities denied that a chargé d'affaires had the authority to charter vessels but stated that, under any circumstances, Fiedler's claim was excessive.

Helper was convinced of the justice of the Fiedler claim and planned the strategy he should use to collect it. He considered seeing Dom Pedro II, the Brazilian emperor, while he was in the United States but decided this course of action would be improper and might prejudice his cause. He decided to go to Brazil and personally plead the case, when told by the Brazilian minister to the United States that the emperor's absence would not hinder a settlement; Princess Izabel, as regent, was endowed with all of the emperor's authority.

Helper alerted the United States minister to Brazil, James H. Partridge, of his impending mission but asked him to make no mention of the claim until after he came. Upon Partridge's advice, he waited until April, 1877, to sail, planning to arrive after the yellow fever season ended in May.

Again traveling as a private citizen, but this time alone, Helper chose to sail on a British vessel. He went first to Europe in order to see the emperor personally. After conferring in London with the Brazilian ambassador to Great Britain, he made a hasty tour of England, Wales, Ireland, and Scotland, then journeyed to France and overtook Dom Pedro II in Paris.

Helper first tried flattery in order to gain an interview and, if possible, favorable action on the claim. "Your Majesty, whose long, wise, honorable and successful reign, will impart strength and lustre to all your dynastic successors" does not need to be told justice should always be done, he wrote. If the Dom would see him, he proposed not only to present a valid case for the Fiedler claim but also to reveal how he planned to spend his fee. This indirect comment was Helper's first reference to the great scheme of an inter-American railway, an ideal that was to dominate his thinking for years.

The emperor refused to see Helper, except socially, during his "customary hour for public receptions." Such a rebuff could not stop Helper from pushing a project dear to his heart. He called on the emperor at the appointed time, finding him "dignified" but "polite." The Dom expressed delight with his visit to the United States, and Helper assured him no foreign visitor had received precedence. At this point Helper brought up the Fiedler claim. The emperor knew nothing of it and could only refer him to the officials at home. "His Majesty seemed to be perfectly candid and impartial about the matter; and, upon the whole, I feel rather pleased and encouraged than otherwise," Helper wrote. In a few days he sailed via Dakar for Rio de Janeiro.[19]

On July 10 Helper arrived in Brazil and began a frustrating five-month sojourn. The American minister had resigned three weeks before, and there was not even a chargé d'affaires present. The new minister, the astute scholar and ante bellum Whig leader of Alabama, Henry W. Hilliard, did not arrive until October 14. In the interim Helper negotiated as best he could, making a basic mistake in connecting the claim with his plans for an inter-American railway. The mysterious manner in which he projected plans for it was not conceived to promote confidence.

In any event, in mid-July Helper wrote to "Her Serene Highness, the Imperial Princess Izabel," reviewing his correspondence with the emperor and asking for payment of the claim. He stated his returns from the claim would be used to promote an enterprise which would be of unlimited value to Brazil. He gave no clue as to its nature but asked that the princess appoint a trusted minister who spoke fluent English, before whom he could lay his plans. The one condition he exacted was that the minister must never reveal or mention the plan except to the princess, the emperor or himself.[20]

A month passed without answer. Unofficially Helper heard the Secretary of the Treasury felt the claim should not be paid, and the United States consul-general stated as long as Brazil continued to be unprosperous, there was no hope for a settlement.

August 23 Helper wrote the Brazilian Secretary of State, Diogo Albuquerque, urging that someone be appointed to discuss the claim and hear his plan, which only "an uncommonly masculine mind" could appreciate. The assistant secretary of state, Cabo de Frio, was chosen to confer with Helper, but after only one meeting Albuquerque terminated the talks on the grounds that a letter of Helper's contained language so severe it could not "be filed among the archives." Furthermore, the secretary declared the claim to be unfounded and the railway scheme impractical.

Unsuccessfully Helper tried to salvage the situation by disclaiming any intention of being rude. Born and reared in a republic, he was accustomed to direct speech which lacked embellishments but was not designed to give offense. Albuquerque was unimpressed by his apologies.

When Dom Pedro II returned in late September, Helper waited two weeks for the ovations to die down and then wrote him again, setting forth the basis of the Fiedler claim. He held that, although it was now worth $32,000, he was seeking to collect only $20,000. If paid, much of this money would be used to initiate the railway project which would profit Brazil as much as any nation. Helper offered to submit a written description of the proposal after the emperor had recognized the validity of the claim. Dom Pedro II refused, forfeiting the opportunity to learn of the plans.[21]

Although there was little hope of success, Helper continued methodically to gather material to strengthen his case. From the *Diario Official de Imperio* he obtained evidence that Goicouria and his associates were official agents of Brazil. He gathered statements from the leading Americans in Rio de Janeiro, expressing their beliefs that the claim was valid. Minister Hilliard, who had become a fast friend of Helper, wrote that an examination of the papers satisfied him "that the claim is at once just and moderate." He felt Fiedler was generous in asking for only $20,000.

On November 17 the Brazilian government returned seventeen vouchers Helper had submitted without even perusing them. Helper, who strongly suspected that Albuquerque and Frio were responsible for the unjust decisions, proposed to Hilliard that the minister call on the emperor and offer arbitration. Hilliard replied he would love to serve as arbiter, but his instructions would not permit. From informal discussions with Frio the minister had concluded the claim could not be collected. "Of course it would be very agreeable to me personally to have you remain here while I stay," he wrote, but collection efforts were a waste of time.[22] Reluctantly Helper had to abandon the immediate attempt to collect the Fiedler claim. In doing so, he retained a hatred of Brazil which was to find expression in his later writings and his plans for his projected railway to avoid Brazil.

Helper was a man of tremendous self-confidence and energy, who, as he failed in Brazil, made plans to cross the Andes to be in Lima well before the Bolivian note came due in March, 1878. On December 1, 1877, he mailed an outline of his railway plan to his brother, Hanson Pinkney Helper, a student at Davidson College, North Carolina. He also enclosed instructions that it was to be submitted to the Senate Foreign Relations Committee if Helper should die on his "second fatiguing and perilous journey on muleback across the continent."[23]

By December 18 Helper was in Buenos Aires, where he spent the holiday season. He was in Santiago, January 19, 1878, after crossing directly from Buenos Aires to Valparaíso, and was in Lima by March 1. Awaiting him was a letter from Colton expressing his surprise and disappointment that there might be difficulty in collecting the March note. He recalled that Helper always had a lower opinion of the Bolivians than he, "declaring them to be a most mongrel and impure race, incapable of constancy to any agreement." Colton believed that Helper would be a match for any opposition, writing if they "overreach you they will have to get up early in the morning."[24]

When March 1, 1878, arrived, Helper and Henry S. Prevost, a commercial agent, called at the Peruvian treasury to collect the draft due at that time. Payment was refused on the grounds that Bolivia contended a mistake had been made in the claim settlement. Daily, Helper and Prevost called at the treasury, which consistently refused payment.

Helper was not a man to demonstrate patience in such a situation. On March 12 he informed the Peruvian Secretary of the Treasury that, if payment were not made by March 29, he would ask the Supreme Court of Peru for a writ of mandamus, address an appeal to the United States Congress or Department of State, and would recommend that the United States government seize Peruvian guano at the port of New York. Furthermore, he would hold Peru responsible for $10,000 damages, plus legal expenses, and seek to collect $78,903.18 in gold from Bolivia to extinguish the claim. Minister Richard Gibbs used all the personal influence at his command in arguments with the foreign minister of Peru but refused to deliver a very strong formal protest, drawn up by Helper March 19.

Helper appealed directly to the attorney-general of Peru, who gave an opinion in his favor, but at this point the Peruvian government began a series of evasive tactics. To each Helper contrived the necessary corrective and continued to press his case. On a technicality the government refused his protest in English, required it "be made out in accordance with various specified formalities," and demanded Helper present copies of certain Bolivian papers. Although the Bolivian legation could have supplied these papers in ten minutes, it refused to do so.

At first Helper tried his usual initial approach, flattery, on the Bolivian minister to Peru, Zoilo Flores, but when this tactic failed, he threatened to prepare a history of the Colton claim, in Spanish, for the Peruvian Congress and ask its aid. He informed the consul-general of Bolivia in Lima that, if the claim were not paid by December 1, he would turn to the United States Congress for aid.

In late May, Peru's president, Manuel Prado, decreed the draft should be paid. Since Helper could give only an alien bond, however, the government refused a settlement. Helper struggled throughout the summer to comply with Prado's decree. He obtained a place for his case on the docket of the Supreme Court of Peru but was unable to get a decision, although he pleaded that he was painfully separated from his family and friends and deserved rapid justice. He requested United States Secretary of State William M. Evarts to instruct Gibbs to make an official bond for him, but the secretary replied he had no authority.

The break in the impasse came when Helper's Peruvian legal representative, Fernando Palacios, became a councilor of state in midsummer. Helper forwarded him a memorial, and he discussed the claim with the president and cabinet. On September 9 the government of Peru "unconditionally accepted" the draft for $19,609.40 in silver. Helper was too exhausted to be more than mildly pleased. He calculated that, if the amount had been paid in March and had earned twelve per cent interest, it would have been worth much more; moreover, his expenses alone had amounted to $5,214.57.[25] It is impossible to ascertain how much of the settlement Helper received personally. Events of his later life indicate that he obtained a considerable portion. Following his return to the United States, he never held a regular job, yet he supported his family and expended thousands of dollars in the promotion of a railway scheme. There is no other apparent source from which he could have obtained the funds he expended.

Regardless of how he and Colton divided the settlement, Helper had performed a minor miracle in settling the claim. Reynolds wrote congratulating him on the victory in a "hard-fought contest, where, during most of the time, the odds were so overwhelmingly against you." Evarts advised Colton, "Mr. Helper seems to have acquitted himself, as your agent, with great zeal and perseverance."

Worn out and homesick, Helper returned immediately. Upon arrival, the strain of his long struggles combined with his usual seasickness confined him for several days in New York City. From his bed he dispatched a memorial to Congress, seeking to recover from Bolivia the additional sum of $78,903.18. Colton acquiesced in this demand but felt that, if the New York manner of compounding interest were used, he should receive $90,000.

Between November, 1878, and January, 1879, Helper was in Washington three times, twice on the way to and from North Carolina, where he visited his mother. Each time he talked with Evarts and other government leaders who told him it would be useless to seek to collect additional money from Bolivia. Reluctantly Helper advised Colton not to undertake additional diplomatic action "until after a man of respectability, education and honor, that is to say, a white man, shall have been elected to the Presidency of that so-called Republic." In Helper's opinion the Bolivian president, General Hilairón Daza, was "an ignorant and unprincipled hybrid, of hazy and hateful hue." He could be counted on "to keep his country constantly in a condition of wild commotion and chaotic repulsiveness and ruin."[26]

But Helper was thoroughly aroused by what he considered to be the lax and corrupt governments of Brazil, Bolivia and Peru. As usual, when frustrated by a major problem, he wrote a book as a possible solution. During 1879 he prepared and published the 475-page volume entitled *Oddments of Andean Diplomacy and Other Oddments.* While briefly outlining his ideas for improved transportation in the Americas, it was devoted primarily to a detailed account of his experiences as a claim agent. He sought to place the people of the United States "on their guard against the habitual unfairness and artifice and faithlessness" of the actual rulers of Latin America as opposed to its potential white leaders. The educated, genteel Latin whites "are the peers if not the paragons, of the politest and highest-toned people in the world," and only by closer relations with the United States could they hope to lead their countries to prosperity and a higher civilization.[27]

Helper's years as a claim agent were full of frustration as well as significance. The laborious mechanics of Latin government were too much for his temperament, and the long periods of negotiation and waiting were extremely trying. His difficulties were compounded by the fact that justice was as unsure as it was elusive. However, despite these tribulations, Helper came to have a great affinity for Latin America. Although, true to his convictions, he despised the governments and nonwhite peoples, he realized the potential of the area and desired its cultural and economic development under United States nurture. The remainder of his life was devoted to this purpose through the promotion of an inter-American railway.

*Chapter Ten*

# Railway Promoter

PREDOMINANCE OF THE United States in the Western hemisphere was a dream that spurred Helper to formulate plans for an inter-American railway extending from Canada to the Argentine. From his earliest contact with Latin America Helper sought to promote better transportation as a first step in economic and cultural penetration. While consul in Buenos Aires, he urged the American government to underwrite a steamship line to South America, and one was established to Rio de Janeiro. Helper wished its extension to the La Plata region and, in 1872, suggested Argentina and the United States grant temporary subsidies for this purpose, believing the stimulation of trade and industry would repay the investment.

At the same time Helper was becoming conscious of the need for an interoceanic canal. Crossing the Andes from Buenos Aires, in 1871, he found every foreign article to be of British or European manufacture and almost all brought to the west coast in British bottoms. To Helper this situation was illogical; because of its location and friendship with republics, the United States should be a commercial leader in all the Americas.[1]

After making a second crossing in 1877, Helper became more convinced than ever of a need for a canal. Everywhere he found goods inferior to those of the United States being sold at prices which this country could more than meet with adequate transportation. Writing to the Mexican consul in New York, Helper proposed that Mexico co-operate with the United States in opening more than one canal. Having crossed the Isthmus of Darien twice and Nicaragua once, he believed either route was practical and had seen reports to indicate Tehuantepec was also. Since the Darien route was much shorter and presented no more difficulties than the others, it should be developed at once. If Mexico would co-operate, the United States could aid in the building of a second canal, as a safety factor, across the Tehuantepec Isthmus.[2]

Always a visionary but never one without a plan, Helper proposed a means by which the United States could finance canal construction. When Secretary of the Navy Richard W. Thompson advocated a better balance should be struck in the size of the United States Navy and merchant marine, Helper challenged him to take the initiative in accomplishing this goal. He felt that $18,000,000 was too much money to spend on a peacetime navy and urged the reduction of the fleet to 38 warships for sea service and 38 cutters for river and harbor patrol, permitting a cut in the navy appropriation of $8,000,000 a year. From this saving, work on an isthmian canal could begin, and $2,000,000 annually, for fifteen years, could be appropriated to develop steamship lines, opening an almost illimitable field for "surplus products and manufactures" of the United States. By advocating this program, Helper assured Thompson, he would become "the most useful and profitable Secretary of the Navy" in American history.[3]

Concern with improved water transportation occupied only a small portion of Helper's thought, and from 1866, he wrote, "scarcely one of my wakeful hours" was free of thoughts of "a longitudinal midland double-tract steel railway from a point far north in North America to a point far south in South America." When he failed to interest Dom Pedro II in his plans, he realized that he had to fight with his own time and money, if he were to succeed.

In New York City in late 1878 Helper conferred with a number of men, all of whom felt his grand design was impractical. Among others he presented his plan to a leading banker who, for years, had been a personal friend, former Governor Edwin D. Morgan. He expressed a warm affection for Helper but, after a week's study, pronounced the railway an impossibility. With these rebuffs Helper left the East for St. Louis where railway men, while not offering any capital, at least did not scorn his ideas.[4]

If his plan were to succeed, Helper realized that some bold means must be used to awaken the imagination of peoples and governments. The only means he knew of achieving this purpose was to publish a book, and to increase interest in it, he conceived the idea of sponsoring a literary contest. From his portion of the Colton claim he resolved to set aside $5,000 to be awarded in prizes for the three best essays and two best poems in the contest. The entries were to deal with the construction and value of a rail line, were to be written in English, and were to be open to people of all nations. The essays were not to exceed in length one hundred pages of "closely-written cap paper" nor to be less than sixty-six. The poems were not to be over 500 lines nor less than 333. By this means Helper hoped to enlist the enthusiasm of the masses of the "Three Americas" in the project and, in his words, to "prove conclusively my own earnestness and confidence in the matter."

It was partially to disseminate news of the contest and to spread his views on a "Three Americas Railway," as he always called the projected line, that Helper published *Oddments of Andean Diplomacy and Other Oddments* in 1879. Much of the preface, as well as the concluding pages of the work, were devoted to the railway.[5]

Helper stated that the volume was issued as a contribution to the "general stock of ideas beginning to actuate the whiter and higher and better portions of the three Americas." The Three Americas Railway was the one means to mitigate and lessen the evils which were all too numerous in Latin America. Helper summarized these evils as:

    1. "A largely preponderating, idle, vicious, and worthless population of negroes, Indians, and bi-colored hybrids."

    2. "The complete, intolerant, and fanatical sway of Roman Catholicism, which . . . may be very justly regarded as the meanest

and most irrational religion ever recognized by any race of white men, Mormonism and Mohammedanism only excepted."

3. A general apathy of the people resulting in the neglect of the agricultural, mechanical, manufacturing and industrial arts.
4. An illiterate stupidity of the masses who devoted much time to playing musical instruments, dancing, gambling, etc.
5. Absolutism and despotism among the upper class minority.
6. General laxity in regard to agreements and widespread malfeasance in public office.
7. In Brazil, "an obstructive monarchy" which was "banefully black and brown and beggarly with Africans, Indians, Mulattoes, and other balefully base and besotted and barbarous with chattel slavery".[6]

With the railway would come much trade and travel from the United States, and investments and direction would develop millions of square miles of fertile lands and precious metals. Tens of thousands of upright, white men in Latin America would "supplant entirely the cumbersomely and worthlessly base and black and brown elements in the vile-visaged and deleterious forms of human rubbish around them."

The beauty of Helper's conception lay in his contention that, while Latin America "will be rendered richer in mind and morals," the United States, through investment and sale of goods "at handsomely remunerative profits," would "be rendered richer in money and manners." Everyone was to gain except the nonwhites and Catholics who were so inferior they deserved displacement.

Helper conceded that the United States was not completely free of all evils itself. "In such Catholic-cursed cities as New York and Cincinnati" power came into the hands of "such detestable miscreants as Tweed, Purcell, Sweeney, Banard, Walsh, Morrissey, and Reilly." The moral senses of "such wretched and despicable negro or semi-negro States as Mississippi, South Carolina, and Louisiana as also in portions of Tennessee" were only half perfect since the population was only half white. But the "gross immoralities" in the United States were "only spasmodic and exceptional; whereas in all South and Central America and Mexico, as indeed in all

Catholic countries, as also in all non-Caucasian countries, they are both regular and general."⁷

After publication of *Oddments of Andean Diplomacy and Other Oddments,* Helper devoted his time completely to the development of the Three Americas Railway. He sent copies of the new work to President Rutherford B. Hayes and members of his cabinet. In sending the book to Mexico and fourteen other Latin American nations, he requested their co-operation in the development of the railway. In particular he asked that they not grant charters or guarantees to railway novices or speculators.⁸

Although Mexico answered in a noncommittal way, Helper was encouraged by the large number of enthusiastic replies from other Latin American governments. Significantly, most of them were contingent upon favorable action by someone else. Guatemala felt that Helper's plan was flattering and assured him that he might "count upon its efficient cooperation, so soon as the scheme shall take proper shape and begin to be put into practice." Salvador proclaimed it had made no concessions. Nicaragua expressed its "good dispositions" toward the project. José Maria Castro of the Costa Rican State Department reported that his country was building a railway from Port Limon on the Atlantic to Puntarenas on the Pacific. He declared that this project would not prevent Costa Rica "from accepting with enthusiasm, and giving its moral support to, the gigantic enterprise here mentioned, so long as there appears to be a fair possibility of carrying it out successfully."

A representative of Colombia was thrilled by the "stupendous and majestic" nature of the projected railway and wrote Helper that he could "confidently rely" on his country's co-operation, as soon as the enterprise was well enough organized to give hopes for its completion. José A. DeCour, in sending Paraguay's "most distinguished consideration," avowed that his state was "animated with the best dispositions in favor" of the railway.⁹

From all areas of the Americas words of praise were poured on Helper for his foresight and courage. No one was more laudatory than Professor James Wood Davidson, author of *Living Writers of the South.* From New York City he wrote Helper, "You are to become the Colossus of *Roads* [*sic*]. . . . Systematic and business-like as are your proceedings, and practical as your extra-ordinary propositions are beginning to appear, yet the scheme, viewed as a whole, is a regular poem in itself." From Asheville, Natt Atkinson wrote that his heart swelled "with emotions of pride when I contemplate the completion of this matchless undertaking; and by no means the less so when I remember that its fore-thoughtful originator is a North Carolinian."

The Reverend Dr. W. C. Bowman of Atlanta felt the railway to be "of unique and preeminent grandeur" and doubted if "another man" besides Helper, "would have thought of it." Helper's presence in South America "as an official and as a lover . . . served to crystalize this mighty conception." L. Placide Canonge, the New Orleans poet, writing in French, described the "huge proposition" as "well worthy of our epoch, so rich in unmatched and meritorious audacities, and so fruitful of wonder-works attempted and accomplished." He advised Helper to pay "no attention to the shallow-brained skeptics, who will only betray their own insignificance by disparaging your splendid project." A Pennsylvania Quaker and textile manufacturer, George W. Taylor, sent his approval, at the same time apologizing for doing so. "I am a member of the Religious Society of Friends," he wrote, "one of whose general practices is to avoid compliments."[10]

From South America came words of praise and encouragement from a number of individuals. Colonel W. Milnor Roberts, engineer-in-chief of Brazil and designer of the St. Louis steel bridge, spoke from first-hand knowledge of railroading. He assured Helper that, although at first his proposal might "be viewed by some as rather visionary, you have properly adopted the very best plan for securing to it the serious attention of practical men." Obviously he felt the railway had merits, since he urged that the line be built through Brazil. "It might be deemed advisable to lay the tract just where Nature calls loudest for it, regardless of all *now-existing* national peculiarities and delinquencies," he wrote, and slavery would be abolished in Brazil before the Three Americas Railway could be constructed.

José Francisco Lopez, a leading member of the Buenos Aires bar, was highly enthusiastic. He petitioned his government to give priority to the Helper program but wrote, "The undertaking is one of such colossal magnitude that it may require a very considerable amount of time and labor to convince the various peoples of Spanish America of its feasibility." He knew the goal was worth the effort, since he completely accepted Helper's racist views. He stated, "Thus far the regenerating and invigorating regions of the North have been inaccessible to South America, the latter being entangled and enslaved by her long-established paganism of idolatry for unworthy persons and dead forms."

Another Argentine, Judge Fenelon Zuviria of the Federal Court of Santa Fe and Cordova, described the railway as a "superb conception." "Neither he who conceived the enterprise, nor those who will execute it," he wrote, "will ever be able to measure either the magnitude or the magnificence of the results which are destined to flow from it." No one could comprehend, in a single effort, the importance of "substituting on an immense continent civilization for barbarism."

At a banquet in Buenos Aires, Judge Zuviria read a letter from Helper describing the projected railway. It was received "with demonstrations of enthusiasm and applause"; among the most pleased were several men who had known Helper when he was in the city.[11]

While listening to these words of praise, Helper continued plans for the literary contest. Upon the suggestion of the chancellor of Washington University, he chose Dr. William T. Harris, superintendent of Public Instruction in St. Louis; Carlos S. Greeley, receiver of the Kansas Pacific Railway; and Thomas Allen, president of the Iron Mountain Railway, to serve as judges. They immediately accepted, but when Dr. Harris was forced to resign, he was replaced by Horace H. Morgan, principal of the St. Louis High School.

The contest closed October 1, 1880, in order that Helper might publish the five winning papers in book form the following year. He hoped, as a result of the enthusiasm engendered, that government guarantees and charters could be obtained and actual railway construction begun by October 14, 1882. At that time, or soon thereafter, he believed 150,000 laborers could be working on the line and the Three Americas Railway completed by 1892, in time to celebrate the four hundredth anniversary of the discovery of America with a great world's fair in St. Louis.

Those connected with the contest soon caught Helper's enthusiasm. All the judges were captivated by the railway program and "the substantial and business-like" way Helper presented it. His banker felt that, once the plan became widely known, it could not "fail to attract the attention and critical examination of all thoughtful and practical Americans." Dr. Harris believed Helper was arousing the interest of the peoples of the Americas to the overriding issue of the times. A great wave of European immigration would continue to come to the Western hemisphere, he wrote. "After it has peopled our own wilderness to the West," it must "spread out laterally to the North and the South," and the Three Americas Railway provided the logical means for its placement and development.[12]

The writers' contest received wide publicity, but by no means was all of it favorable, the most skeptical being that of the New York *Times*. It had heard little of Helper since *The Impending Crisis* caused "such a commotion" in Congress, but it was equally impressed with his proposition "to run a double-track railway from Behring Strait to Cape Horn." This "would be a magnificent undertaking," but the line "would not be much more likely to be built, nor would be more profitable, than a railway to the moon."

The *Times* felt Helper was "suffering from a severe attack of that peculiar enthusiasm which is so characteristic of the people of the Southern states," a disease the same as that which led others to envision additional Saratogas at innumerable trickling mineral springs throughout Dixie. Helper's affliction seemed to have reached a more advanced stage, the *Times* wrote. Nothing equal to his "sublime flights of imagination" had appeared since Edward Fontaine's book "described the inestimable benefits" to be derived from "the application of his method of drainage, called Ekmuzesia, to the desert of Sahara and the swamps of Lake Pontchartrain."

As to Helper's literary contest, the *Times* wrote, "There has been nothing in literature so unique as this since P. T. Barnum offered a prize for the best 'song of greeting to America,' to be sung by Jenny Lind on her arrival here." Although the contest proved Helper's complete sincerity, it wondered if "the half-breeds of the Aleutian Islands and the nomads of Patagonia" would be thrilled by news of "the double track of steel rails which is to bring them the blessings of a civilization which has produced the genius of a Mr. Helper." The *Times* reported, "Mr. Helper is far from being crazy, and his supporters are probably respectable gentlemen and useful members of society," but his plans were impractical. It lamented the fact that Edgar Allan Poe was dead, since he would have made the ideal superintendent of the line.

Despite the rebuffs of the Eastern capitalists and press, Helper continued his literary contest. By its close forty-seven contestants had submitted forty-nine essays and poems. Seven of the entrants were from New York, three from Pennsylvania, two from Massachusetts and one from as far away as Australia. Eleven were women.

All of those connected with the contest were pleased with its results. The judges wrote Helper, "There are few, if any, clear-headed thinkers in this or any other country who will arise from a careful perusal of the five successful papers without giving a hearty assent to the general correctness of your views."

Carlos Greeley felt that they constituted "some of the best writings . . . that he had ever read upon any subject whatever." After reading the winning papers, Helper wrote, "I am more than pleased; I am delighted." "Nor is it the least surprising that all these writers wrote so well; the subject itself having put them at their very best."[13]

Helper wished to get the essays and poems into print quickly. In May, 1881, he wrote the preface for the volume, appropriately entitled *The Three Americas Railway,* almost two-thirds of which was composed of the winning papers.

Accepting as a fact that "the projected Three Americas Railway ought to be built, must be built, and will be built," Helper raised the question as to how this work could be done most expeditiously. Because he had received no encouragement from private capitalists, he urged that it should be built jointly by the sixteen republics it would traverse. Whether or not army engineers should direct the construction was a question which could be resolved later.

Experience had taught Helper that trade, travel and economic development follow the routes of rapid transportation. He knew many Argentine and Chilean merchants who preferred to trade with the United States, but orders to New York or New Orleans were sent via Europe and took six to seven weeks to be delivered with an equal time for reply. United States merchants could not develop markets under such conditions. Establishment of direct steamship lines and the construction of an isthmian canal would put the United States in a competitive position. However, only the regularity and dependability of rail transportation would permit the ultimate development of United States trade.

Helper preferred not to set exact specifications for the route except to stipulate it avoid Brazil. Ideally, engineers would find it possible for the line to proceed along the 28th degree of longitude west from Washington (103° west from Greenwich) from Canada to Mexico. It would be "rectilineal as the straightest street in the most quadrangular city" as it intersected Dakota, Nebraska, Colorado, New Mexico and the Western part of Texas. From the Rio Grande it would make a "bee line" for the City of Mexico and then take as nearly a midland route as possible through the Central American republics. After crossing the Isthmus of Darien into South America, the line would pass east of the Andes "felling the forests and furrowing up the surfaces of Colombia, Ecuador, Eastern Peru and Bolivia, and thence in a nearly straight line, to Rasario, Buenos Ayres" and such other Argentine points as trade might warrant. Branches would connect with the main line at numerous places throughout the Americas. The Three Americas Railway would be more "important than all of the so-called Seven Wonders of the World" combined.

Helper hoped the volume *The Three Americas Railway* would be "an earnest appeal to the plain, practical common-sense of sixteen American republics." He felt its perusal would lead to a demand for the construction of the line as a protection from the "monarchial and ecclesiastical enmities and machinations" all too common in Latin America. As a first step all Americans should vote only for those politicians pledged "in the most unequivocal manner to do everything in their power" to obtain their governments' participation in building the railway. In concentrating on its construction, the great energies of the Latin American people would be aroused and diverted from rebellion and intrigue to a magnificently productive enterprise.[14]

If literary quality of the winning compositions alone could have developed the Three Americas Railway, the line would have been completed even earlier than Helper had dreamed. At Helper's suggestion the winner of the second prize in poetry developed his work into an essay, and Helper was able to present four persuasive prose compositions and one poem. All closely reflected in most details Helper's views as presented in *Oddments of Andean Diplomacy and Other Oddments,* including his racist approach. Yet each possessed its own individuality, and to this day, they form, collectively, one of the strongest arguments for closer relations and improved communications among the states of the Western Hemisphere.

The winner of the $1,300 first prize, in prose, was Frank Frederick Hilder of St. Louis. Railways, he contended, were the most important development of the nineteenth century, and from them the United States had received as many benefits as any country. Yet the construction of the Three Americas Railway would open a fantastic new era of progress for her. He believed that markets would be found for all the United States agricultural and manufacturing surplus in the expanding economy which would develop in Latin America. Interchange of the products of Central America's mines and tropical plantations, alone, would change the way of life of millions of people.

Hilder's views went beyond the economic. By the aid of the railway, he believed "jealousy and ignorance, nurtured by isolation, bigotry and intolerance, will be swept away" from Latin America.

As "better elements" mingled with native populations, Latin nations would rise in the hierarchy of states. In a statement which seems Marxist today he wrote, "There can be no great intellectual, political or social improvement, which is not preceded by corresponding material progress."

After reviewing the engineering needs for the line, Hilder found the greatest area of difficulty to be from the crossing of the Isthmus of Panama to the point where the line would complete its 3,000-foot ascension in Colombia. There was no doubt the engineering was feasible, if money were available. To obtain funds, he proposed that the United States government guarantee five per cent interest on the $300,000,000 he estimated the railway would cost, an annual investment of $15,000,000. This was an insignificant sum to guarantee prosperity for all the Americas and "perfect the principles of the Monroe Doctrine."

Many of Hilder's views were shared by the second-place prize winner, Frederick Anthony Beelen of Courtland-on-the-Hudson, New York. Beelen wrote with authority, since he had lived for many years in Central and South America. Thirty years previous he had seen the effects in Chile when a railway line was opened "in that wonderfully progressive Republic." He predicted that, "unless some new and powerful factor, such as the proposed intercontinental railway, shall be introduced," United States trade with Latin America would continue to languish and warned that British merchants more than anyone else would oppose the line.

From experience, as the leader of a party which explored the headwaters of the Orinoco River, Beelen advocated the railway be built west of the Andes to a point near Copiapo, Chile, where it would cross the mountains into Argentina. Wisely he observed that east of the mountains it would take years to build a population sufficient to support the line. No surveys for railways had been undertaken there, the rivers were as nature made them, and even "roads for wheeled vehicles are almost unknown."

Helper took sharp exception to Beelen's desire for a west coast route. Beelen's arguments against a route east of the Andes could have been applied to the successful transcontinental lines of North

America. "The west coast route will not do," Helper wrote; "It is not sufficiently midland; in fact, it is not midland at all; and besides its being too one-sided, it is too arid, too steep, too sterile."[15]

The third-place prose winner, William Wharton Archer, a young member of the staff of the Richmond *State*, shared Helper's view as to the route of the railway. On its entrance into Colombia, the Andes would be crossed once and for all. Archer held that, since Peru had erected a line where the range was highest, the crossing should present no insurmountable difficulties. "What the enervated Peruvian did the rigorous native of the United States can do, and more," he wrote. He foresaw no difficulties in construction from the neighborhood of Bogotá to Encarnacion in Southern Argentina. In the Peruvian-Ecuador area he felt the railway should go far enough west of the Maranon River "to be out of the reach of its fluctuating tides" but far enough to the east to receive the benefits of the potentially wealthy Amazon Valley.

Archer presented a strong economic argument for the Three Americas Railway as opposed to an isthmian canal. Great Britain already enjoyed a grip on Latin American trade, which he felt a canal would tighten. Furthermore, he contended only $4\frac{1}{2}$ per cent of South American territory could be reached by steamships, even if a canal were opened; whereas, the Three Americas Railway would open 89 per cent of the continent. The history of the United States demonstrated that canal and river navigation offered uncertain transportation as compared to a railway. Archer predicted that one year after the line was opened the United States would have no less than $400,000,000 of commerce with Latin America and that the rewards would be even greater for the states to the South. They would receive new population, business and industry. "Capital is timid, and rightfully so." It would penetrate Latin America only when rapid communication and political stability came as a result of the railway.

The fourth essay, full of practical suggestions and warm praise for Helper, was written by Francis Augustus Deekens of Norwick, Ontario, Canada. "What is called national glory is very often nothing but national dishonor in the truest sense," he wrote. But this would not be the case with the United States' promotion of the Three Americas Railway. Deekens suggested, and Helper appropriated the idea, that the United States government underwrite a preliminary survey of routes for the line. Afterward, if the United States Congress would make substantial land grants, other governments would furnish sufficient labor and goods to build it. Since it would make connections with many cross-lines, he urged a uniform gauge be used throughout the project.

Deekens looked beyond the opening of the Three Americas Railway and suggested the American nations plan ahead. He urged them to see that lands near the line were not "locked up for speculative purpose" but brought quickly into the market. He proposed all governments of the Americas form "a species of Zollverein" designed to remove the crippling tariffs which so greatly disrupted American trade. Influenced by his study of history, he longed for a day when economic co-operation of all the states of Latin America would lead to the formation of a political federation and the end of national conflicts.

Helper received warm tribute from Deekens for his vision and the courage with which he promoted it. If the United States government wisely offered to build the entire line, Deekens felt the soundest decision it could make would be to offer Helper a leading role in the development.[16]

With the publication of *The Three Americas Railway,* Helper sought to bring his plan to fruition. He sent copies of the book to leaders of Congress and the executive branch of the government, following these volumes with a circular containing statements from leading Americans favoring the railway. For example, Senator John Sherman asserted that some lines were already completed which could form part of the larger entity but contended the railway must be operated as a unit. Hiram Barney stated the railway seemed "entirely feasible and more economical and productive of greater results than ocean subsidies."

In 1882 Helper persuaded James B. Belford of Colorado to present a bill in the House of Representatives authorizing the government to publish and distribute 100,000 copies of *The Three Amer-*

*icas Railway* in English and 50,000 copies in Spanish. Unfortunately, although Congress passed a resolution in favor of the publication, the Belford bill was killed in the Committee on Printing.[17]

Helper also induced Senator Francis M. Cockrell of Missouri to introduce a bill providing for the appointment of a commissioner to investigate the possibilities for a line in all South American areas north of Patagonia. His term was for two years, at an annual salary of $8,500, and he was to have an assistant, who was to receive $3,000. This measure was twice defeated but enacted in 1884, when the board of investigation was increased to three. Before the men sailed for Latin America Helper addressed them at the New York Customs House, pleading for a thorough study and pointing out that the future of American trade and the effectiveness of the Monroe Doctrine depended on their success.[18]

While seeking congressional aid, Helper was corresponding with the British financier, Bedford Pim. Pim first learned of Helper's railway plans from a story in the Panama *Star and Herald* and, in 1882, wrote him praising his work. In the summer of 1885 the two men met for dinner at the Gramercy Hotel in New York City, and Pim was so impressed by Helper that he asked him to go to London and convert the Three Americas Railway into a British project. He personally offered Helper an annual salary of $2,000 and an office on Threadneedle Street. Pim was surprised when Helper declined, but anyone who knew his strong American nationalism would not have been.

At the same time William M. Evarts wrote Helper he had concluded that the Three Americas Railway "was feasible and beneficial." He urged that the plans be broadened and the line be extended via ferry into Siberia and Europe. Wisely Helper replied that he dared not expand the scope of his great enterprise. Certainly he felt too weak to furnish plans for four of the world's five continents.

Evarts' letter and Helper's reply were published in a number of newspapers. As a result, ten days afterward Helper received a message from William H. C. Bartlett, former professor of natural and experimental philosophy and engineering at West Point. Bartlett chided Helper and Evarts for neglecting Africa in projecting railways. He contended that a line from the Cape to the mouth of the Nile was logical and desirable. This letter and Helper's reply were reproduced in Europe, and in 1885 Pim wrote and published an article in London, praising Helper's "super-excellent proposition." This was six years before Cecil Rhodes first publicly presented his great railway program. Later Helper disclaimed any honor for himself in conceiving plans for the Cape-to-Cairo line, but he held that the original exponent of the idea was "Bartlett the American."[19]

In November, 1885, Helper undertook another voyage to Latin America. First, as a final effort, he went to Rio de Janeiro, where he met no success whatsoever in an attempt to collect the Fiedler claim. The results were quite different in Buenos Aires, where the Argentine Congress endorsed his concept of a Three Americas Railway. This boosted Helper's hopes, and he sang the praises of Buenos Aires, describing it as "already and at once, in size, business, and elegance, the London and the Paris of the Southern Hemisphere." Within ten to twelve years he believed it and New York could be connected by rail.

While in Buenos Aires Helper heard men were spreading rumors of his death. He believed that their intention was to supplant him in the "superlative endeavor" of his life and vowed "to defend in every respect" his "rightful position" once he returned to the United States.[20]

After his return Helper watched, with keenest interest, the summoning of the first Pan-American Conference. James G. Blaine seemed to have been interested in the Three Americas Railway as early at 1882, when his first attempt at hosting an inter-American meeting failed. Finally, the conference was called in 1889, and one of the United States delegates was Henry Gassaway Davis, a West Virginia railway builder and a strong supporter of Helper's projected line. In his address to the conference, Secretary of State Blaine looked forward to the near future, when North and South America would be joined by rail. The conference, through Davis' influence, endorsed the building of the railway by incorporating existing lines with proposed construction, the complete unit to be

*Hinton Rowan Helper*

run by concessionaires. It urged the member nations to grant land and subsidies for the development and construction of the line.

On recommendation of President Harrison and Blaine, the United States Congress appropriated $65,000 in 1890, 1891 and 1892 for a three-man group, known as the International Railway Commission, to conduct surveys of the proposed routes for the railway and report to the American people. At long last the government was moving to bring Helper's dream to reality.

It is ironic that Helper was not appointed to the commission. Even though he was sixty-one years old and a man with no practical railway experience, he had conceived the great undertaking and given it enough publicity to keep the plan from dying. Like most dreamers, he had spoken unrealistically on some occasions, in order to gain attention. Perhaps because of this reason, Harrison passed over him for three hard-headed businessmen. They were Alexander J. Cassatt, president of the Pennsylvania Railroad who served as chairman; Richard C. Kerens, owner of a Missouri railroad; and Henry G. Davis.

Under their direction three corps, mainly composed of army engineers, surveyed routes for the railway from southwestern Mexico to the border of Bolivia. The United States Congress contributed $260,000 to the project through 1899, including money for the publication of the commission's reports.[21]

Helper, who had returned with his family to live in New York City once the government had taken the initiative in the railway program, was overjoyed with the report. Not only did wise men agree with him on the desirability of the line, but engineers, after years of study, had proven its feasibility. "Dozens if not scores of the most efficient and proficient civil engineers" were almost unanimous in saying the project should proceed at a rapid pace.

Upon publication of the report Helper marveled at the difference in attitude he met everywhere. In a typical gesture he weighed the seven big volumes, replete with plates and maps, finding them to weigh exactly thirty-two pounds, five ounces. Inside they contained 450,000 square inches of type, maps and illustrations. Together they formed "the most elaborate and excellent output of special publications on any single subject ever issued by the Government of the United States." He was understandably pleased when the report recommended that the passage over the elevated plateau which "ties the Cordillas together just north of Timbio and also divides the Atlantic waters from the Pacific" should be named "after Mr. Hinton Rowan Helper, projector of the inter-continental railway."[22]

Although Helper considered the report a vindication, it came too late and brought too few rewards to keep the last decade of his life from being tragic. For years he had spent thousands of dollars, much of his share of the Colton claim, and devoted most of his energy to promoting the Three Americas Railway. By 1899 he was very poor and his long-suffering wife had gone blind. In that year she and their son returned to Buenos Aires, leaving Helper alone.[23]

Helper carried on like the robust character he was. In 1903 the permanent Pan-American Railway Committee recommended that the United States Congress appoint a railway commissioner to Latin America. Henry G. Davis and Andrew Carnegie each contributed $5,000 to supplement the $2,500 appropriated by Congress for the commissioner, and as a result, the distinguished newspaperman, Charles M. Pepper, accepted the position. Before leaving for his new duties, however, he reached an agreement with Carnegie whereby the steel baron agreed to serve as a fiscal agent to raise $200,000,000 to build the railway, if the United States Congress did not provide the money. In 1904 Pepper submitted a report tracing the progress made in building potential units of the line in Latin America and urging rapid completion of the work.[24]

In his great poverty and loneliness and as a result of many defeats and chronic criticism, Helper's mind became obsessed with ideas of conspiracy. Hearing of efforts to raise capital, he decided Carnegie was trying to displace him as promoter of the railway and develop it solely for personal profit without regard for the welfare of the countries and people involved. Within eighteen months' time, Helper presented three letters to Congress in an effort to forestall this development.

Helper pleaded in his memorial of January, 1905, that Congress not permit a private syndicate to build the Three Americas Railway. He feared such a group would take an "undue share of the earnings and profits" of the line and prophesied its functioning would result in "much interruption and dissatisfaction and wrangling and litigation and scandal and strife, and eventually, perhaps, even the horrors of war itself." Helper urged, instead, that the national governments themselves appropriate money and build the railway. Specifically he cautioned the United States government not to place money in the hands of private interests to do the job. "Raw and rough and rude" persons were conspiring "to cast insurmountable obstacles" across the path of rightful procedure and "obtain for themselves unquestionable authority and direction," he warned. In this memorial and another, in December, 1905, Helper advised the Congress not to commit itself until after consulting him, the man who for thirty-eight years had been projecting the railway.[25]

"A certain canny and clandestine combination of insidious and double-dealing conspirators and despoilers" were denounced by Helper in his memorial of June, 1906. They should be condemned as "more sly and vile" than those in New York who had recently wreaked havoc with life insurance funds. "I originated and projected the Three Americas Railway" nearly forty years ago, Helper wrote. Now, as then, it was the best means to improve all the Americas "materially and mentally and morally." It would bring North America an annual commercial increase of $600,000,000, while South America would receive $300,000,000 and Mexico and Central America $200,000,000. This happy result would come only if the railway were developed to aid the peoples and not manipulated to make excessive profits for unjust men. One of the "grafters" had even boasted that his group had $400,000,000 to invest in the line. "He and they are determined to oust me from my position," Helper wrote, "and secure for themselves sole and exclusive control of the whole line from one end to the other." He believed only 3 to 4 per cent of congressmen were "black sheep" and that a majority would never permit such a selfish group to develop the line.

Unfortunately Helper had no official position from which he

could be ousted. In his senility and dreams he had created an imaginary position and used stationery inscribed with the name, "The Three Americas Railway." He threatened to sue those who were attempting to finance the line for $3,500,000 damages and, winning the case, promised to give the proceeds to two or three scientific institutions. He pledged himself never to prostitute his concepts for the great rail line by selling them to anyone. If he ever conveyed them to another, it would be to an upright, public-spirited individual like the now deceased William M. Evarts, William C. Noyes, George C. Curtis, David D. Fields, Charles A. Peabody, or Hamilton Fish.[26]

Obviously, by 1906 Helper had lost his perspective. Yet, to the day of his death he kept his physique, and he was a conspicuous figure in whatever group he found himself. His complexion was now florid and his hair white as cotton, but he continually wore "an expression of unmistakable resolution written all over his countenance" and there was "an air of manifest sincerity in his every utterance." He was often seen in the hotel lobbies of Washington, where he remained continually during the last decade of his life. Much of his time was spent with a group of older men, all of whom "paid the closest attention to what he said, and . . . accorded him something very nearly like deference." In the last days of his life his subject of conversation was often the depravity of man and the evil influence of novel reading.[27]

It is easy to understand how Helper could feel bitter. He had spent thousands of dollars and much of his life to promote the Three Americas Railway. Not only was the line failing to emerge as he had planned, but he, as its originator and directing genius, was completely ignored. Without any income he was forced to subsist on the loans he could obtain from friends. In 1904 one of his benefactors, Fred E. Woodward, tried to collect $10 he had loaned Helper. In a hand, shaking with grief and embarrassment, Helper replied that he could not repay the loan at the time. "It is quite right and proper for you to require payment of the $10, with interest, which I owe you," Helper wrote. "It humiliates and grieves me beyond expression that I cannot call immediately and hand it to you—so small is the amount in comparison with $73,000, which is equitably and validly overdue to me."

Since neither the Fiedler claim nor the additional sum Helper contended Bolivia owed Colton was settled, Helper was not able to repay this small loan. For a man of his sensitivity and pride, his correspondence about it over a two-year period formed one of the most distressing episodes of his career. In March, 1906, when Woodward again requested repayment, Helper pledged every effort to do so as quickly as possible. He wrote, "In strict truth, however, I am still so sorely crippled financially because of gross and persistent injustice long practiced against me, to the extent of seventy-odd thousand dollars, that it is quite impossible for me to pay anything at this time."[28]

Conditions grew worse instead of better. In March, 1908, he was forced from his humble quarters at 806 Twelfth Street and moved to even more humble quarters at 628 Pennsylvania Avenue. Usually he would leave his drab room early in the morning, walk for hours, and subsist on one or two meals during the day. Fortunately the downtown hotel lobbies gave him some area in which to rest and find warmth in winter. During the sessions of Congress its halls also afforded a haven.

Despite his poverty Helper never abandoned the Three Americas Railway. In the last days of his life he tried to borrow $1,500 from a number of congressmen in order to flood Europe with pamphlets advocating its construction. When rebuffed, he referred to himself as the "second Christopher Columbus," his favorite historical hero. This brought the sneers of his auditors upon the now obviously senile man.

At last weary and bankrupt, mentally as well as financially, Helper concluded that suicide was the best solution to his problems. On March 8, 1909, he prepared for this act with the meticulousness which had characterized most of his life's work. On his table he placed letters to George R. Starkweather, a friend and interpreter in the city post office, and the Treasurer of the United States urging construction of the Three Americas Railway. He barricaded the door to his room and stopped up the keyhole "with his well-worn coat." Afterward, he placed a towel around his neck and turned on the gas. The next morning, March 9, at 10:00, his body was discovered by a maid. At first it was taken to the morgue, but his friends and the city of Washington arranged a decent burial in an unmarked grave in Forest Lake Cemetery.[29]

After his death Helper received a notoriety he had not known since 1860. *The Literary Digest* headlined its obituary story, "A Forgotten Hero of Slavery Days." It recalled that *The Impending Crisis* had been "a real factor in promoting the election of Lincoln" and "did a work in molding public opinion that had been impossible for such a book as 'Uncle Tom's Cabin.'" *The Nation* saw Helper as a prophet unappreciated in his own time, stating "What Mr. Helper foresaw for the South in the event of the abolition of slavery all came to pass in his lifetime—the diversification of industry, the springing up of manufactures, the opening of mines, the development of commerce, the spread of education." The Washington *Evening Star* described Helper as a "venerable man" who had practically abandoned the literary field to develop "his railway project." Perhaps the Charlotte *Observer* came nearer a succinct description when it wrote, "Mr. Helper was a man of distinct intellectual brilliancy and decided views on the question of slavery and the negro." "Tillman in his palmiest days of bitterness on the negro question could not even approach Helper."[30]

Although tragedy did dog his last days, Helper had led an eventful and full life. It was his misfortune that the great event of his career, the publication and wide circulation of *The Impending Crisis,* came before he reached middle age. But, throughout his life, he felt justifiably proud that he had struck a mighty blow in behalf of free white labor.

In his latter years Helper had concentrated on the development of the Three Americas Railway to the exclusion of almost everything else. One should never forget that, to Helper, this was the means to an end—the one way to destroy the inferior, non-Caucasian, Catholic civilization of Latin America and replace it with the sort of people and culture which predominated in the United States. In the process he predicted all of the Americas would grow commercially and industrially.

Undoubtedly, Helper's motives were immoral and fantastic, but the goal of closer co-operation and multilateral development of the American states was far in advance of his time. A railway committee of the Pan-American Conference and the succeeding Organization of American States continued to promote an inter-American railway until 1950, indicating that Helper's dream was more than illusion. The Pan-American highway has been largely completed, and as late as 1951, a historian wrote, in regard to a railway line from the United States to the Argentine, "Most of the Latin American republics are determined that it shall be completed."[31] It may be that the greater concern with Latin America in our own day, because of the pressures of international Communism, will result in the type of co-operation of the Americas which Helper envisioned.

Because of his zeal, his particular combination of abolitionism and racism and of Latin sympathies and anti-Catholicism, Helper has often been dismissed as a mere "mad" man. Except in the last few years of his life this description is unjust. His views were probably those of many of his class and section and, indeed, of many nineteenth-century Americans. His uniqueness lay in his ability to concentrate on one issue and forcefully to present his ideas.

# NOTES

CHAPTER ONE

1. Jethro Rumple, *A History of Rowan County, North Carolina*, ed. J. J. Burner (Salisbury, 1916), 6, 29.

2. James S. Brawley, *The Rowan Story, 1753–1953* (Salisbury, 1953), 150, 153, 172–73, 179–80, 182–83. It is more than coincidental that Rowan County was a Unionist stronghold in 1860 and that it and its neighboring counties produced not only Helper but also Benjamin Sherwood, Professor Benjamin S. Hedrick, and Daniel Reaves Goodlow, a group of the South's most forceful antislavery leaders. See John S. Bassett, *Anti-Slavery Leaders of North Carolina (Johns Hopkins University Studies in Historical and Political Science,* ed. Herbert B. Adams, Series XVI [Baltimore, 1898]), 11–12.

3. David R. Barbee, "Hinton Rowan Helper," *Tyler's Historical Quarterly and Genealogical Magazine,* XV (January, 1934), 145; New York *Times,* January 10, 1860.

4. Hinton R. Helper, *Nojoque* (New York, 1867), 11; *id., Noonday Exigencies in America* (New York, 1871), 157. Helper's only comment on the slaves—Judy, Jimsy, Joe, and Jack—was that they were "black as jet" and "as ink in color as the juice of Japan."

Barbee, "Helper," *loc. cit.,* 147–48, felt that he had a true copy of Jacob Helper's will made in 1808 in which he left 200 acres of land to his wife, Catherina, to be divided at her death between his two sons, David and Daniel. Since she outlived both sons, Barbee believed Daniel lived out his days as a tenant on his mother's land. Also he questioned whether Daniel held any slaves, since he was unable to locate his will.

5. Bassett, *Anti-Slavery Leaders,* 11–12; Mrs. Mattie Mooring to Barbee, in Barbee, "Helper," *loc. cit.,* 150; William Polk, "The Hated Helper," *The*

*South Atlantic Quarterly,* XXX (April, 1931), 180; Samuel A. Ashe, *et al.* (eds.), *Biographical History of North Carolina* (Greensboro, 1917), VIII, 204–205.

6. Barbee, "Helper," *loc. cit.,* 170; New York *Times,* January 10, 1860.

7. Hinton R. Helper, *The Land of Gold* (Baltimore, 1855), 16–18, 46–96, 109–13, 178–214.

8. *Ibid.,* 237.

9. Robert G. Cleland, *A History of California: The American Period* (New York, 1922), 276–77.

10. Gertrude Atherton, *California, An Intimate History* (New York, 1914), 143–48; Cleland, *A History of California,* 296.

11. Helper, *Land of Gold,* 248–53.

12. Atherton, *California,* 191. For a complete history of the 1851 committee see Mary F. Williams, *History of the San Francisco Committee of Vigilance of 1851 (University of California Publications in History,* Vol. XII [Berkeley, 1921]). Miss Williams also has published the *Papers of the San Francisco Committee of Vigilance of 1851 (Publications of the Academy of Pacific Coast History,* Vol. IV [4 vols.; Berkeley, 1919]).

13. Helper, *Land of Gold,* 147–59.

14. *Ibid.,* 179, 214–20, 226–36.

15. *Ibid.,* v; Barbee, "Helper," *loc. cit.,* 152; New York *Times,* January 10, 1860.

16. Helper, *Land of Gold,* v, vi, 13–28, 217, 221–22, 268–79, 283.

17. Helper, *Noonday Exigencies in America,* 159–61; New York *Tribune,* January 20, 1860; Jay B. Hubbell, *The South in American Literature, 1607–1900* (Durham, 1954), 403; *Southern Literary Messenger,* XXI (September, 1855), 576.

18. William H. Gerke, "Negro Slavery Among the Germans in North Carolina," *North Carolina Historical Review,* XIV (October, 1937), 321; Helper, *Noonday Exigencies in America,* 161–62, 203–04; Bassett, *Anti-Slavery Leaders,* 13–14, Polk, "Hated Helper," *loc. cit.,* 181.

CHAPTER TWO

1. Gilbert H. Barnes, *The Anti-Slavery Impulse, 1830–1844* (New York, 1933), *passim;* Arthur Y. Lloyd, *The Slavery Controversy, 1831–1860* (Chapel Hill, 1939), *passim;* Kenneth M. Stampp, "The Fate of the Southern Anti Slavery Movement," *The Journal of Negro History,* XXVIII (January, 1943), 10–22. Professor Stampp holds that the rise of abolitionism has been given overdue emphasis for the change in the Southern attitude toward slavery.

A portion of Chapters II–IV appeared in the author's "Hinton Rowan Helper and *The Impending Crisis,*" *The Louisiana Historical Quarterly,* XL (April, 1957), 133–45.

2. This attack was entitled *Inquiry into the Causes which have Retarded the Accumulation of Wealth and Increase of Population in the Southern States in which the Question of Slavery is Considered in a Politico-Economic Point of View*. By a Carolinian. After the war Goodlow returned to North Carolina and in 1867 and 1868 edited the Raleigh *Register*, which was published by Harvey Hogan Helper, the abolitionist brother of Hinton Rowan Helper. Stephen B. Weeks, "Anti-Slavery Sentiment in the South; With Unpublished Letters from John Stuart Mill and Mrs. Stowe," *Publications of the Southern History Association*, II (April, 1898), 118–23; E. Merton Coulter (ed.), *The Course of the South to Secession. An Interpretation by Ulrich Bonnell Phillips* (New York, 1939), 113, hereinafter cited as Phillips, *South to Secession*. In *The Southern Platform: or, Manual of Southern Sentiment on the Subject of Slavery*, published in 1858, Goodlow sought to bring together all "that the most eminent Southern Revolutionary characters have left us" on the subject of slavery.

3. Clement Eaton, *Freedom of Thought in the Old South* (Durham, 1940), 47, 186; Phillips, *South to Secession*, 113; see also the 1847 publication of Henry Ruffner, *Address to the People of West Virginia; showing that Slavery is Injurious to the Public Welfare; and that it may be Gradually Abolished without Detriment to the Rights and Interests of Slaveholders*.

4. Eaton, *Freedom of Thought*, 222; Lorenzo D. Turner, "Anti-Slavery Sentiment in American Literature Prior to 1865," *The Journal of Negro History*, XIV (October, 1929), 491; *History of the United States from the Compromise of 1850 to the McKinley-Bryan Campaign of 1896* (New York, 1920), II, 375–76, hereinafter cited as Rhodes, *History of the United States;* Avery O. Craven, *The Growth of Southern Nationalism (A History of the South*, eds. Wendell Holmes Stephenson and E. Merton Coulter, Vol. VI [Baton Rogue, 1953]), 250; Polk, "Hated Helper," *loc. cit.*, 181; Joint Committee of North Carolina English Teachers Association and North Carolina Library Association, *North Carolina Authors; A Selective Handbook (University of North Carolina Library Extension Publications*, Vol. XVIII [Chapel Hill, 1952]), 56.

5. J. Carlyle Sitterson, *The Secession Movement in North Carolina (The James Sprunt Studies in History and Political Science*, Vol. XXIII [Chapel Hill, 1939]), 81–82, 110, 117, 128–29.

6. Benjamin Brawley, *A Short History of the American Negro* (New York, 1937), 61, 63.

7. Willis D. Weatherford and Charles S. Johnson, *Race Relations, Adjustment of Whites and Negroes in the United States* (New York, 1934), 296.

8. Allen Nevins, *The Emergence of Lincoln* (New York, 1950), I, 214.

9. Hinton R. Helper, *The Impending Crisis of the South: How to Meet It* (New York, 1857), dedication and v-vi.

10. *Ibid.*, 11–12. See Appendix for a complete summary of Helper's statis-

tics and Table I, in particular, for a comparison of New York and Virginia, as given by Helper. Henceforth in this chapter Roman numeral citations refer to tables in the Appendix.

11. *Ibid.,* 12–19, 22–25, 32, II, III.
12. *Ibid.,* 33–53, 55, 59–61, IV, V, VI.
13. *Ibid.,* 71–73, 75–76, VIII.
14. *Ibid.,* 83–84, 90–92, 123–30, XXII.
15. *Ibid.,* 139, 142, 146, 147, XII.
16. *Ibid.,* 285–97, 302–06, XIV–XXIX, XXXI.
17. *Ibid.,* 331–35, 347, XXV.
18. *Ibid.,* 381–96, 402–06.
19. Jesse Macy, *The Anti-Slavery Crusade, A Chronicle of the Gathering Storm (The Chronicles of America,* ed. Allan Johnson, Vol. 28 [New Haven, 1919]), 138.
20. Nevins, *The Emergence of Lincoln,* I, 213; Polk, "Hated Helper," *loc. cit.,* 180; review of A. B. Hart's *American Patriots and Statesmen from Washington to Lincoln,* in *William and Mary Historical Quarterly,* XXV (January, 1917), 220; Craven, *Growth of Southern Nationalism,* 250.
21. Helper, *The Impending Crisis,* 40–45.
22. *Ibid.,* 85, 109–10, 125–26, 146.
23. *Ibid.,* 81, 111, 116, 120. In Helper's opinion, "A freesoiler is only a tadpole in an advanced state of transformation; an abolitionist is the full and perfectly developed frog."
24. *Ibid.,* 120–21, 128–29, 141, 149, 397.
25. *Ibid.,* 149–56, 178.
26. *Ibid.,* 101–03, 145, 157–91 *passim,* 330, 356, 363, 367.
27. To John F. Mercer, September 9, 1786; to LaFayette, April 5, 1783.
28. Helper, *The Impending Crisis,* 193-97.
29. *Ibid.,* 195–213.
30. *Ibid.,* 237–41, citing a letter to Elias Boudinot, November 17, 1819.
31. *Ibid.,* 246–80 *passim.*
32. *Ibid.,* 413.
33. Rupert B. Vance, "Racial Competition for the Land," in Edgar T. Thompson (ed.), *Race Relations and the Race Problem* (Durham, 1939), 101; A.N.J. Den Hollander, "The Tradition of 'Poor Whites,' " in W. T. Couch (ed.), *Culture in the South* (Chapel Hill, 1934), 420.
34. Louis P. A. d'Orleans, *History of the Civil War in America* (Philadelphia, 1875), I, 87.
35. Robert E. Spiller, *et al., Literary History of the United States* (New York, 1948), 567.
36. See Chapter VII which deals with Helper's post-war books.
37. Of all Southern writers Helper is the only one to accept the theory that it was "the blight of slavery" which stifled the development of a Southern

literature. See Jay B. Hubbell, "Literary Nationalism in the Old South," in *American Studies in Honor of William Kenneth Boyd,* ed. David K. Jackson (Durham, 1940), 206; also Hubbell, *The South in American Literature, 1607-1900,* 402-04. Helper's indictment of the slaveholders for the South's failure to provide schools, libraries, and other cultural training schools for the masses is fully developed.

38. Montrose J. Moses, *The Literature of the South* (New York, 1910), 213; Henry H. Simms, *A Decade of Sectional Controversy, 1851-1861* (Chapel Hill, 1942), 157-58; Ulrich B. Phillips, *American Negro Slavery* (New York, 1918), 350.

CHAPTER THREE

1. New York *Daily Tribune,* July 13, 1857.
2. Cited in James W. Wall, "Hinton Rowan Helper and *The Impending Crisis*" (Master's thesis, University of North Carolina, 1949), 53.
3. Cited in Theodore V. Theobald, "Hinton Rowan Helper and *The Impending Crisis*" (Master's thesis, Columbia University, 1949), 22-24.
4. *Carolina Watchman,* June 23, 30, August 11, 18, 25, 1857.
5. Washington *Union,* August 5, 1857.
6. Bassett, *Anti-Slavery Leaders,* 16.
7. *Congressional Globe,* 36 Cong., 1 sess., 147-48.
8. *Carolina Watchman,* April 20, 1858; Hugh T. Lefler, *Hinton Rowan Helper, Advocate of A "White America" (Southern Sketches,* No. 1 [Charlottesville, 1935]), 21-22.
9. A. B. Burdick to Helper, September 27, 1858, in William Henry Anthon Journal Book of Letters Relative to the Publication of *The Impending Crisis* (New York Public Library, New York City), hereinafter cited as Anthon Book. The author used a microfilm copy of this book.
10. Helper to F. P. Blair, Sr., November 4, 1858; Helper to Daniel R. Goodlow, November 13, 1858, Blair–Lee Papers (Princeton University, Princeton, N. J.). These and other citations to this collection are used with the permission of the owner, P. Blair Lee, Philadelphia.
11. Tentative circular, dated November 15, 1858; *ibid.;* Helper to William H. Anthon, November 25, 1858, Anthon Book; circular in New York *Daily Tribune,* December 4, 1858. The earlier circular required sixteen dollars contributions for a name listing and receipt of copies.
12. New York *Daily Tribune,* December 4, 1858.
13. *Ibid.,* December 18, 1858, citing Lemuel Jewell to Anthon, December 6, 1858, and Benjamin S. Hedrick to Anthon, December 14, 1858.
14. D. L. Gregory to Helper, January 29, 1859; Edward Harris to Helper, February 7, 1859; Gerritt Smith to Helper, February 7, 1859, Anthon Book.
15. William M. Chance to Helper on letter, Nicholas Brown to Anthon,

February 9, 1859; Bradford R. Wood to Helper, February 9, 10, 1859; John
Norton to Helper, February 15, 1859; Samuel May to Helper, February 19,
1859, *ibid.* Obviously, many of the New England contributors were motivated
to contribute by a philanthropic concern for the slaves. Helper, of course, had
no such concern.

16. E. G. Dudley to Helper, March 24, 1859; E. M. Davis to Helper, n. d.;
W. A. Buckingham to Helper, April 2, 1859, *ibid.*

17. New York *Daily Tribune,* March 16, 1859; Theobald, "Hinton Rowan
Helper," 45, points out Banks's absence among the endorsers.

18. List of contributors appended to Hinton Rowan Helper's *The Compendium of the Impending Crisis* (New York, 1859).

19. New York *Daily Tribune,* December 26, 1859.

20. Helper, *The Impending Crisis,* 1857 edition, 103–05, 108–09, 118–
20, 150–56, 158, 161, 171, 178; 1860 edition, 89, 91–100, 118–26, 129, 139;
*The Compendium,* 1–100.

21. New York *Daily Tribune,* December 27, 1859.

22. *The Compendium* was able to pack much of the larger editions into its
214 pages since, instead of 33, it had 44 lines per page. While its writing was
largely that of the 1860 edition, its tables were based mainly on the 1857
edition. There were numerous minor variations in the quotations given from
experts in all three editions. A notable addition in *The Compendium* (140–
71) and 1860 edition (263–319) was "Testimony of Our Contemporaries."
Included here were quotations from "Abram Lincoln," Edward Bates,
Owen Lovejoy, John Sherman, and many others. The two later editions were
dedicated to Cassius M. Clay, Francis P. Blair, Jr., Benjamin S. Hedrick, all
Southerners, and to the "Non-slaveholding whites of the South, generally."

23. Lewis Tappan to Helper, September 9, 1859, Anthon Book.

24. Jesse Wheeler to Helper, September, 1859; Helper to Anthon, September 6, October 3, 29, November 16, 1859, *ibid.*

25. William Garrison to Helper, November 21, 1859; Cassius M. Clay to
Helper, November 27, 1859, *ibid.*

26. Joseph Medill to Helper, May 23, November 26, 1859; Helper to Anthon, October 29, 1859, *ibid.*

27. New York *Herald,* November 26, 1859. This argument was virtually
repeated by the Richmond *Semi-Weekly Examiner,* December 2, 1859.

28. W. B. Thomas to Helper, December 8, 1859; William Still to Helper,
December 12, 1859; J. A. Hopkins to Helper, December 11, 1859; S. B. Beman
to Helper, December 15, 1859, Anthon Book.

29. New York *Daily Tribune,* December 26, 1859.

30. William Garrison to Helper, December 17, 1859; Thomas Crua to
Helper, Anthon Book. The date of the last letter appears to be January 13,
1859, but internal evidence would indicate it was January 13, 1860.

31. Helper, *Noonday Exigencies in America,* 79; Ashe, *et al., Biographical
History of North Carolina,* VIII, 207.

32. Wall, "Hinton Rowan Helper," 50–52.

33. Sarah A. Wallace and Frances E. Gillespie (eds.), *The Journal of Benjamin Moran, 1857–1865* (Chicago, 1948), I, 641. Entry is for February 25, 1860.

34. Emerson Fite, *The Political Campaign of 1860* (New York, 1911), 45–56; Bassett, *Anti-Slavery Leaders,* 22; letter to the *National Era* as cited in Eaton, *Freedom of Thought in the Old South,* 139.

35. Eaton, *ibid.,* 139–41; Bassett, *Anti-Slavery Leaders,* 25–26; Wall, "Hinton Rowan Helper," 48.

36. Carl Sandburg, *Abraham Lincoln, The Prairie Years* (New York, 1926), II, 115–22; Robert W. Winston, *Andrew Johnson, Plebeian and Patriot* (New York, 1928), 108, 115, 133; W. E. Burghardt Du Bois, *Black Reconstruction* (New York, 1935), 242, 244; George F. Milton, *The Age of Hate, Andrew Johnson and the Radicals* (New York, 1930), 90.

CHAPTER FOUR

1. William E. Woodward, *Years of Madness* (New York, 1951), 58.

2. Rhodes, *History of the United States,* II, 417.

3. Roy F. Nichols, *The Disruption of American Democracy* (New York, 1948), 270–73.

4. Ollinger Crenshaw, "The Speakership Contest of 1859–1860, John Sherman's Election a Cause of Disruption," *Mississippi Valley Historical Review,* XXIX (December, 1942), 323.

5. *Congressional Globe,* 36 Cong., 1 sess., 2.

6. *Ibid.,* 4, 16–18; *Carolina Watchman,* December 20, 1859. The Salisbury newspaper lamented, "The Whigs and Americans are the only pacificators in the House."

7. *Congressional Globe,* 36 Cong., 1 sess., 21, 546, 548.

8. John Sherman to William T. Sherman, December 24, 1859, in Rachel Sherman Thorndike (ed.), *The Sherman Letters: Correspondence Between General and Senator Sherman from 1837 to 1891* (New York, 1894), 75.

9. Cited in William P. Trent, *et al.* (eds.), *The Cambridge History of American Literature* (New York, 1917–21), IX, 344. "Yet, strange to say, the particular passage which called forth this remark was a quotation from the Virginia Debates of 1831."

10. *Anti-Abolition Tracts No. 3* (New York, 1866), 18, hereinafter cited as *Tract No. 3.*

11. *DeBow's Review,* XXVII (1860), 239; Sitterson, *Secession Movement in North Carolina,* 156.

12. New York *Herald,* December 3, 12, 1859; January 4, 5, 7, 21, 26, 1860.

13. Richmond *Semi-Weekly Examiner,* December 2, 1859; Washington *States and Union,* December 7, 14, 17, 1859.

14. *Congressional Globe,* 36 Cong., 1 sess., 21, 49, 148, 161.

15. *Ibid.,* 22–24, 200, 343, 458, 468.

16. *Ibid.,* 263–64, 308–11, 357–58, 492, 503.

17. *Ibid.,* 167, 216, 270.

18. See Crenshaw, "Speakership Contest," 332; *Congressional Globe,* 36 Cong., 1 sess., 224.

19. Letters of January 29, 1860, and December 20, 1859, to Miles in Miles Papers (Southern History Collection, University of North Carolina), Chapel Hill, N. C.), cited in Crenshaw, "Speakership Contest," 333–34.

20. *Congressional Globe,* 36 Cong., 1 sess., 408.

21. Avery O. Craven, *The Coming of the Civil War* (New York 1942), 411; John S. Wise, *The End of An Era* (New York, 1899), 118, 135.

22. Selma *Daily State Sentinel,* February 28, 1860; Richmond *Semi-Weekly Enquirer,* December 16, 1859.

23. Quotations are from the Reading (Pa.) *Gazette and Democrat,* January 28, 1860; *Cheshire Republican,* January 25, 1860; and Pottsville *Democratic Standard,* January 28, 1860, as cited in Lawrence T. Lowrey, *Northern Opinion of Approaching Secession, October 1859–November 1860* (John S. Bassett and Sidney B. Fay, eds., *Smith College Studies in History,* Vol. III [July, 1918]), 229.

24. Washington *States and Union,* December 10, 17, 1859.

25. *Tract No. 3,* 21, 22.

26. *Harper's Weekly,* III (January 14, 1860), 18; (November 12, 1859), 722; (December 16, 1859), 802.

27. *Congressional Globe,* 36 Cong., 1 sess., 40–41. Greeley commenting on Kellogg's speech wrote, "It was the most pitiable exhibition that it was ever my misfortune to endure the sight of." See New York *Tribune,* December 8, 1859.

28. *Congressional Globe,* 36 Cong., 1 sess., 145–46, 195, 224–29, 585–86.

29. *Ibid.,* 5–6.

30. New York *Tribune,* December 5, 7, 8, 1859.

31. Rhodes, *History of the United States,* II, 428; New York *Tribune,* January 11, 25, 1860.

32. New York *Times,* December 9, 11, 1859; January 10, February 2, 1860.

33. *Congressional Globe,* 36 Cong., 1 sess., 41, 236, 315.

34. They were Hickman and Swartz of Pennsylvania and Reynolds of New York. See Rhodes, *History of the United States,* II, 382, and Nichols, *Disruption of American Democracy,* 272.

35. This was Pennsylvania's Hickman. See *Congressional Globe,* 36 Cong., 1 sess., 349.

36. *Ibid.,* 3, 52, 134, 158, 165, 169, 175, 188–89, 196, 208, 235, 242, 269, 274, 286, 337.

37. *Ibid.,* 47, 188, 216, 437, 444, 465, 481, 587, 607, 612–15, 619–20, 634.

38. Washington *States and Union,* December 14, 1859.

39. *Congressional Globe,* 36 Cong., 1 sess., 634–38, 650; Rhodes, *History of the United States,* II, 382.

40. New York *Tribune,* January 2, 1860; Lefler, *Hinton Rowan Helper,* 25; Rhodes, *History of the United States,* II, 378; Fite, *Political Campaign of 1860,* 33–34.

41. New York *Herald,* January 22, 1861, citing a letter of December 7, 1859.

42. *Harper's Weekly,* IV (February 11, 1860), 82; Bigler to Robert Tyler, December 16, 1859, in Lyon G. Tyler, *Letters and Times of the Tylers* (Richmond, 1884–96), II, 255.

43. John B. McMaster, *A History of the People of the United States from the Revolution to the Civil War* (New York, 1921), VIII, 429–31.

44. *Acts of the Seventh Biennial Session of the General Assembly of Alabama* (Montgomery, 1860), 689.

45. New York *Tribune,* December 10, 15, 1859; *Harper's Weekly,* III (December 31, 1859).

46. Richmond *Semi-Weekly Examiner,* December 13, 1859.

47. A Southerner, *Fanaticism and Its Results: or, Facts versus Fancies* (Baltimore, 1860), 23.

48. New York *Herald,* February 2, 1860.

49. Cited in Crenshaw, "Speakership Contest," 327.

50. The Richmond *Examiner,* February 14, 1860, cited in Dwight L. Dumond, *Southern Editorials on Secession* (New York, 1931), 35–37.

51. New Orleans *Bee,* February 9, 1860, in Dumond, *Southern Editorials on Secession,* 30.

52. It is interesting to see the comments of French E. Chadwick, *Causes of the Civil War, 1859–1861* (A. B. Hart, ed., *The American Nation,* Vol. XIX [New York, 1906]), 92.

53. New York *Herald,* January 22, 1861. The estimated distribution of *The Impending Crisis* was determined in the following way: 25,000 copies of *The Compendium* were ordered by the New York Committee in October 1859; approximately 37,000 were distributed by the New York *Tribune* during the Speakership Contest; this leaves 13,000 copies as the figure for the circulation of the regular editions, a small number for so prominent a work. See pages 56-57.

CHAPTER FIVE

1. Hereinafter cited as Beebe, *A Review.* This work was published at Beebe's newspaper office in 1860, and copies were sold for twenty-five cents each.

2. Hereinafter cited as Shade, *A Book for the "Impending Crisis!"* It was published in Washington in 1860 by Little, Morris and Co. at the office of the *National Democratic Quarterly Review.* Pages 62–73 specifically challenge the Helper arguments.

3. Hereinafter cited as Wolfe, *Crisis Dissected.* The publisher was J. T. Lloyd.

4. They were "S. Bocock and R. M. T. Hunter of Virginia, John Cochran of New York, Charles H. Larabee of Wisconsin, Stephen A. Douglas of Illinois, and Jabez L. M. Curry of Alabama." See Wolfe, *Crisis Dissected,* introduction.

5. *Ibid.*

6. Hereinafter cited as Peissner, *The American Question.* This work was published in New York City by H. H. Lloyd and Co. in 1861. It contained 146 pages.

7. *Ibid.,* 9–11.

8. The full title was *Southern Wealth and Northern Profits As Exhibited in Statistical Facts and Official Figures: Showing the Necessity of Union to the Future Prosperity and Welfare of the Republic,* hereinafter cited as Kettell, *Southern Wealth.* This work was published in New York City in 1860 by George W. and John A. Wood.

9. *Ibid.,* 40–45.

10. Peissner, *The American Question,* 21; *The Union: Being a Condemnation of Mr. Helper's Scheme, with A Plan for the Settlement of the "Irrepressible Conflict,"* By One Who Has Considered Both Sides of the Question (New York, 1860), 7, hereinafter cited as *The Union;* Shade, *A Book for the "Impending Crisis!"* 68–69; Wolfe, *Crisis Dissected,* 49; "The Raid of John Brown and the Progress of Abolition," *The Southern Presbyterian Review, Conducted by An Association of Ministers in Columbia, South Carolina,* XII (January, 1860), n. 803, hereinafter cited as *So. Presby. Review,* XII.

11. The 1850 returns showed Georgia to have 208,710 head of horses and mules, 1,097,528 cows, work oxen and other cattle, 560,435 sheep and 2,729,052 swine. *So. Presby. Review,* XII, n. 800.

12. Beebe, *A Review,* 16–17, 54–60.

13. Helper, *The Impending Crisis,* 286–96. All references in this chapter are to the 1857 edition.

14. *Ibid.,* 304; Kettell, *Southern Wealth,* 101, 120–24; Beebe, *A Review,* 54; Peissner, *The American Question,* 51.

15. Helper, *The Impending Crisis,* 140–41; Edward A. Pollard, *Black Diamonds Gathered in the Darkey Homes of the South* (New York, 1959), 25, 48, 81.

16. *The Southern Literary Messenger,* XXVI (June, 1858), 418; XXVII (July, 1858), 18, 93. A present-day writer has well stated the viewpoint of these people by holding that in the North an "industrial white slavery was

established which had many of the worst features of human bondage."
Marked by child labor and the sweat shop, it "created horrors that never
once attached to black . . . slavery." See David R. Barbee, "Hinton Rowan
Helper's Mendacity," *Tyler's Historical Quarterly and Genealogical Magazine*, XV (January, 1934), 232.

17. Wolfe, *Crisis Dissected*, 62, 149, 153.

18. Beebe, *A Review*, 6, 39; Helper, *The Impending Crisis*, 145.

19. Wolfe, *Crisis Dissected*, n. 125.

20. *The Union*, 27.

21. Helper, *The Impending Crisis*, 125–29, 159–61; W. W. Handlin,
*American Politics* (New Orleans, 1864), 37; E. W. Reynolds, *The True
Story of the Barons of the South* (Boston, 1862), 34.

22. Beebe, *A Review*, 34. A modern writer has well expressed a standard
argument when he wrote that the slave system made the South more democratic than free society. Since its aristocracy was based on the inferiority
of a colored class, true democracy could exist among the whites, according
to this reasoning. As evidence, this writer pointed out that all Southern
white men were called "Mister," regardless of their wealth, education, culture, or physical condition. See Barbee, "Helper's Mendacity," *loc. cit.*, 231.

23. MS Diary, March 1, 1860, in Library of Congress, cited in Nevins,
*Emergence of Lincoln*, I, 213; Beebe, *A Review*, 34; George Lunt, *The
Origin of the Late War* (New York, 1866), 325.

24. Wolfe, *Crisis Dissected*, 78; Beebe, *A Review*, 9, 37; Peissner, *The
American Question*, 53; "Problems of Free Society," *Southern Literary
Messenger*, XXVII (August, 1858), 94.

25. "American Slavery in 1857," *Southern Literary Messenger*, XXV (August, 1857), 84; Pollard, *Black Diamonds*, 53.

26. "Southern and Northern Civilization Contrasted," *Russell's Magazine*,
I (May, 1857), 98, 103.

27. Helper, *The Impending Crisis*, 154–59; Wolfe, *Crisis Dissected*, 38;
Peissner, *The American Question*, 75, 77.

28. *So. Presby. Review*, XII, 798–99, 803; Wolfe, *Crisis Dissected*, 78, 121;
Lunt, *Origin of the Late War*, 326; Beebe, *A Review*, 27, 34, 62.

29. "American Slavery in 1857," *loc. cit.*, 87.

30. Peissner, *The American Question*, 55; *The Union*, 28–30, agreed with
Helper that, short of emancipation, there was nothing ahead but servile
war. It advocated compensated emancipation but opposed the plan to give
each freedman sixty dollars on the grounds that inexperience would cause
the Negro to squander his money to his own detriment. It felt that transporting the freedman to Liberia was a Utopian ideal. The best program, it
believed, would be to encourage the servants to stay with their masters after
emancipation and provide government support to care for the aged and
infirm.

31. Helper, *The Impending Crisis,* 188–280.

32. Brownlow wondered if these facts should be disclosed until after Edward Everett had finished his project to restore Mt. Vernon, as it would end the contributions of antislavery men. W. G. Brownlow and Abram Pryne, *Ought American Slavery to Be Perpetuated?* (Philadelphia, 1858), 199.

33. Beebe, *A Review,* 40, 44, 46; Peissner, *The American Question,* 62.

34. *So. Presby. Review,* XII, 800.

35. Peissner, *The American Question,* 73; Wolfe, *Crisis Dissected,* 204, 210–13; Beebe, *A Review,* 47–52. The following portions of Scripture were cited as proof of the Biblical sanction of slavery: Leviticus 30: 44–46; Ezra 2:55–58; Nehemiah 2:10; Job 1:14–17; Proverbs 19:10, 29:19–21, 30:10; Isaiah 11, 18, 20; St. Matthew 8:5–13; 18:23–34; St. Luke 7:2–9; St. John 4:51; Acts 21:27–28; I Timothy 6: 1–5.

36. Peissner, *The American Question,* 13.

37. Shade, *A Book for the "Impending Crisis!"* 68.

38. Beebe, *A Review,* 10–11.

39. Helper, *The Impending Crisis,* 23, 284 ff.; Peissner, *The American Question,* 27–30; Beebe, *A Review,* 54.

40. Wolfe, *Crisis Dissected,* 128, 138, 164.

41. Brownlow and Pryne, *Ought American Slavery to Be Perpetuated?* 260–67.

42. Shade, *A Book for the "Impending Crisis!"* 62–67; Beebe, *A Review,* 60–61; Kettell, *Southern Wealth,* 61–62, 72–77, 126.

43. Edward A. Pollard, *The Lost Cause* (New York, 1866), 57–58. A modern writer has answered Helper's contention (*The Impending Crisis,* 23) that to the very grave the South was dependent on Northern products, including drugs, coffins, shrouds, hearses, and tombstones. David R. Barbee ("Helper's Mendacity," *loc. cit.,* 228–29) held that the 1850 census answered all of Helper's arguments at this point. "There were no manufacturing druggists in any State in the Union in that year," he wrote. If manufacturing chemists made drugs, the South had an ample number, 229; but in that era physicians frequently manufactured their own drugs. It was true that Southerners were buried in their own clothes. "That decent custom prevails even today, for respectable families refuse to permit the burial of their dead in shrouds." If not buried on their premises, Southerners were carried to churchyards in their own carriages. They were handmade, as there "were no dealers in carriages in the South in 1850 who purchased their goods from any [Northern] manufacturer." Alabama had 12 coach and carriage factories; Georgia, 73; Kentucky, 32; Louisiana, 13; Virginia, 79; Tennessee, 26; Mississippi, 20; Missouri, 137; Maryland, 52; North Carolina, 78. While in 1850 marbleworks were not listed among the manufacturing plants, yet from 1850 to 1860 there were many announcements of Southern marblecutters in the newspapers.

44. Helper, *The Impending Crisis*, 70; Beebe, *A Review*, 13.
45. *So. Presby. Review*, XII, 801–802; Peissner, *The American Question*, 22.
46. Helper, *The Impending Crisis*, 71–72; *So. Presby. Review*, XII, 799; Beebe, *A Review*, 13–14.
47. Helper, *The Impending Crisis*, 38, 123–35; Beebe, *A Review*, 23, 28, 59.
48. Peissner, *The American Question*, 17; Wolfe, *Crisis Dissected*, 50–52; Beebe, *A Review*, 28; *The Union*, 27.

CHAPTER SIX

1. Phillips, *American Negro Slavery*, 391.
2. Ralph B. Flanders, *Plantation Slavery in Georgia* (Chapel Hill, 1933), 85, 213, 217, 225; Charles S. Sydnor, *Slavery in Mississippi* (New York, 1933), 196–97; Lewis C. Gray, *History of Argiculture in the Southern United States to 1860* (Washington, 1933), I, 471, 474, 476–78.
3. Thomas P. Govan, "Was Plantation Slavery Profitable?" *Journal of Southern History*, VIII (November, 1942), 516–23.
4. Alfred E. Conrad and John R. Meyer, "The Economics of Slavery in the Ante Bellum South," *The Journal of Political Economy*, XLVI (April, 1958), 96, 103, 106–12, 114, 116–18.
5. Kenneth M. Stampp, *The Peculiar Institution, Slavery in the Ante-Bellum South* (New York, 1956), 383, 388, 403–04, 410, 417; Orville W. Taylor, *Negro Slavery in Arkansas* (Durham, 1958), 121, 127–28.
6. J. Carlyle Sitterson, *Sugar Country, The Cane Sugar Industry in the South, 1753–1950* (Lexington, 1953), 175, 180–83; Paul W. Gates, *The Farmer's Age: 1815–1860* (*The Economic History of the United States*, Vol. III [New York, 1960]), 154.
7. Phillips, *American Negro Slavery*, 401; Flanders, *Plantation Slavery in Georgia*, 85, 213, 217, 225; Govan, "Was Plantation Slavery Profitable?" *loc. cit.*, 512; Stanley M. Elkins, *Slavery, A Problem in American Institutional and Intellectual Life* (Chicago, 1959), 231.
8. In the Appendix the author has collated Helper's figures with those of the Census of 1850 and noted his few errors.
9. Robert R. Russell, *Economic Aspects of Southern Sectionalism, 1840–1861* (New York, 1960), 47.
10. Stampp, *The Peculiar Institution*, 393–94, 399; Conrad and Meyer, "The Economics of Slavery . . . ," *loc. cit.*, 100–01, 111; Gates, *The Farmer's Age*, 294.
11. Eugene D. Genovese, "The Significance of the Slave Plantation for Southern Economic Development," *Journal of Southern History*, XXVIII (November, 1962), 427, 435–37.

12. Mississippi is an exception to this generalization, but 43.79 per cent of her nonslaveholders' land ownership in the sample counties is undetermined in 1860. See Frank L. Owsley, *Plain Folk of the Old South* (Baton Rogue, 1949), 156–58, 164, 166, 168, 174–75, 179–80, 185, 191, 197–98, 206–08, 220–21, 224, 226–27.

13. Robert R. Russell, "The General Effects of Slavery upon Southern Economic Progress," *Journal of Southern History,* IV (February, 1938), 46, conceded this point, although he apologized for slavery. Of course, his work came before Owsley's.

14. John H. Franklin, *From Slavery to Freedom, A History of American Negroes* (2d ed.; New York, 1956), 185–86.

15. Conrad and Meyer, "The Economics of Slavery . . . ," *loc. cit.,* 119–20; Stampp, *The Peculiar Institution,* 389, 427. This suggests that much race antagonism may have arisen not from hatred of the physical presence of the black man but revulsion to his status as a slave. Franklin, *From Slavery to Freedom,* 195.

16. Richard B. Morris, "The Measure of Bondage in the Slave States," *Mississippi Valley Historical Review,* XLI (September, 1954), 220, 223–25, 228–30. Clement Eaton, "Slave-Hiring in the Upper South: A Step toward Freedom," *ibid.,* XLVI (March, 1960), 663, 677–78, writes, "behind the facade of increasing values of slave property there had been at work for at least two decades [before 1860] a slow and subtle erosion of the base of the institution." He believed this was strongest in the upper South, where hiring "instead of purchase was inevitably loosening the bonds of an archiac system." Eaton contended the hiring system was the main means of introducing the slave into the town and industry and was a step toward freedom. Slavery was so different in nature in the upper South that this thesis needs also to be examined in the lower South. Eaton pointed out that extra wages were often paid hired slaves in the upper South. Was this true elsewhere? Without the war would an expansion of this system have overcome some of slavery's evil effects on white labor?

17. Russell, "General Effects of Slavery . . . ," *loc. cit.,* 41–44.

CHAPTER SEVEN

1. New York *Herald,* January 10, 1861; Barbee, "Helper," *loc. cit.,* 162–64.

2. Helper to Lincoln, January 21, 1861; William H. Anthon to Lincoln, January 21, 1861; Edgar Ketchum to Lincoln, January 21, 1861; W. D. Noyes to Lincoln, January 21, 1861, Appointment Office Files (Department of State, Washington, D.C.). All of these letters are cited in William P. Dale, II, "Hinton Rowan Helper and Latin America" (Master's thesis, Duke University, Durham, N.C., 1935), 16, and Barbee, "Helper," *loc. cit.,* 161–62.

Notes

211

3. Helper to Salmon P. Chase, July 25, 1861, Chase Papers (Library of Congress [microfilm], Washington, D.C.).

4. Helper to Abraham Lincoln, November 1, 1861, Lincoln Papers (Library of Congress [microfilm], Washington, D.C.).

5. Helper to Chase, November 5, 1861, Chase Papers. In the dotage of old age Helper incorrectly convinced himself that he had turned down the consulate at Aix-la-Chapelle to take the Buenos Aires post, even though it paid five hundred dollars per year less. Referring to Lincoln, he wrote, "When my homely faced but wise-headed and noble-hearted friend" offered him the consulate at either Aix-la-Chapelle or Buenos Aires, he asked for a day to think it over. "Returning to the White House the next day a few minutes in advance of the particular time specified," Helper saluted Lincoln and told him he would go to Buenos Aires. Lincoln supposedly expressed amazement, stating that Aix-la-Chapelle was "a fine city, rich and renowned in history, and . . . in near neighborship with the greatest centers of civilization in Europe." On the other hand, Buenos Aires was little known except in South America. To this observation Helper replied that his choice was based on the fact that he could accomplish more in Buenos Aires "by cooperation in expanding commercial relations." This apocryphal account of his appointment was written by Helper in 1906 and is part of a letter published as Senate Document No. 504, 59 Cong., 1 sess., 3–4.

It seems highly probable that Helper had come to believe this account. He had, at the time of writing this letter, spent so many years working to improve trade with Latin America that its promotion had become a sacred object with him. How could he better have projected himself as the prophet of such an enterprise than to have challenged the wisdom of the now venerated Lincoln in choosing to go to the Argentine?

6. Helper to William H. Seward, November 16, 1861, in Despatches from United States Consuls in Buenos Aires, X (January 20, 1861–May 26, 1865). File microcopies of records in the National Archives: No. 70, Roll 11, hereinafter cited as Despatches, X.

7. Seward to William H. Hudson, May 25, 1866, and Helper to Seward, October 19, 1865, in Despatches from United States Consuls in Buenos Aires, XI (June 3, 1865–November 9, 1867). File microcopies of records in the National Archives: No. 70, Roll 12, hereinafter cited as Despatches, XI.

8. *Senate Document,* No. 504, 59 Cong., 1 sess., 4–5; Helper to Seward, December 7, 14, 1861, January 4, March 11, 1862; Henry W. Hoffman to Chase, September 12, 1862; James Kean to Messrs. Hugh Jenkins and Co., September 3, 1862; Hugh Jenkins and Co. to Hoffman, September 3, 1862; *id.* to Seward, January 27, 1863, Despatches, X.

9. Helper to Seward, November 14, 1861, April 14, July 28, August 7, 1862, September 16, 1863; Helper to Chase, July 28, August 7, 1862, September 16, 1863, *ibid.*

10. Helper to Seward, June 26, September 27, December 26, 1862, August 26, September 11, 1863, March 30, August 23, 1864, *ibid.*

11. *Id.* to *id.,* September 5, 1865, Despatches, XI.

12. *Id.* to *id.,* August 28, 1862, October 15, 1864, Despatches, X; Hudson to Seward, September 12, 1865, Despatches, XI.

13. Helper to Chase, November 4, December 11, 1863; Helper to Seward, November 23, December 11, 1863, Despatches, X.

14. Helper to Seward, June 13, 1863, April 25, 1864; Helper to Capt. Oliver S. Glisson, February 10, 1864, *ibid.*

15. Helper to Robert Kirk, October 24–25, 1862; Helper to Seward, December 26, 1862, February 1, 1865, *ibid.*

16. Helper to Edward Folmer, October 21, 1865; Helper to Seward, November 4, December 15, 1865, July 21, 1866, Despatches, XI. When the "La Portena" was sold, it was replaced on the run between Buenos Aires and Montevideo by the American steamer, "La Oriental."

17. Helper to Seward, November 25, 1862, Despatches, X; Buenos Aires *Standard,* November 16, 1862, *ibid.*

18. Resolutions of May 31, 1865; Helper to Seward, June 3, 21, 1865; American Citizens to Andrew Johnson, June 15, 1865, Despatches, XI.

19. Buenos Aires *Standard,* July 6, 1865; Helper to Seward, July 6, 1865, *ibid.*

20. Buenos Aires *Standard,* October 26–27, 1864; Helper to Seward, October 15, November 5, December 27, 1864, February 27, 1865, Despatches, X; *id.* to *id.,* August 21, 1866, Despatches, XI.

21. *Id.* to *id.,* May 28, June 26, August 19, October 14, 1862; Helper to Chase, August 19, 1862, Despatches, X.

22. Helper to Seward, December 10, 24, 1864, February 25, April 17, 1865; Buenos Aires *Standard* dispatch from Montevideo, December 21, 1864, *ibid.*

23. Helper to Seward, August 12, 25, September 26, 1865, January 11, May 31, August 11, September 11, 14, October 5, 1866; Helper to Rufino de Elizalde, August 8, 1866; Elizalde to Helper, August 10, 1866; Helper to Charles A. Washburn, August 10, 1866; Washburn to Helper, August 10, 1866, Despatches, XI.

24. Helper to Seward, March 3, December 10, 1863, January 11, May 25, December 2, 1864, Despatches, X.

25. *Id.* to *id.,* May 14, June 5, 1865; Lisbon Pizarro to Helper, May 11, 1865; Helper to Isaac Newton, May 13, June 30, August 31, 1865, April 24, 1866, Despatches, XI; Helper to Pizarro, May 13, 1865, Despatches, X, and April 7, 1866, Despatches, XI.

26. Helper to Seward, June 6, 1865, February 24, 1866; Helper to Spencer F. Baird, May 26, 1865, Despatches, XI; Helper to Francis A. Stout, December 26, 1863; Helper to Don Estevan Ram y Rubert, May 9, 1864; Rubert to Helper, May 23, 1864, Despatches, X.

27. Helper to Seward, July 13, 1863, *ibid.*, August 15, 1865, Despatches, XI; Buenos Aires *Standard*, August 3, 1865.

28. Helper to Seward, February 27, March 13, 1863, Despatches, X, October 19, 1865, Despatches, XI.

29. Helper to Chase, July 8, December 24, 1863, Despatches, X.

30. Robert C. Kirk and Charles A. Washburn, copy of letter to Seward, undated; Helper to Seward, January 8, May 11, July 20, December 31, 1864, February 15, 1865; Helper to Charles Sumner and Henry Wilson, May 7, 1864; Helper to the Senators and Representatives of the United States Congress, December 31, 1864, *ibid.*

31. Helper to Seward, May 25, 1865, *ibid.*, October 19, 1865, March 5, May 14, 1866, Despatches, XI. Three additional papers to Congress pleading for a raise are enclosed.

32. *Id.* to *id.*, October 20, November 20, 1866, February 15, 1867; Madison E. Hollister to Seward, October 8, 1866, January 24, 1867, *ibid.* Hollister of Ottawa, Illinois, received an appointment to replace Helper in early October. He arrived in Buenos Aires January 14, 1867.

33. Helper to Seward, February 4, 1867; Julian Allen to Seward, February 4, 1867, *ibid.*

34. N. P. Banks to Seward, March 2, 1867, *ibid.;* Dale, "Helper and Latin America," 39–40, 44, citing Hamilton Fish to Zachary Chandler.

CHAPTER EIGHT

1. Barbee, "Helper," *loc. cit.*, 167–68.

2. Helper to editor of the *National Intelligencer*, January 22, 1869, in Hinton R. Helper, *The Negroes in Negroland; the Negroes in America; and Negroes Generally* (New York, 1868), 249–50.

3. Burdick to Helper, July 9, 1869, cited in Helper, *Noonday Exigencies in America*, 204–05. Louis Filler, *The Crusade Against Slavery, 1830–1860* (New York, 1960), 255, notes that in a copy of *The Impending Crisis* in a St. Louis library Helper wrote, "For proof that this work was *not* written in behalf of negroes—as has been erroneously stated—but in behalf of the *whites* rather see" [here follows twenty-two enumerated citations].

4. Helper, *Nojoque*, dedication.

5. *Ibid.*, 37–62, 81–89, 99, 113, 115, 155, 160, 176.

6. Helper, *Negroes in Negroland*, xiii, xiv.

7. Helper, *Nojoque*, 193, 209–16, 376–90.

8. Helper, *Negroes in Negroland*, 171–72.

9. Dumas Malone, *Jefferson the Virginian* (*Jefferson and His Times*, Vol. I [Boston, 1948]), 267.

10. Helper, *Negroes in Negroland*, 174–75.

11. *Ibid.*, 180; Helper, *Nojoque,* 37.

12. Richard Hofstadter, "Abraham Lincoln and the Self-Made Myth," *The American Political Tradition and the Men Who Made It* (New York, 1948), 109–10.

13. Helper, *Negroes in Negroland,* ix–x.

14. Hinton R. Helper, *Oddments of Andean Diplomacy and Other Oddments* (St. Louis, 1879), 291–314, quoting a letter to Senator Augustus S. Merriman, June 29, 1877, hereinafter cited as *Oddments.*

15. Helper, *Nojoque,* 63, 209, 238–39, 250–51, 352, 372.

16. Helper, *Negroes in Negroland,* 238–39.

17. Robert F. Durden, *James Shepherd Pike, Republicanism and the American Negro, 1850–1882* (Durham, 1957), viii, 31–35, 161–66, 201–02, 215–19. As a Republican, Pike also was probably influenced by a desire for his party to control the Southern states. By 1870–71 he had begun the process of removing his endorsement of the Negro vote. See *ibid.,* 185.

18. Helper, *Negroes in Negroland,* vii, 239–48.

19. Helper, *Noonday Exigencies in America,* v–xi.

20. *Ibid.,* 15–18. Citations are of the New York *Times,* March 9, 1869, the New York *Tribune,* December 26, 1870, and the New York *Herald,* April 11, 1869.

21. *Noonday Exigencies in America,* 19–23, 27–28, 37, 41, 46–47, 49, 51–52, 54–55, 57–58, 71–72.

22. *Ibid.,* 74–78.

23. Helper's attitude of imperialism was not a departure from his previous writings. In *Nojoque* (160–61) he proposed a scheme whereby the nations of the world would be reduced in number but increased in size and improved in form. Among others, he proposed that Norway and Sweden should go to Russia, and Germany would receive Switzerland, Holland and Denmark. Spain would receive Portugal; France would get Belgium and Luxembourg. Great Britain would annex Ireland and "all of the comparatively out-of-the-way islands of the world." The great United States would obtain "the whole of North America, from Behring's Strait in the north to the Isthmus of Darien in the south, and from Cape Race in the east to Vancouver's Island in the west;" as well as Cuba, Haiti, Jamaica, Puerto Rico, and the remaining West Indian islands. South America would be parceled out among New Granada, Brazil, and Chile. Asia would be divided among a half dozen European and American powers and placed "under the exclusive control of Caucasian-blooded people." With the "superior races" everywhere in control, Helper looked for the millenium on earth.

24. John R. Commons, *et al., History of Labour in the United States* (New York, 1921), II, 114, 118–19, 129, 134, 136, 145, 149, 152–55.

25. Ashe, *et al., Biographical History of North Carolina,* VIII, 213; *The Southern Review,* II (October, 1867), 489, VIII (July, 1870), 226–27.

26. *War of Races* (Richmond, 1867), 11–14.
27. E. R. Carter (Negro), *The Black Side* (Atlanta, 1894), vi–viii.
28. Helper, *Noonday Exigencies in America,* 96, 105.
29. Hofstadter, "Abraham Lincoln," *loc. cit.,* 110–11, 113, 116, 129–32.
30. Morris, "The Measure of Bondage in the Slave States," *loc. cit.,* 229–30.

CHAPTER NINE

1. Memorial of Colton to the United States Congress; Helper to Casimiro Corral, November 1, 1871, *Oddments,* 29–31. Henceforth in this chapter all page citations, unless otherwise indicated, refer to *Oddments.*
2. Fish to Helper, December 21, 1870, 34.
3. Corral to Helper, November 4, 1871; affidavits of Commandant Juan Mariano Mujia, November 9, 1871, and Col. Juan Ondarza, December 23, 1871, 37–43.
4. Corral to Helper, January 4, 1872; Helper to Corral, January 16, 1872, 44–45; Leopold Markbreit to Fish, November 30, 1872, Despatches from Bolivia, Vol. VI, cited in Dale, "Helper and Latin America," 52; Decree of the Bolivian Government, February 1, 1872, 49.
5. Markbreit to Helper, March 31, July 3, 1872; Helper to Markbreit, June 14, August 7, 1872, 53–54, 58–60.
6. Helper to Corral, No. 1, February 15, 1873, 68–71.
7. Fish to Helper, December 11, 1872; Leonard Myers to Helper, December 20, 1872; Helper to Fish, February 28, 1873, 76–78, 97–100, 102.
8. Helper to Tomas Frias, February 15, 1873; Helper to Corral, No. 2, February 15, 1873; Frias to Helper, April 17, 1873; Helper to Narcisco Campero, April 18, 1873, 73–74, 79, 102. The author only infers that Helper was accompanied by his family on this trip.
9. Page 23. Later observations and correspondence were added to this pamphlet to form the first portion of *Oddments.*
10. Colton Memorial, 83–89.
11. Helper to Simon Cameron, December 15, 1873, January 7, 1874; Helper to Corral, January 3, February 5, 1874, 81–82, 106–11.
12. Henry A. Blythe to Helper, February 23, 1874; Fredrick L. Olmstead to Helper, March 14, 1874; H. G. Onderdonk to Helper, March 19, 1874; John C. Smith to Helper, March 27, 1874, 116–20.
13. Helper to Fish, February 5, 1874, 111–15.
14. Pages 25, 129–40; Helper to the Senate Foreign Relations Committee, Fish to Cameron, May 27, 1874, 125.
15. Reproduced, 154–61. This was Senate Bill 1156, Report 531.
16. Helper to Cameron, March 17, 1875; Helper to Robert M. Reynolds,

March 8, August 30, 1875; Reynolds-Frias Settlement, May 10, 1875, 161–63, 168, 174–76.

17. Helper to Reynolds, April 14, 1876; Helper to Richard Gibbs, May 29, 1876; Colton to Fish, June 6, 1876; Fish to Colton, June 8, 1876; Helper to Fish, October 21, 1876; John L. Cadwalader to Helper, October 23, 1876, 177–78, 180–82, 184–85.

18. Helper to Fish, November 30, 1876, February 20, 1877; Helper to Prevost and Co., December 1, 1876, February 27, 1877, March 21, 1877; F. W. Seward to Reynolds, September 15, 1877; Reynolds to Helper, September 24, 1877; Helper to William M. Evarts, November 10, 1877, 188–89, 191–95, 198–201.

19. Edward Jordan to Helper, May 6, 1876; Helper to Jordan, May 2, 1876, April 13, May 30, 1877; Helper to Dom Pedro II, May 9, 1877; Secretary Aranjo to Helper, May 11, 1877; Helper to Aranjo, May 13, 1877, 342–56, 374–82.

20. Helper to Evarts, August 6, 1877; Helper to Henry W. Hilliard, October 15, 1877; Helper to Izabel, July 21, 1877, 383–86, 429.

21. Helper to Jordan, August 6, 1877; Helper to Diogo Velho Cavalcanti de Albuquerque, August 23, September 5, 1877; Albuquerque to Helper, August 23, September 4, 1877; Helper to Evarts, August 24, 1877; Helper to Cabo de Frio, August 28, 1877; Helper to Dom Pedro II, October 11, 12 (undispatched), 1877, 389–95, 398–406, 413–26.

22. Hilliard to Helper, November 20, 23, December 1, 1877; Helper to Hilliard, November 22, 29, 1877, 430–33, 435–37.

23. Helper to Senate Foreign Relations Committee, Helper to Hanson Pinkney Helper, December 1, 1877, 438–40.

24. Helper to Evarts, December 18, 1877, January 19, 1878; Helper to Richard W. Thompson, February 22, 1878; Colton to Helper, December 29, 1877, 202–03, 277–79, 441–45.

25. Helper to Garcia, March 12, 1878; Protest against Peru and Bolivia, March 19, 1878; Gibbs to Helper, April 2, 1878; Helper to Evarts, April 19, May 20, 1878; Helper to Zoilo Flores, April 23, May 16, 1878; Helper to Joaquin P. Lanfranco, May 20, 1878; Evarts to Helper, June 17, 1878; Helper to Members of the Supreme Court of Peru, June 6, 1878; Helper to Fernanco Palacios, July 8, 1878; Memorial Letter to Peru, September 2, 1878; Helper to Gibbs, September 9, 1878, 204–06, 209–11, 219–30, 232–34, 239–40, 255–61.

26. Reynolds to Helper, October 23, 1878; Evarts to Colton, May 28, 1878; Helper to Evarts, October 31, 1878; Colton to Helper, November 23, 1878, January 21, 1879, 231, 263–67.

27. Pages 16–17. *Oddments of Andean Diplomacy and Other Oddments* was dedicated not to "the somnolent, short-sighted and shallow-souled subjects of Monarchial Portuguese Brazil" which were not "yet in accord with

the whiter and freer and better ideas and institutions of the New World . . .
Nor in the least to the bigoted and fanatical adherents of the absurd, befool-
ing and baneful religion of Rome, to which the repeated revolutions and
wreck and ruin of so many of the commonwealth of South and Central
America, and the illiteracy and poverty and decadence of Italy, Spain, Portugal, Ireland, Poland, and other Catholic countries of Europe, are in the main
attributable," whose doctrines are false, whose creed is one "of most insidious
and pernicious idolatry, hypocrisy, superstition and knavery."

Rather it was dedicated to "the more liberal, enlightened and progressive
citizens of Republican Spanish America, among whom he [Helper] has had
the good fortune to find the best friend he ever had—his wife."

Helper warned his readers that some "people not generally reckoned in the
category of idiots" read books without first reading the title page, dedication,
preface, etc. He asked that no one take such liberties with this book.

CHAPTER TEN

1. Helper to Julius White, August 1, 1872, in Helper, *Oddments,* 273–77.
Helper obtained from Dr. Francis Lieber his poem, "The Central American
Ship Canal. From the Atlantic to the Pacific. An Ode to the American
People." This poem was written as a result of a passage in President Polk's
State of the Union Message of 1847. See Helper to Lieber, August 30, 1872,
and Lieber to Helper, September 2, 1872, *ibid.,* 319–20.

2. Helper to Richard W. Thompson, February 22, 1878; Helper to John
F. Cahill, September 1, 1879, *ibid.,* 280, 324–27. In a kind letter in which
Cahill referred to Helper as a man identified with all major movements to
develop Spanish-American resources, the Mexican consul gave his reasons
for preferring the Tehuantepec route over the Darien. He held the Darien
route would require tunneling and many excavations. It was known for "the
very notorious and fatal unhealthfulness of the climate. The Darien route
was 1,000–1,200 miles greater distance from Atlantic and Gulf ports than
Tehuantepec. He believed its advocacy by Europeans showed it would aid
European trade more than American. See Cahill to Helper, September 3,
1879, *ibid.,* 328–30.

3. Helper to Thompson, February 22, 1878, *ibid.,* 277–85. Helper believed
New Orleans was the only "convenient and proper port" for the concentration of the Southern trade because of its closer proximity, nearness to the
Midwest and warm climate. Helper's letter was reproduced in the *South
Pacific Times,* which described him as a man famous "for the peculiar and
forcible combination of anti-negro and anti-slavery views advanced in his
work entitled *The Impending Crisis of the South.*"

Helper (to Thompson, July 10, 1879, *ibid.,* 286–91) called the Secretary's

attention to various extravagant purchases and wasteful storage of goods by
the navy at Rio de Janeiro, Callao, and Lima.

4. *Ibid.,* 10; *Senate Document,* No. 504, 59 Cong., 1 sess., 14.

5. Helper to St. Louis Bank of Commerce, Cyrus B. Burnham, July 18,
1879; Helper to Thomas Allen, Carlos S. Greeley, and William T. Harris,
July 25, 1879, Helper, *Oddments,* 460, 462–65.

6. *Ibid.,* 12–13.

7. *Ibid.,* 13–20.

8. Helper to Rutherford B. Hayes, December 27, 1879; Helper to Secretary
of State of Mexico, November 1, 1879, in Hinton R. Helper, *The Three
Americas Railway* (New York, 1881), 415, 417.

9. Helper to Secretary of State of Mexico, September 7, 1880; Government
of Guatemala to Helper, December 3, 1879; Manuel T. Morales to Helper,
January 14, 1880, February 22, 1881; Nicaraguan Department of State to
Helper, October 14, 1880; Louis Carlos Rico to Helper, June 5, 1880; José A.
DeCour to Helper, December 10, 1880, *ibid.,* 421, 424, 426–30.

10. James Wood Davidson to Helper, February 2, 1881; Natt Atkinson to
Helper, January 12, 1880; Dr. W. C. Bowman to Helper, January 5, 1880;
L. Placide Canonge to Helper, December 18, 1879, April 23, September 24,
1880; George W. Taylor to Helper, July 12, 1880, *ibid.,* 435–37, 444–57.

11. W. Milnor Roberts to Helper, March 4, 1881; José Francisco Lopez to
Helper, February 25, 1880; Fenelon Zuviria to Helper, August 23, 1880,
*ibid.,* 456–61, 464–67.

12. Helper to William G. Eliot, July 11, 1879; Eliot to Helper, July 12, 1879;
Helper to Cyrus B. Burnham, July 18, 1879; Burnham to Helper, July 19,
1879; Helper to Allen, Greeley, and Harris, July 25, 1879; Harris, Greeley,
and Allen to Helper, September 25, 1879, Helper, *Oddments,* 458–72, 475;
Harris to Helper, July 28, 1879, *ibid.,* 474, and August 12, 1880, Helper,
*Three Americas Railway,* 32; Helper to Horace H. Morgan, August 27, 1880;
Morgan to Helper, August 28, 1880, *ibid.,* 34–35; New York *Times,* January
13, 1881.

13. *Ibid.,* March 26, May 31, 1880, January 14, 21, 1881; Helper, *Three
Americas Railway,* 12–13, Committee of Judges to Helper, *ibid.,* January 8,
1881, 36–37.

14. *Ibid.,* 3–13.

15. New York *Times,* January 21, 1881; Helper, *Three Americas Railway,*
44–138, 207.

16. New York *Times,* January 14, 1881; Helper, *Three Americas Railway,*
139–202, 207–76, 281–95. Frank Deyeaux Carpenter, a government engineer
from New York on temporary duty in Washington, D.C., won the first prize
in poetry. His poem, "Zone to Zone," concluded with these lines, referring to
Helper:

So may the railway run
That he may live to hear this message given

To all the waiting nations 'neath the sun;
The golden spike which marks the end is driven;
The Three Americas are joined in one.

17. New York *Times,* March 14, 1882, October 23, 1883.

18. Dale, "Helper and Latin America," 130–31.

19. *Senate Document,* No. 504, 59 Cong., 1 sess., 10–12.

20. New York *Times,* July 24, 1886; Dale, "Helper and Latin America," 133. After failing to collect the Fiedler claim in 1885, Helper began work on an anti-Brazilian book. In 1888 he sought copyright of the following title: *Braganza in Besetment: Decadence of American Monarchy: Destined Disruption of an Empire; A Direful Doom Encompassing Brazil! Soon Afterward, However, to be Rightfully and Resplendedly Succeeded by the Redemptive and Renovating Republic of Amazon.* Due to the fall of the House of Braganza in 1889 and Helper's concern with the Three Americas Railway, the book was abandoned. See note of August 13, 1888, by Helper, Miscellaneous Papers, New York Public Library.

21. John A. Caruso, "The Pan American Railway," *The Hispanic America Historical Review,* XXXI (November, 1951) 611–19. Caruso believed Helper may have first obtained his concept of a Three Americas Railway from U.S. Minister to Peru, Francis Thomas. In 1872 Thomas "sent to the State Department an official despatch urging that the government build a trunk-line from some point on the Southern Pacific Railroad through Latin America to Cuzco or to Santiago." Helper was through Lima in the same year this dispatch was sent. This conflicts with Helper's account of his origin of the plan. Caruso wrote, "In any case, Helper was the first to give the project wide-spread publicity."

22. *Senate Document,* No. 504, 59 Cong., 1 sess., 13–16. The titles of the sections of the *Report of the Intercontinental Railway Commission* indicate the scope of the survey. They are: Vol. I, part 1, *Condensed report of transactions and of surveys in Central and South America, 1891–1898;* Vol. 1, part 2, *Report of surveys and explorations made by Corps 1 in Guatemala, Salvador, Honduras, Nicaragua and Costa Rica, 1891–1893;* Vol. 2, *Report of surveys and explorations made by Corps 2 in Costa Rica, Colombia and Ecuador, 1891–1893;* Vol. 3, *Report of surveys and exploration made by Corps 3 in Ecuador and Peru, 1891–1892.*

23. Dale, "Helper and Latin America," 160; Barbee, "Helper," *loc. cit.,* 169.

24. Caruso, "Pan American Railway," *loc. cit.,* 620–25. It appears only to have been because of Roosevelt's interest in the Panama Canal that the government did not take the initiative in developing the railway at this time.

25. *Senate Document,* No. 108, 58 Cong., 3 sess., 1–3; *Senate Document,* No. 92, 59 Cong., 1 sess., 1–5.

26. *Senate Document,* No. 504, 59 Cong., 1 sess., 1–2, 9–10, 19–21.

27. Barbee, "Helper," *loc. cit.,* 170, citing "Savoyard," *In the Pennyrile of Old Kentucky, and Men, Things and Events* (Washington, 1911), 118–19.

28. Helper to Fred E. Woodward, June 20, 1904, March 31, 1906, Fred E. Woodward Papers, Library of Congress.

29. Washington *Evening Star,* March 9, 1909; Washington *Post,* March 10, 1909. The *Post* contended that Helper's widow lived with two children in Chicago. The Charlotte *Observer,* March 10, 1909, reported, "It was learned today that Helper's wife, who was a Spanish woman, Marie Rodriguez, before marriage, is now blind and living in Buenos Ayres." Helper was survived by two nephews, Alexander Helper of Baltimore and Daniel Ott Helper of Mockville, N.C., and a niece, Mrs. E. W. Mooring of Mockville.

30. *Literary Digest,* XXXVIII (April 3, 1909), 569–71; *The Nation,* LXXXVII (March 11, 1909), 254 (*The Nation* did not understand Helper's racist views, however.); Washington *Evening Star,* March 9, 1909; Charlotte *Observer,* March 10, 1909.

31. Caruso, "Pan American Railway," *loc. cit.,* 625–39.

# Bibliography

I. PAPERS

William Henry Anthon Book of Letters Relative to the Publication of *The Impending Crisis*. New York Public Library.
Blair-Lee Papers, Princeton University.
Buenos Aires Consular Despatches, 1811–1906. Vols. X, XI. National Archives Microfilm Rolls 11 and 12.
William J. Bryan Papers. Library of Congress.
Salmon P. Chase Papers. Library of Congress.
John Hay Papers. Library of Congress.
Abraham Lincoln Papers. Library of Congress.
Miscellaneous Papers. New York Public Library.
William H. Seward Papers. Library of Congress.
John T. Sherman Papers. Library of Congress.
Fred E. Woodward Papers. Library of Congress.

II. GOVERNMENT DOCUMENTS

*Acts of the Seventh Biennial Session of the General Assembly of Alabama Held in the City of Montgomery, Commencing on the Second Monday in November, 1859*. Montgomery, 1860.
*Congressional Globe*, 35 Cong., 1 sess. Washington, 1858.
*Congressional Globe*, 36 Cong., 1 sess. Washington, 1860.
De Bow, J. D. B. *Statistical View of the United States, Embracing its Territory, Population—White, Free Colored, and Slave—Moral and Social Condition, Industry, Property, and Revenue; The Detailed Statistics of*

*Cities, Towns, and Counties; Being A Compendium of the Seventh Census, to which Are Added the Results of Every Previous Census, Beginning with 1790, in Comparative Tables, with Explanatory and Illustrative Notes, Based upon the Schedules and Other Official Sources of Information.* U.S. Census Office, Seventh Census. Washington, 1854.

International Railway Commission, *Report.* 7 vols. Washington, 1892–98.

*Senate Document,* No. 108, 58 Cong., 3 sess. January 20, 1905.

*Senate Document,* No. 92, 59 Cong., 1 sess. December 18, 1905.

*Senate Document,* No. 504, 59 Cong., 1 sess. June 25, 1906.


III. NEWSPAPERS, PERIODICALS, AND JOURNALS


Charlotte *Observer,* March 10, 1909.

*De Bow's Review,* XXII–XXVII (1857–60).

*Harper's,* XIX, XX (1859–60).

*Harper's Weekly,* III, IV (1859–60).

*Literary Digest,* XXXVIII (April 3, 1909).

Lynchburg *Republican Tri-Weekly,* 1859.

*The Nation,* LXXXVII (March 11, 1909).

New York *Daily Tribune,* 1857–61.

New York *Herald,* 1857–61.

New York *Times,* 1857–1909.

Richmond *Semi-Weekly Examiner,* 1859–60.

Salisbury *Carolina Watchman,* 1857–60.

Selma (Alabama) *Daily Sentinel,* February, 1860.

*The Southern Literary Messenger,* XXV–XXVII (1857–58).

*The Southern Review,* II–VIII (1867–1870).

Washington *Evening Star,* March 9, 1909.

Washington *Post,* March 10, 1909.

Washington *States and Union,* 1859–60.

Washington *Union,* 1857.

*William and Mary Quarterly,* New Series, XXV (1917).


IV. ARTICLES


"American Slavery in 1857," *Southern Literary Messenger,* XXV (August, 1857).

Barbee, David R. "Hinton Rowan Helper," *Tyler's Historical Quarterly and Genealogical Magazine,* XV (January, 1934).

Barbee, David R. "Hinton Rowan Helper's Mendacity," *Tyler's Historical Quarterly and Genealogical Magazine,* XV (January, 1934).

Caruso, John A. "The Pan American Railway," *The Hispanic America Historical Review,* XXXI (November, 1951).

Conrad, Alfred H., and John R. Meyer. "The Economics of Slavery in the Ante Bellum South," *The Journal of Political Economy,* XLVI (April, 1958).

Crenshaw, Ollinger. "The Speakership Contest of 1859–1860, John Sherman's Election A Cause of Disruption," *Mississippi Valley Historical Review,* XXIX, No. 3 (December, 1942).

Crenshaw, Ollinger. "The Psychological Background of the Election of 1860 in the South," *The North Carolina Historical Review,* XIX (July, 1942).

Eaton, Clement. "Slave Hiring in the Upper South: A Step toward Freedom," *Mississippi Valley Historical Review,* XLVI (March, 1960).

Genovese, Eugene D. "The Significance of the Slave Plantation for Southern Economic Development: The Retardation of Demand," *Journal of Southern History,* XXVIII (November, 1962).

Gerke, William H. "Negro Slavery Among the Germans in North Carolina," *The North Carolina Historical Review,* XIV, No. 4 (October, 1937).

Gilbert, Benjamin F. "The Life and Writings of Hinton Rowan Helper," *The Register of the Kentucky Historical Society,* LIII (January, 1955).

Govan, Thomas P. "Was Plantation Slavery Profitable?" *Journal of Southern History,* VIII (November, 1942).

Holbrook, Stewart H. "Hinton Helper and His Crisis," *The American Mercury,* LX (January, 1945).

Morris, Richard B. "The Measure of Bondage in the Slave States," *Mississippi Valley Historical Review,* XLI (September, 1954).

Polk, William. "The Hated Helper," *The South Atlantic Quarterly,* XXX No. 2 (April, 1931).

"Problems of Free Society," *Southern Literary Messenger,* XXVII (August, 1858).

"The Raid of John Brown and the Progress of Abolition," *The Southern Presbyterian Review,* XII (January, 1860).

Russell, Robert R. "The General Effects of Slavery upon Southern Economic Progress," *Journal of Southern History,* IV (February, 1938).

"Southern and Northern Civilization Contrasted," *Russell's Magazine,* I (May, 1857).

Stampp, Kenneth M. "The Fate of the Southern Antislavery Movement," *The Journal of Negro History,* XXVIII (January, 1943).

Stampp, Kenneth M. "The Southern Refutation of the Proslavery Argument," *The North Carolina Historical Review,* XXI (January, 1944).

Weeks, Stephen B. "Anti-Slavery Sentiment in the South; With Unpublished

Letters from John Stuart Mill and Mrs. Stowe," *Publications of the Southern History Association,* II (April, 1898).

V. PUBLISHED BOOKS AND UNPUBLISHED UNIVERSITY THESES

Alderman, Edwin A., and Armistead C. Gordan. *J. L. M. Curry, A Biog-
raphy.* New York, 1911.
Alderman, Edwin A., and Joel C. Harris, *et al.* (eds.). *Library of Southern
Literature.* 16 vols. Atlanta, 1907.
*Anti-Abolition Tracts. No. 3. The Abolition Conspiracy to Destroy the
Union; or, A Ten Years' Record of THE "Republican Party." The
Opinions of William Lloyd Garrison, Wendell Phillips, . . . etc.* New York,
1866.
Ashe, Samuel A., Stephen B. Weeks, Charles L. Van Noppen (eds.).
*Biographical History of North Carolina, From Colonial Times to the
Present.* 8 vols. Greensboro, 1917.
Atherton, Gertrude. *California, An Intimate History.* New York, 1914.
Barnes, Gilbert H. *The Anti-Slavery Impulse, 1830–1844.* New York, 1933.
Bassett, John S. *Anti-Slavery Leaders of North Carolina. (Johns Hopkins
University Studies in Historical and Political Science,* ed. Herbert B.
Adams, Series XVI, No. 6.) Baltimore, 1898.
Beebe, Gilbert J. *A Review and Refutation of Helper's "Impending Crisis."*
Middleton, N.Y., 1860.
Brawley, Benjamin. *A Short History of the American Negro.* New York,
1937.
Brawley, James S. *The Rowan Story, 1753–1953, A Narrative History of
Rowan County, North Carolina.* Salisbury, 1953.
Brownlow, W. G., and Abram Pryne. *Ought American Slavery To Be Per-
petuated? A Debate Between W. G. Brownlow and Abram Pryne.* Phila-
delphia, 1858.
Carter, Rev. E. R. (Negro). *The Black Side. A Partial History of the Business,
Religious, and Educational Side of the Negro in Atlanta, Ga.* Atlanta,
1894.
Cate, Wirt A. *Lucius Q. C. Lamar, Secession and Reunion.* Chapel Hill, 1935.
Chadwick, French E. *Causes of the Civil War, 1859–1861.* (A. B. Hart, ed.,
*The American Nation: A History,* Vol. XIX.) New York, 1906.
Cleland, Robert G. *A History of California: The American Period.* New
York, 1922.
Coleman, J. Winston, Jr. *Slavery Times in Kentucky.* Chapel Hill, 1940.
Commons, John R., *et al. History of Labour in the United States.* 4 vols.
New York, 1921.
Couch, W. T. (ed.) *Culture in the South.* Chapel Hill, 1934.

Coulter, E. Merton (ed.) *The Course of the South to Secession. An Interpretation by Ulrich Bonnell Phillips.* New York, 1939.

Coulter, E. Merton. *The South During Reconstruction, 1865–1877.* (E. Merton Coulter and Wendell H. Stephenson, eds., *A History of the South,* Vol. VIII.) Baton Rouge, 1947.

Cox, Oliver C. *Caste, Class, & Race. A Study in Social Dynamics.* Garden City, 1948.

Craven, Avery O. *The Coming of the Civil War.* New York, 1942.

Craven, Avery O. *The Growth of Southern Nationalism, 1848–1861.* (E. Merton Coulter and Wendell H. Stephenson, eds., *A History of the South,* Vol. VI.) Baton Rouge, 1953.

Dale, William P., II. "Hinton Rowan Helper and Latin America." Unpublished master's thesis, Duke University, 1935.

Davidson, James W. *The Living Writers of the South.* New York, 1869.

d'Orleans, Louis P. A. *History of the Civil War in America.* 4 vols. Philadelphia, 1875.

Du Bois, W. E. Burghardt. *Black Reconstruction. An Essay toward A History of the Part Which Black Folk Played in the Attempt to Reconstruct Democracy in America, 1860–1880.* New York, 1935.

Dumond, Dwight L. (ed.). *Southern Editorials on Secession.* New York, 1931.

Durden, Robert F. *James Shepherd Pike, Republicanism and the American Negro, 1850–1882.* Durham, 1957.

Eaton, Clement. *Freedom of Thought in the Old South.* Durham, 1940.

Elkins, Stanley M. *Slavery, A Problem in American Institutional and Intellectual Life.* Chicago, 1959.

Filler, Louis. *The Crusade Against Slavery, 1830–1860.* New York, 1960.

Fite, Emerson. *The Political Campaign of 1860.* New York, 1911.

Flanders, Ralph B. *Plantation Slavery in Georgia.* Chapel Hill, 1933.

Franklin, John H. *From Slavery to Freeedom, A History of American Negroes.* 2d ed. New York, 1956.

Gates, Paul W. *The Farmer's Age: 1815–1860.* (*The Economic History of the United States,* Vol. III.) New York, 1960.

Gilmer, John H. *War of Races. By whom it is sought to be brought about. Considered in two letters with copious extracts from the recent work of Hilton [sic] R. Helper.* Richmond, 1867.

Goodlow, Daniel R. *The Southern Platform: or, Manual of Southern Sentiment on the Subject of Slavery.* Boston, 1858.

Gray, Lewis C. *History of Agriculture in the Southern United States to 1860.* 2 vols. Washington, 1933.

Green, Fletcher M. (ed.). *Essays in Southern History Presented to Joseph Gregoire de Roulhac Hamilton, Ph.D., LL.D., by his Former Students at the University of North Carolina.* Chapel Hill, 1949.

Handlin, W. W. *American Politics, A Moral and Political Work, Treating of the Causes of the Civil War, The Nature of Government and the Necessity for Reform.* New Orleans, 1864.

Helper, Hinton R. *The Compendium of The Impending Crisis.* New York, 1859.

Helper, Hinton R. *The Impending Crisis of the South: How to Meet It.* New York, 1857, 1860.

Helper, Hinton R. *The Land of Gold. Reality Versus Fiction.* Baltimore, 1855.

Helper, Hinton R. *The Negroes in Negroland; the Negroes in America; and Negroes Generally. Also the Several Races of White Men, Considered As the Involuntary and Predestined Supplanters of the Black Race.* New York, 1868.

Helper, Hinton R. *Nojoque: A Question for A Continent.* New York, 1867.

Helper, Hinton R. *Nojoque Une Grave Question Pour Un Continent.* Traduction française précédée d'une Introduction, avec notes, par L. Placide Canonge. Nouvelle-Orleans, 1867.

Helper, Hinton R. *Noonday Exigencies in America.* New York, 1871.

Helper, Hinton R. *Oddments of Andean Diplomacy and Other Oddments.* St. Louis, 1879.

Helper, Hinton R. *The Three Americas Railway.* New York, 1881.

Henneman, John Bell (ed.). *The South in the Building of the Nation.* 13 vols. Richmond, 1913.

Hofstadter, Richard. *The American Political Tradition and the Men Who Made It.* New York, 1948.

Hubbell, Jay B. *The South in American Literature, 1607–1900.* Durham, 1954.

Jackson, David K. (ed.). *American Studies in Honor of William Kenneth Boyd.* Durham, 1940.

Jackson, Walter M. *The Story of Selma.* Birmingham, 1954.

Joint Committee of North Carolina English Teachers Association and North Carolina Library Association. *North Carolina Authors: A Selective Handbook. (University of North Carolina Library Extension Publications,* Vol. XVIII, No. 1.) Chapel Hill, October, 1952.

Kettell, Thomas P. *Southern Wealth and Northern Profits, As Exhibited in Statistical Facts and Official Figures: Showing the Necessity of Union to the Future Prosperity and Welfare of the Republic.* New York, 1860.

Kunitz, Stanley, and Howard Haycroft. *American Authors, 1600–1900. A Biographical Dictionary of American Literature.* New York, 1938.

Lefler, Hugh T. *Hinton Rowan Helper, Advocate of A "White America." (Southern Sketches,* No. 1.) Charlottesville, 1935.

Lloyd, Arthur Y. *The Slavery Controversy, 1831–1860.* Chapel Hill, 1939.

Lowrey, Lawrence T. *Northern Opinion of Approaching Secession, October, 1859–November, 1860.* (John S. Bassett and Sidney B. Fay, eds., *Smith*

*College Studies in History,* Vol. III, No. 4.) Northampton, Mass., July, 1918.

Lunt, George. *The Origin of the Late War: Traced from the Beginning of the Revolt of the Southern States.* New York, 1866.

McMaster, John B. *A History of the People of the United States from the Revolution to the Civil War.* 8 vols. New York, 1921.

Macy, Jesse. *The Anti-Slavery Crusade, A Chronicle of the Gathering Storm.* (Allen Johnson, ed., *The Chronicles of America,* Vol. 28.) New Haven, 1919.

Malone, Dumas. *Jefferson the Virginian.* (*Jefferson and His Time,* Vol. I.) Boston, 1948.

Mayes, Edward. *Lucius Q. C. Lamar: His Life, Times and Speeches, 1825–1893.* Nashville, 1896.

Milton, George F. *The Age of Hate, Andrew Johnson and the Radicals.* New York, 1930.

Moses, Montrose J. *The Literature of the South.* New York, 1910.

Mrydal, Gunnar (with the assistance of Richard Sterner and Arnold Rose). *An American Dilemma, The Negro Problem and Modern Democracy.* 2 vols. New York, 1944.

Nevins, Allen. *The Emergence of Lincoln.* 2 vols. New York, 1950.

Nicolay, John G., and John Hay. *Abraham Lincoln, A History.* 10 vols. New York, 1917.

Nichols, Roy F. *The Disruption of American Democracy.* New York, 1948.

Oates, William C. *The War Between the Union and the Confederacy and Its Lost Opportunities.* New York, 1905.

Owsley, Frank L. *Plain Folk of the Old South.* Baton Rogue, 1949.

Peissner, Elias. *The American Question in Its National Aspect. Being Also an Incidental Reply to Mr. H. R. Helper's "Compendium of the Impending Crisis of the South."* New York, 1861.

Perkins, Howard C. (ed.). *Northern Editorials on Secession.* 2 vols. New York, 1942.

Phillips, Ulrich B. *American Negro Slavery, A Survey of the Supply, Employment and Control of Negro Labor as Determined by the Plantation Regime.* New York, 1918.

Pollard, Edward A. *Black Diamonds Gathered in the Darkey Homes of the South.* New York, 1859.

Pollard, Edward A. *The Lost Cause: A New Southern History of the War of the Confederates. Comprising A Full and Authentic Account of the Rise and Progress of the Late Southern Confederacy—The Campaigns, Battles, Incidents, and Adventures of the Most Gigantic Struggle of the World's History. Drawn from Official Sources, and Approved by the Most Distinguished Confederate Leaders.* New York, 1866.

Pryor, Mrs. Roger A. *Reminiscences of Peace and War.* New York, 1904.

Reynolds, E. W. *The True Story of the Barons of the South, or the Rationale of the American Conflict.* Boston, 1862.

Rhodes, James F. *History of the United States from the Compromise of 1850 to the McKinley-Bryan Campaign of 1896.* 8 vols. New York, 1920.

Rippy, J. Fred. *The Historical Evolution of Hispanic America.* New York, 1932.

Robert, Joseph C. *The Road from Monticello, A Study of the Virginia Slavery Debate of 1832.* Durham, 1941.

Rumple, Rev. Jethro. *A History of Rowan County, North Carolina, Containing Sketches of Prominent Families and Distinguished Men, with an Appendix,* ed. J. J. Bruner. Salisbury, 1916.

Russell, Robert R. *Economic Aspects of Southern Sectionalism, 1840–1861.* New York, 1960.

Sandburg, Carl. *Abraham Lincoln: The Prairie Years.* 2 vols. New York, 1926.

Shade, Louis. *A Book for the "Impending Crisis!" Appeal to the Common Sense and Patriotism of the People of the United States. "Helperism" Annihilated! The "Irrespressible Conflict" and Its Consequences!* Washington, 1860.

Shanks, Henry T. *The Secession Movement in Virginia, 1847–1861.* Richmond, 1934.

Simms, Henry H. *A Decade of Sectional Controversy, 1851–1861.* Chapel Hill, 1942.

Sitterson, J. Carlyle. *The Secession Movement in North Carolina. (The James Sprunt Studies in History and Political Science,* Vol. XXIII) Chapel Hill, 1939.

Sitterson, J. Carlyle. *Sugar Country, The Cane Sugar Industry in the South, 1753–1950.* Lexington, 1953.

Smith, Theodore C. *Parties and Slavery, 1850–1859.* (A. B. Hart, ed., *The American Nation: A History,* Vol. XVIII.) New York, 1906.

A Southerner. *Fanaticism and Its Results: or, Facts versus Fancies.* Baltimore, 1860.

Spiller, Robert E., Willard Thorp, Thomas H. Johnson, and Henry S. Canby. *Literary History of the United States.* New York, 1948.

Stampp, Kenneth M. *The Peculiar Institution, Slavery in the Ante-Bellum South.* New York, 1956.

*Studies in Southern History and Politics Inscribed to William Archibald Dunning.* New York, 1914.

Sydnor, Charles S. *Slavery in Mississippi.* New York, 1933.

Taylor, Orville W. *Negro Slavery in Arkansas.* Durham, 1958.

Theobald, Theodore V. "Hinton Rowan Helper and *The Impending Crisis.*" Unpublished master's thesis, Columbia University, 1949.

Thorndike, Rachel S. (ed.). *The Sherman Letters: Correspondence Between General and Senator Sherman from 1837 to 1891.* New York, 1894.

Trent, William P., John Erskin, Stuart P. Sherman, and Carl Van Doren. (eds.). *The Cambridge History of American Literature.* 4 vols. New York, 1917–21.

Thompson, Edgar T. (ed.). *Race Relations and the Race Problem, A Definition and An Analysis.* Durham, 1939.

Trexler, Harrison A. *Slavery in Missouri, 1804–1865.* (*John Hopkins University Studies in Historical and Political Science,* Series XXXII) Baltimore, 1914.

Turner, Lorenzo D. *Anti-Slavery Sentiments in American Literature Prior to 1865.* Washington, 1929.

Tyler, Lyon G. *Letters and Times of the Tylers.* 3 vols., Richmond, 1884–1896.

*The Union: Being a Condemnation of Mr. Helper's Scheme, with A Plan for the Settlement of the "Irrepressible Conflict."* By One Who Has Considered Both Sides of the Question. New York, 1860.

Villard, Oswald G. *John Brown, 1800–1859. A Biography Fifty Years After.* New York, 1911.

Wall, James W. "Hinton Rowan Helper and *The Impending Crisis.*" Unpublished master's thesis, University of North Carolina, 1949.

Wallace, Sarah A., and Frances E. Gillespie (eds.). *The Journal of Benjamin Moran, 1857–1865.* 2 vols. Chicago, 1948.

*War of Races. Letter of John H. Gilmer, Esq. to "Messrs. Thos. Wood, John J. Bocock, W. T. Early and others, forming the Committee to Report Resolutions, &c., to the Ablemarle Meeting held 1st day of July."* Richmond, 1867.

Weatherford, Willis D., and Charles S. Johnson. *Race Relations, Adjustment of Whites and Negroes in the United States.* New York, 1934.

Weaver, Herbert. *Mississippi Farmers, 1850–1860.* Nashville, 1945.

Wilgus, Alva C. *The Development of Hispanic America.* New York, 1941.

Williams, Mary F. *History of the San Francisco Committee of Vigilance of 1851.* (*University of California Publications in History,* Vol. XII.) Berkeley, 1921.

Wilson, James G., and John Fiske (eds.). *Appleton's Cyclopaedia of American Biography.* Vol. III. New York, 1888.

Winston, Robert W. *Andrew Johnson, Plebeian and Patriot.* New York, 1928.

Wise, John S. *The End of An Era.* New York, 1899.

Wolfe, Samuel M. *Helper's Impending Crisis Dissected.* Philadelphia, 1860.

Woodward, C. Vann. *Origins of the New South, 1877–1913.* (E. Merton Coulter and Wendell H. Stephenson, eds., *A History of the South,* Vol. IX.) Baton Rouge, 1951.

Woodward, William E. *Years of Madness.* New York, 1951.

# Appendix

## The Impending Crisis

NOTE.—The page citations are to the 1857 edition of *The Impending Crisis*. The table and page citations in brackets refer to the source from which Helper obtained his information in J. D. B. DeBow (ed.), *Seventh Census of the United States, 1850* (Washington, 1854). Where there are no bracketed citations, Helper used sources other than the census.

I. Comparison of New York and Virginia (11–14)
   [XII, 40]
   A. Population:

|      | New York  | Virginia  |
|------|-----------|-----------|
| 1790 | 340,120   | 748,308   |
| 1850 | 3,097,394 | 1,421,661 |

   B. Exports and imports:
      [Imports start, 1821, CCVIII, 186, 187]

|         |            | 1791        | 1852          |
|---------|------------|-------------|---------------|
| Exports: |           |             |               |
|         | New York   | $2,505,465  | $87,484,456   |
|         | Virginia   | 3,130,865   | 2,724,657     |
| Imports: |           | 1790        | 1853          |
|         | New York   | about equal | $178,270,999  |
|         | Virginia   | about equal | 399,000       |

   C. Returns from manufacturing, mining, and mechanical arts, 1850:
      [CXCV, 179]

|          |               |
|----------|---------------|
| New York | $237,597,249  |
| Virginia | 29,705,387    |

231

D. Real and personal property, 1850:
[CCXIV, 190]
New York                    $1,080,309,216
Virginia                     391,646,438 (not including slaves)

E. Cash value of all farms, farm implements, and machinery, 1850:
[CLXXXIII, 169]
New York                    $576,631,568
Virginia                     223,423,315

II. Comparison of Massachusetts and North Carolina (14–17) [XII, 40]

A. Population:

|              | Massachusetts | North Carolina |
|--------------|---------------|----------------|
| 1790         | 378,717       | 393,751        |
| 1850         | 994,514       | 869,039 (including 288,548 slaves) |

B. Physical area:
[VIII, 36]
Massachusetts               7,800 sq. mi.
North Carolina              50,704 sq. mi.

C. Returns from manufacturing, mining, and mechanical arts, 1850:
[CXCV, 179]
Massachusetts               $151,137,155
North Carolina               9,111,245

D. Cash value of all farms, farm implements, and machinery, 1850:
[CLXXXIII, 169]
Massachusetts               $112,285,931
North Carolina               71,823,298

E. Real and personal property:
[CCXIV, 190]
Massachusetts               $573,342,286
North Carolina               226,800,472 (including slaves)

F. Illiterate white and free colored persons, 1850:
Massachusetts               1,861
North Carolina              80,083

III. Comparison of Pennsylvania and South Carolina (18–20)

A. Imports of Philadelphia and Charleston:
Philadelphia    (1854)      $21,963,021
Charleston      (1855)       1,750,000

B. Returns from mining, manufacturing, and the mechanical arts, 1850:

[CXCV, 179]

| | |
|---|---|
| Pennsylvania | $155,044,910 |
| South Carolina | 7,063,513 |

C. Cash value of all farms, farm implements, and machinery, 1850:

[CLXXXIII, 169]

| | |
|---|---|
| Pennsylvania | $422,598,640 |
| South Carolina | 86,518,038 |

D. Real and personal property, 1850:

[CCXIV, 190]

| | |
|---|---|
| Pennsylvania | $729,144,998 |
| South Carolina | 288,257,694 (including slaves) |

E. Income of public schools:

[CXLV, 142]

| | |
|---|---|
| Pennsylvania | $1,348,249 |
| South Carolina | 200,600 |

F. Public libraries:

[CLXVII, 159]

| | |
|---|---|
| Pennsylvania | 393 |
| South Carolina | 26 |

G. Newspapers:

[CLXII, 156]

| | |
|---|---|
| Pennsylvania | 310 with circulation of 84,898,672 |
| South Carolina | 46 with circulation of 7,145,930 |

IV. Comparison of agricultural production, bushel measure products, 1850

[CLXXXV, 170–74]

A. Free states—Tables I, III, V, VII (39)

| | Bushels | | |
|---|---|---|---|
| Wheat | 72,157,486 | @ $1.50 | $108,236,229 |
| Oats | 96,590,371 | .40 | 38,636,148 |
| Indian corn | 242,618,650 | .60 | 145,571,190 |
| Potatoes (I&S) | 59,033,170 | .38 | 22,432,604 |
| Rye | 12,574,623 | 1.00 | 12,574,623 |
| Barley | 5,002,013 | .90 | 4,501,811 |
| Buckwheat | 8,550,245 | .50 | 4,275,122 |
| Beans & peas | 1,542,295 | 1.75 | 2,699,015 |
| Clover & grass seeds | 762,265 | 3.00 | 2,286,795 |
| Flax seeds | 358,923 | 1.25 | 448,647 |
| Garden products | | | 3,714,605 |
| Orchard products | | | 6,332,914 |
| | 499,190,041 | valued as above | $351,709,703 |

B. Slave states—Tables II, IV, VI, VIII (39)

|  | Bushels |  |  |
|---|---|---|---|
| Wheat | 27,904,476 | @ $1.50 | $41,856,714 |
| Oats | 49,882,799 | .40 | 19,953,191 |
| Indian corn | 348,992,282 | .60 | 209,395,369 |
| Potatoes (I&S) | 44,847,420 | .38 | 17,042,019 |
| Rye | 1,608,240 | 1.00 | 1,608,240 |
| Barley | 161,970 | .90 | 145,716 |
| Buckwheat | 405,357 | .50 | 202,678 |
| Beans & peas | 7,637,227 | 1.75 | 13,365,147 |
| Clover & grass seeds | 123,517 | 3.00 | 370,551 |
| Flax seeds | 203,484 | 1.25 | 254,355 |
| Garden products |  |  | 1,377,260 |
| Orchard products |  |  | 1,355,827 |
|  | 481,766,889 | valued as above | $306,927,067 |

Difference in bushels:     17,423,152
Difference in value:     $44,782,636

V. Comparison of leading Southern crops with the Northern hay crop, 1850 (53)
[CLXXXV, 172, 174]

A. Southern crops:

|  |  |  |  |
|---|---|---|---|
| Cotton | 2,445,779 bales | @ $32.00 | $78,264,928 |
| Tobacco | 185,023,906 lbs. | .10 | 18,502,390 |
| Rice (rough) | 215,313,497 lbs. | .04 | 8,612,539 |
| Hay | 1,137,784 tons | 11.20 | 12,743,180 |
| Hemp | 34,673 tons | 112.00 | 3,883,376 |
| Cane sugar | 237,133,000 lbs. | .07 | 16,559,310 |
|  |  |  | $138,605,723 |

B. Hay crop of the free states:

| 12,690,982 tons | @ $11.20 | 142,138,998 |
|---|---|---|
| Sundry products of the slave states |  | 138,605,723 |
| Balance in favor of the free states |  | $3,533,275 |

VI. Comparison of agricultural production, twelve principal pound measure products, 1850
[CLXXIV, 172–74]

A. Free states—Tables IX, XI, XIII, XV (61–65)

|  | Pounds |  |  |
|---|---|---|---|
| Hay | 28,427,799,680 | @ $ .01–.02 | $142,138,998 |
| Hemp | 443,520 | .05 | 22,176 |
| Hops | 3,463,176 | .15 | 519,476 |
| Flax | 3,048,278 | .10 | 304,827 |

| | | | |
|---|---|---|---|
| Maple sugar | 32,161,799 | .08 | 2,572,943 |
| Tobacco | 14,752,087 | .10 | 1,475,208 |
| Wool | 39,647,211 | .35 | 13,876,523 |
| Butter and cheese | 349,860,783 | .15 | 52,479,117 |
| Beeswax and honey | 6,888,368 | .15 | 1,033,255 |
| | 28,878,064,902 | valued as above | $214,422,522 |

B. Slave states—Tables X, XII, XIV, XVI (61–65)

*Pounds*

| | | | |
|---|---|---|---|
| Hay | 2,548,636,160 | @ $ .01-.02 | $ 12,743,180 |
| Hemp | 77,667,520 | .05 | 3,883,376 |
| Hops | 33,780 | .15 | 5,067 |
| Flax | 4,766,198 | .10 | 476,619 |
| Maple sugar | 2,088,687 | .08 | 167,094 |
| Tobacco | 185,023,906 | .10 | 18,502,390 |
| Wool | 12,797,329 | .35 | 4,479,065 |
| Butter and cheese | 68,634,224 | .15 | 10,295,133 |
| Beeswax and honey | 7,964,760 | .15 | 1,194,714 |
| Cotton | 978,311,600 | .08 | 78,264,928 |
| Cane sugar | 237,133,000 | .07 | 16,599,310 |
| Rice (rough) | 215,313,497 | .04 | 8,612,539 |
| | 4,338,370,661 | valued as above | $155,223,415 |

Difference in pounds: 24,539,694,241
Difference in value: $59,199,108

VII. Comparison of actual crop yield per acre, 1850 (summary, 70)
[CXCIII, 178]
Free states—Table XVI*; slave states—Table XVII

| | *Free states* | *Slave states* |
|---|---|---|
| Wheat | 12 bu. per acre | 9 bu. per acre |
| Oats | 27 | 17 |
| Rye | 18 | 11 |
| Indian corn | 31 | 20 |
| Irish potatoes | 125 | 113 |

\* Apparently through error, there are two Tables XVI.

VIII. Comparison of farms and domestic animals, 1850 (summary, 72)
[CLXXXV, 171]
A. Free states—Table XVIII

Value of livestock............................$  286,376,541
Value of animals slaughtered................       56,990,237
Value of farms, farming implements, and
    machinery .............................  2,233,058,619
                                            $2,576,425,397
B. Slave states—Table XIX
Value of Livestock...........................$  253,723,687
Value of animals slaughtered.................       54,388,337
Value of farms, farming implements, and
    machinery .............................  1,183,995,274
                                            $1,492,107,338
Balance in favor of the free states............$1,084,318,059

IX. Extent to which the agricultural interest of the free states predomi-
    nates over that of the slave states (72)
    [Tables IV, VI, VII]
        Difference in the value of bushel-measure
            products ...............................$   44,782,636
        Difference in the value of pound-measure
            products ..................................       59,199,108
        Difference in the value of farms and domestic
            animals ..................................  1,084,318,059
                                                    $1,188,299,803

X. Comparison of wealth, real and personal property, 1850
        (summary, 80)                          _
    [CCXIV, 190]
    Free states—Table XX; Slave states—Table XXI
    A. Entire wealth of free states                $4,102,172,108
    B. Entire wealth of slave states (with Negroes)   2,936,090,737
        Balance in favor of free states            $1,166,081,371

XI. Comparison of area and population, 1850 (143–45)
    [VIII, 36; summary gives slave states as 851,508*]
    A. Area—Tables XXII, XXIII:

|  | Sq. mi. | Acres |
|---|---|---|
| Slave states | *851,448 | 544,926,720 |
| Free states | 612,597 | 392,062,082 |
| Balance in favor of slave states | 238,851 | 152,864,638 |

    B. Population—Tables XXIV, XXV:
        [XII, 40]

|  | *Whites* | *Total* |
|---|---|---|
| Free states | 13,233,670 | 13,434,922 |
| Slave states | 6,184,477 | 9,612,976 |
| Balance in favor of free states | 7,049,193 | 3,821,946 |

XII. Distribution of slave ownership, 1850 (146)
[XC, 95]
A. Number of slaveholders and hirers (including additional entries for ownership or employment in more than one county or state): 347,525
B. Number of slaves possessed by each owner or hirer:

| | |
|---|---|
| 1 | 68,820 |
| 1 under 5 | 105,683 |
| 5 under 10 | 80,765 |
| 10 under 20 | 54,595 |
| 20 under 50 | 29,733 |
| 50 under 100 | 6,196 |
| 100 under 200 | 1,479 |
| 200 under 300 | 187 |
| 300 under 500 | 56 |
| 500 under 1000ʻ | 9 |
| 1000 & over | 2 |

XIII. Comparison of tonnage, exports, and imports, 1855 (283)
A. Free states—Table XXVI

| *Tonnage* | *Exports* | *Imports* |
|---|---|---|
| 4,252,615 | $167,520,693 | $236,847,810 |

B. Slave states—Table XXVII

| *Tonnage* | *Exports* | *Imports* |
|---|---|---|
| 855,517 | $107,480,688 | $ 24,586,528 |

XIV. Comparison of manufactures, 1850 (284)
[CXCV, 179. Alabama is incorrectly given as $4,538,878. It should be $4,528,878.]
Free states—Table XXVIII; Slave states—Table XXIX

| | *Value of annual products* | *Capital invested* | *Hands employed* |
|---|---|---|---|
| Free states | $842,586,058 | $430,240,051 | 780,576 |
| Slave states | 165,413,027 | 95,029,879 | 161,733 |

XV. Comparison of miles of canals and railroads, 1854–57 (285)
[CCXIII, 189]
Free states—Table XXX; Slave states—Table XXXI

|              | Canal miles 1854 | Railroad miles 1857 | Cost of railroads 1855 |
|--------------|------------------|---------------------|------------------------|
| Free states  | 3,682            | 17,855              | $538,313,647           |
| Slave states | 1,116            | 6,859               | 95,252,581             |

XVI. Comparison of bank capital, 1855—Table XXXII (286)

| Free states  | $230,100,340 |
|--------------|--------------|
| Slave states | 102,078,940  |

XVII. Comparison of militia forces, 1852—Table XXXIII (286)

| Free states  | 1,381,843 |
|--------------|-----------|
| Slave states | 792,876   |

XVIII. Comparison of post office operations, 1855 (287)
Free states—Table XXXIV; Slave states—Table XXXV

|              | Stamps sold | Total postage collected | Cost of transporting mails |
|--------------|-------------|-------------------------|----------------------------|
| Free states  | 1,719,513   | $4,670,725              | $2,608,295                 |
| Slave states | 666,845     | 1,553,198               | 2,385,953                  |

XIX. Comparison of public schools, 1850 (288)
[CXLV, 142]
Free states—Table XXXVI; Slave states—Table XXXVII

|              | Number | Teachers | Pupils    |
|--------------|--------|----------|-----------|
| Free states  | 62,433 | 72,621   | 2,769,901 |
| Slave states | 18,507 | 19,307   | 581,861   |

XX. Comparison of libraries other than private, 1850 (289)
[CLXVII, 159]
Free states—Table XXXVIII; Slave states—Table XXXIX

|              | No.    | Vols.     |
|--------------|--------|-----------|
| Free states  | 14,911 | 3,888,234 |
| Slave states | 695    | 649,577   |

XXI. Comparison of newspapers and periodicals published, 1850 (290)
[CLXII, 156]
Free states—Table XL; Slave states—Table XLI

|              | No.   | Copies printed annually |
|--------------|-------|-------------------------|
| Free states  | 1,790 | 334,146,281             |
| Slave states | 704   | 81,038,693              |

XXII. Comparison of illiterate white adults, 1850 (291)
[CXLIX, 145]
Free States—Table XLII; Slave states—Table XLIII

|  | *Native* | *Foreign* | *Total* |
|---|---|---|---|
| Free states | 248,725 | 173,790 | 422,515 |
| Slave states | 493,026 | 19,856 | 512,882 |

XXIII. Comparison of national political power, 1857 (292)
Free states—Table XLIV; Slave states—Table XLV

|  | *Senators* | *Representatives* | *Electoral votes* |
|---|---|---|---|
| Free states | 32 | 144 | 176 |
| Slave states | 30 | 90 | 120 |

XXIV. Comparison of popular vote for President, 1856 (293)
Free states—Table XLVI; Slave states—Table XLVII

|  | *Rep.* *Fremont* | *Am.* *Fillmore* | *Dem.* *Buchanan* | *Total* |
|---|---|---|---|---|
| Free states | 1,340,618 | 393,590 | 1,224,750 | 2,958,958 |
| Slave states | 1,194 | 479,465 | 609,587 | 1,090,246 |

XXV. Comparison of the value of churches, 1850—Table XLVIII (294)
[CXL, 138. Figures for slave states are one column off.]

| Free states | $67,773,477 |
|---|---|
| Slave states | 21,674,581 |

XXVI. Comparison of number of patents issued on new inventions, 1856—Table XLIX (294)

| Free states | 1,929 |
|---|---|
| Slave states | 268 |

XXVII. Comparison of contributions to the Bible and Tract Cause, 1855 (295)
Free states—Table L; Slave states—Table LI

|  | *Bible Cause* | *Tract Cause* |
|---|---|---|
| Free states | $319,667 | $131,972 |
| Slave states | 68,125 | 24,725 |

XXVIII. Comparison of contributions to the Missionary Cause and the Liberian Colonization Cause, 1855–56 (296)
Free states—Table LII; Slave states—Table LIII

|  | *Missionary Cause* | *Colonization Cause* |
|---|---|---|
| Free states | $502,174 | $51,930 |
| Slave states | 101,934 | 27,618 |

XXIX. Comparison of deaths, 1850 (297)
[Vary slightly from CVIII, 105; some may be drawn from CX, 107]
Free states—TableXLIV; Slave states—Table LV

|              | No. of deaths | Ratio to No. living |
|--------------|---------------|---------------------|
| Free states  | 184,249       | 72.91               |
| Slave states | 133,865       | 71.82               |

XXX. Free white male persons over fifteen years of age engaged in agricultural and other outdoor labor in the slave states, 1850–Table XLVI (298)
[Since Free Negro is included in DeBow's CXXX, 128, these figures are somewhat lower than census comp.]

| No. engaged in agriculture | No. engaged in other outdoor labor | Total |
|----------------------------|------------------------------------|-------|
| 803,052                    | 215,968                            | 1,019,020 |

XXXI. Comparison of intersectional migration, 1850—Table LVII (304)
[CXX, 116–17]

| Natives of slave states in free states | Natives of free states in slave states |
|-----------------------------------------|------------------------------------------|
| 609,223                                 | 205,924                                  |

XXXII. Value of slaves at $400 per head, 1850—Table XLVIII (306)
[LXXII, 83]
$1,280,145,600
Value of Southern real and personal property, less the value of the slaves at $400 per head
[LXXII, 83; CXIV, 190]
$1,655,945,137

XXXIII. William Henry Hurlbut's summary furnished *The Edinburgh Review* with information on the influence of the South in the national government (316)

|                            | No. of Southerners |
|----------------------------|--------------------|
| Presidents                 | 11 out of 16       |
| Judges of the Supreme Court| 17 out of 28       |
| Attorneys-General          | 14 out of 19       |
| Presidents of the Senate   | 61 out of 77       |
| Speakers of the House      | 21 out of 33       |
| Foreign ministers          | 80 out of 134      |

XXXIV. Comparison of the agricultural values revealed in the comptrollers' reports of New York and North Carolina, 1856 (324)

|  | New York | North Carolina |
|---|---|---|
| Acres of Land | 30,080,000 | 32,450,560 |
| Valued at | $1,112,133,136.00 | $98,800,636.00 |
| Avg. value per acre | $36.97 | $3.06 |

XXXV. Comparison of the population and wealth of nine Northern and nine Southern cities, as revealed by replies from their mayors and city clerks and the Chicago *Tribune* (347)

A. Nine "Free Cities":

|  | Population | Wealth | Wealth per capita |
|---|---|---|---|
| New York | 700,000 | $511,740,492 | $731 |
| Philadelphia | 500,000 | 325,000,000 | 650 |
| Boston | 165,000 | 249,162,500 | 1,510 |
| Brooklyn | 225,000 | 95,800,440 | 425 |
| Cincinnati | 210,000 | 88,810,734 | 422 |
| Chicago | 112,000 | 171,000,000 | 1,527 |
| Providence | 60,000 | 58,064,516 | 967 |
| Buffalo | 90,000 | 45,474,476 | 505 |
| New Bedford | 21,000 | 27,047,000 | 1,288 |
|  | 2,083,000 | $1,572,100,158 | $754 |

B. Nine "Slave Cities":

|  | Population | Wealth | Wealth per capita |
|---|---|---|---|
| Baltimore | 250,000 | $102,053,839 | $408 |
| New Orleans | 175,000 | 91,188,195 | 521 |
| St. Louis | 140,000 | 63,000,000 | 450 |
| Charleston | 60,000 | 36,127,751 | 602 |
| Louisville | 70,000 | 31,500,000 | 450 |
| Richmond | 40,000 | 20,143,520 | 503 |
| Norfolk | 17,000 | 12,000,000 | 705 |
| Savannah | 25,000 | 11,999,015 | 480 |
| Wilmington | 10,000 | 7,850,000 | 785 |
|  | 787,000 | $375,862,320 | $477 |